Scripture, Tradition,
and Infallibility

Also by Dewey Beegle:
Moses, the Servant of Yahweh

Scripture,

Tradition,

and Infallibility

DEWEY M. BEEGLE

Professor of Old Testament
Wesley Theological Seminary

WILLIAM B. EERDMANS PUBLISHING COMPANY
Grand Rapids, Michigan

BS
480
B363
1973

Copyright © 1973 by Wm. B. Eerdmans Publishing Company
All rights reserved
Printed in the United States of America

Library of Congress Cataloging in Publication Data

Beegle, Dewey M
  Scripture, tradition, and infallibility.

  Published in 1963 under title: The inspiration of Scripture.
  Bibliography: p.
  1. Bible—Inspiration. 2. Revelation. 3. Bible and tradition.
  I. Title.
BS480.B363 1973   220.1'3   73-78218
ISBN 0-8028-1549-9

Permission has been granted to quote from the following sources (in addition to those credited in the footnotes):

Biblical Inspiration by Bruce Vawter. Copyright © 1972 Bruce Vawter. Reprinted by permission of The World Publishing Company.

Catholic Theories of Biblical Inspiration Since 1810: A Review and Critique by James Tunstead Burtchaell. Published by the Syndics of the Cambridge University Press. Reprinted by permission.

The Early Church by Oscar Cullmann, edited by A. J. B. Higgins. Published in the U.S.A. by The Westminster Press, 1956. Used by permission.

Holy Writ or Holy Church by George H. Tavard. Copyright © 1959 by George H. Tavard. Reprinted by permission of Harper & Row, Publishers, Inc.

Infallible? An Inquiry by Hans Küng. Copyright © 1966 by Darton, Longman & Todd Ltd. and Doubleday & Company, Inc. Reprinted by permission of Doubleday & Company, Inc.

The Interpretation of Scripture by James D. Smart. Copyright © MCMLXI, W. L. Jenkins. Used by permission of The Westminster Press.

Old and New in Interpretation by James Barr. Copyright © 1966 by SCM Press Ltd., London. Reprinted by permission of Harper & Row, Publishers, Inc.

The Resurrection of Jesus of Nazareth by Willi Marxsen. Used by permission of Fortress Press.

"Scripture, Tradition, and the Church: An Ecumenical Problem" by Josef Geiselmann, from *Christianity Divided*, edited by Callahan, Oberman and O'Hanlon. © Sheed and Ward Inc., 1961.

To my wife
 MARION
Her love and faith aided me greatly
in writing the original book and
her encouragement lightened the task
of making the expanded revision.

249169

Foreword

When the first edition of this work appeared in 1963, under the title *The Inspiration of Scripture*, it excited a wide diversity of reaction within the American evangelical tradition to which it belonged. One of the best known evangelical journals in the United States featured it critically under the heading "Yea, hath God said?"—a question to which the only reply can be "Yea, God hath said." Another evangelical journal, equally well known, reviewed it more positively under the caption "Accepting the Scriptures Without Panic."

In the first edition, Dr. Beegle argued as an evangelical with fellow-evangelicals. He still does so, but has extended his range to include the Roman Catholic situation since Vatican Council II. Roman Catholics and evangelical Protestants have both had to tackle problems of revelation and inspiration, and it is interesting to mark the degree of convergence between the two approaches, as each has moved along its own lines. The role of tradition on the evangelical side, as Dr. Beegle shows, has been no less influential than in the Roman communion—perhaps even more influential from the very fact of its being so largely unrecognized for what it is.

It might be well if on both sides we gave up the use of

theological clichés and loaded terminology and tried to express in nontechnical language what is really involved in the truth of Scripture. It is useless to affirm that the Bible is the Word of God just because we have heard someone else say so, or because we have been told that this is the orthodox thing to say. If, on the other hand, we affirm the Bible to be the Word of God because God speaks to us in this volume as he does in no other, then we speak of what we know. Similarly, if we come to the Bible with ideas of revelation and inspiration that we have learned from others, we may find ourselves in difficulties when we try to square them with the text. But if we allow our understanding of biblical revelation and inspiration to be shaped by the evidence that the Bible itself provides, in all the variety of its contents, we shall not be exposed to the charge of excessively *a priori* reasoning, nor shall we be perturbed by those biblical passages discussed by Dr. Beegle which are difficult to accommodate to certain preconceived notions. Some of them indeed present problems of exegesis, but if so, it is the established methods of exegesis that will lead to their solution.

It is, of course, important to aim, by means of all the resources of textual criticism, at recovering as far as possible the *ipsissima verba* of the sacred writers. But Dr. Beegle points out that the believer who wishes to know the will of God and the way of life from the Bible has no need to wait until the "autographic" text is conclusively determined. When the New Testament writers, for example, appeal to the authority of the Old Testament, they appeal to such texts or versions as lay ready to hand in the first century A.D. For practical purposes the situation is still the same for the majority of Bible readers who are concerned with the everyday issues of Christian faith and life.

If we appeal to the "autographic" texts, we should consider the implications of the fact that for some of the most important books of the Bible autographs never existed. There was no autograph of the Epistle to the Romans in the proper sense—that is, no copy written by Paul himself. Paul dictated, and Tertius copied. Indeed, the early textual history of the epistle suggests that more

copies than one may have been made at Paul's direction—
not only the primary one, but others, naturally lacking the
personal greetings at the end, for other churches that
would be glad to have this definitive exposition of the
gospel. When a letter was intended to go to a number of
different places, it is conceivable that several simultaneous
copies were made by as many amanuenses at one dictation.

Another issue to be borne in mind is the difference
between trying to establish the earliest canonical form and
meaning of the text and trying to get behind it to a
precanonical stage. This issue has been debated in relation
to the New English Bible—especially the Old Testament
part of the work. But it can be easily illustrated by
reference to the Pauline epistles. The earliest *canonical*
text of these epistles dates from the time when they were
collected into the *corpus Paulinum*. But they had a separate existence of some decades before that. The textual
critic, pursuing his discipline for its own sake, will endeavor to get behind the *corpus Paulinum* to the mid-first-
century text (say) of Romans, but is this quest relevant for
the church's concern with canonical Scripture? In my
mind the answer is not in doubt; but it should be recognized that the question is a real and relevant one.

By the "singular care and providence" of God, the text
of Scripture has come down to us in such substantial
purity that even the most uncritical edition of the Hebrew
and Greek, or the most incompetent (or even the most
tendentious) translation of such an edition, cannot effectively obscure its essential message or neutralize its saving
power. But those who are most eager to let that message
make its full saving impact will be foremost to eliminate
every obstacle of scribal inaccuracy, translational defect,
or presuppositions and attitudes at variance with the Bible's testimony to itself, so that men and women may hold
in their hands and receive in their hearts the form of words
that conveys as faithfully as possible the revelation of God
"as originally given" through prophet and sage, and made
incarnate in Jesus Christ.

Dr. Beegle's first edition was largely a demolition job.
Here he has rearranged and amplified his material, given

the work a new and more comprehensive title, and struck a more positive note. He does not ask his readers to agree with him but to take his arguments seriously. In particular, I endorse as emphatically as I can his deprecating of a Maginot-line mentality where the doctrine of Scripture is concerned. The Word of God is something alive and active, not least when it bursts the confining bands in which our well-meant definitions try to enclose and protect it, and manifests its power to overcome opposition and lead on to fresh enterprises in the cause of Christ those who bring to it the response of obedience and faith.

F. F. BRUCE

Contents

Preface

The first edition of this book was published in 1963 under the title *The Inspiration of Scripture*. At the time there was a growing dissatisfaction with established institutions, especially the church. The malaise spread through out culture and in some instances resulted in virtual rebellion against all authority. This spirit permeated the church to such an extent that in many congregations the biblical ideas of revelation, inspiration, and authority were considered relics of the past. Any desire to discuss the subjects was taken as proof of irrelevancy.

Conditions may have to get worse before they get better, but there are signs that this sickness of the sixties is beginning to pass. Not a few, both youth and adults, are searching seriously for ultimate reality, and some are rediscovering the Bible. God is indicating again that neither he nor his claims are dead. Because of this renewed interest and the continuing concern of biblically oriented Christians, there is still a need for discussion of inspiration. Since, however, this biblical idea is intertwined with revelation, canonicity, tradition, and authority, an adequate discussion of one facet of the cluster of concepts necessarily involves consideration of the others.

Moreover, in the light of Vatican II and the more ecumenical spirit prevailing between Roman Catholics and Protestants, it seemed imperative to treat the cluster of ideas from the perspective of both traditions. Accordingly, Roman Catholic discussions of inerrancy, tradition, and infallibility have been considered at length along with the Protestant views. Of course, these additional concerns necessitated a change in the title of the book. Hopefully, this study will help inform each tradition about the common problems and solutions found in both.

Some themes are discussed in two or three different chapters, and so the book may seem repetitious at times. However, the varying insights derived from different perspectives will enhance and clarify the many-faceted aspects of Scripture and tradition. To ease the task of the readers, references to sources cited and quoted appear as footnotes at the bottom of the page instead of being grouped by chapters at the end of the book. For those interested in doing further research, a bibliography of books and articles consulted has been appended at the end of the book along with the scriptural and general indexes.

F. F. Bruce, Rylands Professor of Biblical Criticism and Exegesis, Manchester University, England, has written a foreword, and to him go heartfelt thanks for his concern about the book and its purposes. Deep gratitude is also expressed to my colleague Bruce C. Birch for reading page proofs and preparing the indexes.

DEWEY M. BEEGLE

Washington, D.C.

Chapter One

The Biblical Concept of Revelation

"The doctrine of inspiration," according to James Orr (1844-1913), "grows out of that of revelation, and can only be made intelligible through the latter."[1] Because of the accuracy of this insight, the most meaningful attempt to understand the cluster of concepts associated with the inspiration of Scripture is to begin with the idea of revelation.

The Problem of Method

Basic to the theory of modern research is the principle that an investigation of a problem must begin with the data of the primary sources dealing with the issue. This is a valid procedure; therefore our first task is to ascertain the various aspects of revelation as stated in Scripture. The success of this study depends on the degree to which we understand what is being said. We must acknowledge at the outset that there are some limitations in such an investigation because, in spite of our desire to be perfectly objective, each of us brings (often unconsciously) some presuppositions to the task of interpretation. But this need not

1. *Revelation and Inspiration*, p. 197.

be a significant defect since careful attention to method can reduce the lack of objectivity to a minimum.

Deduction and Induction

The human mind is capable of two basic processes of reasoning. One of these is the *deductive* method. It starts with an assumption or generalization from which are deduced details or particulars. The other approach is the *inductive* method. It begins with facts or details from which a generalization or principle is formulated.

The two methods of reasoning are well illustrated by archaeology. In excavating an ancient mound (*tell*) with its many layers of superimposed cities, the primary task is to dig down through these various strata, labeling all the objects and pottery according to the stratum in which they were discovered. When these facts are correlated the archaeologist observes that the pottery, for example, of a certain stratum has form and features about it that distinguish it from the pottery of other strata. In other words, each stratum tends to have its own type or class of pottery. This process of observation and inductive reasoning from facts to generalization is called "stratigraphy."

On the other hand, when the archaeologist comes across the same type of pottery while excavating another mound, he makes the deduction that the stratum in which the pottery was found dates from the same general period as the similar stratum in the first mound. This deductive reasoning from the generalization of pottery form to certain facts about the pottery is called "typology."

The accurate archaeological results of the last fifty years can be attributed to careful application of both of these methods of reasoning, and it has become increasingly apparent that adequate solutions to complex problems necessitate both induction and deduction. If handled properly, therefore, the two methods are complementary: a valid deduction should result in details that accord with the observable facts, and correct observation and relating of details should lead to a sound generalization.

The Priority of Inductive Reasoning

Granting the propriety and necessity of both kinds of reasoning, this does not mean that one is free to begin resolving the problem with whichever method happens to strike his fancy at the moment. The best results are obtained when induction precedes deduction. The history of archaeological activity makes this quite evident. Early attempts at interpreting the data often led to conflicting conclusions because the assumptions of certain archaeologists either distorted their observation of the facts or made it impossible for them to detect some of the pertinent details. Order came out of chaos when priority was given to inductive reasoning, and the same can be said for all other realms of science.

In the early stages of the struggle between science and Christianity, the church in general shied away from the inductive method on the grounds that it was not applicable to the realm of Scripture and theology. Only with the aid of the Holy Spirit, so it was claimed, could one understand the Bible. But this objection failed to see that there are two levels of understanding: content and experience. True, one cannot fully comprehend the concept of love until one experiences love for another person. Yet it is perfectly possible for a person who has not had this experience to have a great deal of factual knowledge about love by observing lovers and reading books on the subject. Similarly, the secular scholar may not have the faith to believe and experience the claims of the Bible, but if he is sensitive and does not permit his presuppositions to push the evidence aside, he can understand on the level of factual knowledge the content of the declarations. If this were not true, then all preaching to unbelievers would be fruitless. A person without faith in God can understand the essential message of the gospel. The ultimate issue is whether he exercises his will in obedience to the claim of God. It is very important, therefore, to distinguish between knowledge as content and knowledge as experience.

At the level of factual knowledge any intelligent person

with proper methods of interpretation and acquaintance with life in the ancient Near East can discern what the Bible is all about. The message is not hidden or esoteric, and there is no need to have the aid of the Holy Spirit in the inductive process. Where that aid is absolutely necessary is in the act of acceptance of the will of God. Without such help there is a rationalization that slides around the confrontation of the claim, or an attempt to postpone a decision, or even an outright refusal to respond positively to the challenge to choose. But the basis of all these reactions is the fact that the will of God is known. As Mark Twain wisely observed, the parts of the Bible that cause the most trouble are those we understand, not those we fail to comprehend.

Another objection to the inductive method has been the tendency in the liberal wing of the church for the historical-grammatical method of biblical interpretation to undercut, rather than support, confidence in the Bible and faith in God. Unfortunately, this condition is still far too prevalent. The failure, however, has not been in the method of interpretation, but in the application of the method. Rather than approaching all the biblical data with empathy, the so-called "scientific mind" has often dismissed a great deal of the evidence with the allegation that such ideas were prescientific and not in accord with reality. The criterion for this judgment has been the interpreter's limited realm of experience. Because the experiences of the biblical characters tended to be outside of his, he could not believe them. Furthermore, this disbelief resulted in a refusal even to try to understand the biblical proclamations.

This one-eyed approach was actually pseudoscientific because the data it did accept were wrenched from their theological contexts. Over and above all else, the Bible is a theological book—it speaks of God and his relation to man. It is a fatal error not to recognize this fact. Accordingly, the proper use of the inductive method demands observation of the theological presuppositions and claims of Scripture along with the data that fit into the so-called scientific category of human, nontheological history. It is recognized that the biblical writers did not set forth their views of revelation with the detail and completeness of systematic theologians, but insofar as they expressed themselves in this regard, their statements are primary data for consideration. Every claim they make for revelation is a relevant fact, and so is every discussion related to the concept of revelation.

By induction, therefore, we do *not* mean an investigation of Scripture to determine whether or not we will believe its message. Some have found Christ in this way, but for the vast majority of Christians the act of faith preceded any systematic attempts to determine the validity and meaning of Scripture. In this study, accordingly, the priority of inductive reasoning means that it is the first method to be employed in the interpretation of the Bible.

Finally, the most conclusive argument in favor of the inductive method is that without it there is no way for Scripture to correct traditions where they have misinterpreted passages in the Bible. The reader who comes to the Bible with the conviction (usually nurtured by his theological tradition) that he has the true understanding of what is being conveyed has made Scripture the prisoner of his own interpretation. The freedom of the Holy Spirit to correct and instruct is possible only when we come to the Bible with an openness that expects to receive new insight for amending and deepening our fellowship with God and his son Jesus Christ. In short, the inductive method (when properly understood and applied) is an honest approach to Scripture that resolves at all costs to let God's Written Word speak for itself.

The Term "Revelation" in the Bible

The specific Old Testament (OT) term meaning "to reveal" is the Hebrew verb *galah*. Its root meaning is "to uncover, strip away," and so it signifies the act of opening to view what has been hidden. At times it refers to the stripping of clothes as a means of humiliation; for example, Isaiah 47:3, "Your nakedness shall be uncovered, and your shame shall be seen." *Galah* appears about twenty-three times in connection with God's manifestation of himself or the communication of his message. In such cases obstacles to perception, hearing, and sight are removed. While under the influence of the Spirit of God, Balaam declares, "The oracle of him who hears the words of God, who sees the vision of Shadday ["the Mountain One," usually translated "the Almighty"], falling yet having his eyes uncovered" (Num. 24:4). In the story of God's call to young Samuel the narrator comments, "Now Samuel did not yet know Yahweh, and the word of Yahweh had not yet been revealed to him" (1 Sam. 3:7); but later on he notes, "Yahweh appeared again at Shiloh, for Yahweh revealed himself to Samuel at Shiloh by the word of Yahweh" (1 Sam. 3:21).

When God makes a covenant with David and his lineage, David declares, "For you, O Yahweh of hosts, the God of Israel, have uncovered the ear of your servant, saying, 'I will build you a house [or, dynasty]'" (2 Sam. 7:27). Isaiah the prophet claimed, "Yahweh of hosts has revealed himself in my ears" (Isa. 22:14), and this explicit affirmation of all the prophets is summed up in the conviction of Amos, "For the Lord Yahweh does nothing without revealing his secret [or, plans] to his servants the prophets" (Amos 3:7).

It is an interesting fact that eight of the twenty-three occurences of *galah* (in the sense of revelation) appear in the book of Daniel, and seven of these in chapter 2. Here the stress is on the secret interpretation of Nebuchadnezzar's dream, a prediction of "what will be in the latter days" (2:28). After the key to the dream has been made known, the king exclaims to Daniel, "Your God is indeed God of gods and Lord of lords and a revealer of secrets [or, mysteries], for you have been able to reveal this secret" (2:47).

The New Testament (NT) equivalent of *galah* is the Greek verb *apokaluptō* ("to uncover, disclose, reveal"), which occurs twenty-six times. After Peter's confession at Caesarea Philippi that Jesus is the Christ, Jesus explains, "Blessed are you, Simon Bar-Jona, for flesh and blood have not revealed this to you, but my Father who is in heaven" (Matt. 16:17).

While the OT has no derivative noun from *galah*, the NT has the noun *apokalupsis* ("revelation"), which occurs eighteen times. Concerning the gospel he preaches, Paul affirms, "I did not receive it from man, nor was I taught it. But it came through a revelation of Jesus Christ" (Gal. 1:12). He states that he went up to Jerusalem the second time "by revelation" (Gal. 2:2). In discussing the issue of speaking in tongues Paul informs the Corinthians that his speaking in tongues would mean nothing without an interpretation resulting in "some revelation or knowledge or prophecy or teaching" (1 Cor. 14:6). In the church at Corinth, moreover, the various members have "a hymn, a lesson, a revelation, a tongue, or an interpretation" (1 Cor. 14:26). "God is not a God of confusion, but of peace," Paul declares; thus in order that there may be genuine edification for all, he urges that they speak "one by one." Accordingly, if a revelation comes to someone seated, then the one who has the floor is to yield to the one with the new insight (1 Cor. 14:30).

The NT counterpart to Daniel, where revelation is depicted as a forecast of future events, is the book of Revelation: "The revelation of Jesus Christ, given to him by God in order that he might show his servants what must happen shortly" (1:1).

Terms and Expressions Associated with Revelation

While it is recognized that the terms "to reveal" and "revelation" are relatively sparse, considering the extensive amount of material in the Bible, there are numerous terms and expressions associated with the idea of revelation. As noted earlier, one of these is "secret, mystery." During and after the exile in Babylonia, a number of Jews despaired of expecting God's redemptive activity in the normal course of history. For them the only hope was the culmination of the age, when God would fulfil his promises to his people and restore justice and peace. Although "secret" (Heb.

sod) in Amos 3:7 seems to refer to God's redemptive plans in the course of history, the concept came increasingly to signify the hidden purpose of God concerning the last days, and so in Daniel 2 the "secret" (Aram. *raz*) is a prediction of what God will do at the end of the age.

In the NT the term *musterion* (from which the English word "mystery" derives) occurs twenty-seven or twenty-eight times. In answering the disciples' question "Why do you speak to them in parables?" Jesus remarks, "It has been given to you to know the secrets [mysteries] of the kingdom of heaven" (Matt. 13:11). Paul speaks of his gospel as being "the revelation of the mystery which was kept secret for long ages" (Rom. 16:25). This secret (mystery), made known by the Spirit, is Paul's insight that "the Gentiles are fellow heirs [with the Jews], members of the same body, and sharers of the promise in Christ Jesus" (Eph. 3:6). The "mystery of the faith" (1 Tim. 3:9) and "mystery of our religion" (3:16) clearly refer to the apostolic teaching about Christ as the newly revealed content of faith.

Another way of expressing the idea of revelation was the verb "to manifest, show oneself" (Gk. *phaneroō*) and its related noun "manifestation." Jesus was God "manifested in the flesh" (1 Tim. 3:16), "made manifest at the end of the times" (1 Pet. 1:20). In 1 John 1:2 the author declares, "The life was made manifest and we saw it." The various gifts of the Christians at Corinth were "the manifestation of the Spirit" (1 Cor. 12:7). During the years in the wilderness God made himself known to the Israelites by means of a cloud (Heb. *anan*, Ex. 40:38). The more original meaning of the term was "manifestation," and so the cloud was thought of as "the manifestation of Yahweh."

Yet another term associated with revelation is "glory." A cloud, as "the glory of Yahweh," appeared in the wilderness (Ex. 16:10). Also it settled on Mt. Sinai (Ex. 24:16). Yahweh spoke of his plagues on the Egyptians as being "my glory and my signs" (Num. 14:22). Thus God's acts in behalf of his people were signs of his glory. According to the psalmist, "The heavens declare the glory of

God" (Ps. 19:1). In his vision in the temple Isaiah heard the seraphim chanting, "Holy, holy, holy is Yahweh of hosts. The whole earth is full of his glory" (Isa. 6:3). The theme of Yahweh's glory appears many times in the OT, and it carries over as a dominant idea in the NT: "So the Word became flesh and dwelt among us, full of grace and truth. We have seen his glory, glory befitting the Father's only son" (John 1:14).

In Psalm 29:2 the psalmist exhorts, "Ascribe to Yahweh the glory of his name." It was a well-known tradition among the Israelites that the name "Yahweh," most likely meaning "He causes [all things] to be," was made known to Moses by revelation at the burning bush (Ex. 3:15). In another context God says to Moses, "I appeared to Abraham, to Isaac, and to Jacob as El Shadday [God Almighty], but by my name Yahweh I did not make myself known to them" (Ex. 6:3). In the ancient Near East a name was thought to express the character of the person bearing it. From the times of Moses, therefore, "Yahweh" became the personal designation for the creative, sovereign God of Israel. From this name developed the idea of God's universal control. "It is he who sits enthroned on the vaulted roof of the earth whose inhabitants are like grasshoppers. He stretches out the skies like a curtain and spreads them like a tent to dwell in. He brings princes to nothing, and makes the earth's rulers as nothing" (Isa. 40:22-23). "Have you not known, have you not heard? Yahweh is the everlasting God, the Creator of the limits of the earth. He neither faints nor grows weary. His understanding is unsearchable" (Isa. 40:28).

Even the names of God's servants and their children could convey God's message and point to his glory. "Isaiah" (meaning "Yahweh is salvation") and his sons "Shear-jashub" ("A remnant shall return") and "Mahershalal-hash-baz" ("The spoil speeds, the plunder hastens") were walking sermons because of their names. Accordingly, Isaiah could say, "I and the children whom Yahweh has given me are signs and portents in Israel" (Isa. 8:18).

Luke 8:20 informs us that Jesus, on meeting the Gerasene demoniac, asked him, "What is your name?" He replied, "Legion," because many demons had entered him. Jesus, praying to God, says, "I have manifested your name to the men you have given me out of the world" (John 17:6). He could do this because, as he claimed to Philip, he had a unique relationship with God: "He who has seen me has seen the Father" (John 14:9). In speaking about God's judgment Joel states, "All who call upon the name of Yahweh shall be delivered [saved]" (2:32), and Paul quotes the passage in Romans 10:13. In numerous other passages "the name" is associated with God's communication of himself.

One of the most commonly used terms in expressing the concept of revelation is the verb "to know" (Heb. *yada*, Gk. *ginōskō*). Throughout the Bible it is a comprehensive word including both experiential and factual knowledge. On being confronted by Moses, Pharaoh retorts, "Who is Yahweh, that I should obey him and let Israel go? I do not know Yahweh" (Ex. 5:2). From that moment the showdown struggle between Pharaoh and Moses becomes Yahweh's school for instructing both the Israelites and the Egyptians. Yahweh promises, "I will take you for my people and I will be your God. You shall know that I am Yahweh, your God" (Ex. 6:7). Moreover, Yahweh declares, "The Egyptians shall know that I am Yahweh when I extend my hand [power] over Egypt and bring out the Israelites from among them" (Ex. 7:5).

The experience of knowing another person always results in some factual knowledge whether the participants formulate it explicitly or not. A favorite expression of the prophets for designating this content of experience is "the word of Yahweh": "Hear the word of Yahweh, you rulers of Sodom! Listen to the teaching [Heb. *torah*] of our God, you people of Gomorrah!" (Isa. 1:10). *Torah*, often translated "law" in the older versions, has the broader meaning of "teaching, instruction": "For instruction comes from Zion and the word of Yahweh out of Jerusalem" (Isa. 2:3). The eternal authority of God's revelation is affirmed in Isaiah 40:8, "The grass withers, the flower fades, but the word of our God endures forever." In his desire to experience God's revelation, one of the psalmists implores, "Make your ways known to me, O Yahweh. Teach me your paths" (Ps. 25:4).

There are a number of other terms associated with the concept of revelation. Beyond the nouns noted above ("revelation, word, teaching, name, glory, prediction, wisdom, manifestation, and path or way"), there are numerous biblical examples where the following nouns are used to express the idea of revelation: "commandment, announcement, proclamation, promise, knowledge, counsel, truth, tradition, testimony, covenant, appearance, and light." Over and above the verbs "to reveal, prophesy, foretell, speak, and know," there are examples of the verbs "to appear, lead (guide), open, shine, bear witness, promise, and proclaim." The fact that so many terms and expressions are used to describe the biblical idea of revelation is an indication of both the complexity of the concept and the tenacity with which it was held throughout the various periods of biblical history. The author of the book of Hebrews was certainly correct when he claimed that God had spoken "in many and various ways" (1:1).

Channels of Revelation

God employed many different channels, as well as ways, in communicating his message. A classic passage is Jeremiah 18:18: "Come, let us plot against Jeremiah because instruction shall not perish from the priest, nor counsel from the wise, nor the word from the prophet." In a similar vein Ezekiel 7:26 notes, "They seek a vision from the prophet, but instruction perishes from the priest, and counsel from the elders." These verses indicate that by late seventh century B.C. the traditional concept of God's revelation was threefold: (1) the prophet with "the word" and "visions"; (2) the priest with "instruction" concerning God's teaching or law; and (3) the wise man or elder with "counsel."

Concerning the regular prophet God states, "I, Yahweh, make myself known to him in a vision, I speak with him in a dream" (Num. 12:6). Yahweh even "put a word" in the mouth of Balaam, the Syrian seer (Num. 23:5). Moses, however, was a special kind of prophet, and when Aaron and Miriam challenged his authority Yahweh said, "With him I speak clearly, mouth to mouth" (Num. 14:8). In the intimate call of Jeremiah, Yahweh touches his mouth, explaining, "I have put my words in your mouth" (Jer. 1:9). Time and again the prophets claim, "The word of Yahweh came to me," or "Thus says Yahweh." They have an absolute conviction that their messages come from Yahweh.

The priests also claimed that the regulations concerning the ritual and cult were given by God (Lev. 1:1). In addition to his sacrificial duties the priest was to instruct the people (Deut. 33:10; 2 Chron. 17:8-9). In crucial situations the chief priest was to ascertain the will of God by the "Urim and Thummim" (Num. 27:21; Deut. 33:8; 1 Sam. 28:6). Moreover, the levitical priests, along with the judges, held court at times by interpreting the case law and passing sentence (Deut. 17:8-9). In some degree all of these functions of the priest involve God's special guidance.

While the Israelite wise man or elder seldom claims that his insights come directly from Yahweh, it is implicit that God does reveal himself in the practical affairs of life. This basic assumption is made explicit in Proverbs 2:6: "For Yahweh gives wisdom. Knowledge and understanding come from his mouth." It is felt that the experience of the covenant relationship with Yahweh adds a depth of insight not plumbed in the wisdom of neighboring cultures: "Awe of Yahweh is the beginning of knowledge [wisdom]" (Prov. 1:7; 9:10).

Whereas the most prominent channel of revelation in the OT was the prophet, his NT counterpart was the apostle. It was quite natural that those persons specially called and trained by Jesus would exercise the greatest authority in the church. According to Paul, the priority of roles performed by members of the church was: apostles, prophets, teachers, miracle-workers, healers, helpers, administrators, and speakers in tongues (1 Cor. 12:28). Although there is a difference in rank, the first three roles pertain to the teaching ministry and each is considered as a channel of revelation.

Judaism defined the close of the Hebrew canon as the time when the spirit of prophecy ceased to function. The moving of the Spirit of God in the early church reinstated the role of the prophet. Some prophets from Jerusalem visited Antioch and "one of them named Agabus stood up and predicted by the Spirit that there would be a great famine over all the world. This took place in the days of Claudius" (Acts 11:28). Apparently the same Agabus came down from Judea to the home of Philip the evangelist in Caesarea, where Paul was staying. After tying Paul's hands and feet with Paul's own belt, he predicted in the name of the Holy Spirit that the Jews in Jerusalem would arrest Paul and turn him over to the Gentiles (Acts 21:11).

This role of short-range prediction picked up one of the facets of the classical OT prophets. About 735 B.C. Isaiah assured Ahaz that before the child Immanuel would know how to distinguish good from evil, the territory of Rezin, king of Damascus, and Pekah, king of Israel, would be devastated (Isa. 7:16). Within three years Tiglath-pileser III overran Syria and the northern part of Israel, thus bringing to pass the prediction of Isaiah. In the struggle to authenticate his word against that of the false prophet Hananiah, Jeremiah predicted that Hananiah would die within a year (Jer. 28:16), and his word came true in two months (Jer. 28:1, 17).

The role of the teacher in the NT is not spelled out in detail, but in all likelihood it was similar to the teaching ministry of the priests. He probably instructed church members about the OT and its role in preparing for Jesus Christ. Most certainly he taught the apostolic tradition about Jesus, and quite possibly he had a share in interpreting the gospel and making it relevant to the local conditions of the church in question.

The Range and Means of Revelation

In some cases the channel of revelation is not conscious of any rational effort on his part and the message is attributed completely to Yahweh. At the burning bush, for example, Yahweh communicated his message directly to Moses (Ex. 3:2-17). In one tradition Moses is credited with writing the Decalogue on the tablets of stone (Ex. 34:28), but another tradition claims that the tablets were "written with the finger of God" (Ex. 31:18). Moses undoubtedly inscribed the tablets, but the tradition that God wrote them is valid in the sense that Moses was conscious of such help in formulating the Ten Commandments that he felt God's finger had guided him.

But in the attempt to live by the Decalogue, the stipulations of the covenant, there arose the need for interpretations and setting of guidelines. When situations required further information about God's will, Moses resorted to the tent of meeting, and there Yahweh spoke to him "face to face, as a man speaks to his friend" (Ex. 33:11). In due time these decisions grew into a collection of case law. At the renewal of the covenant at Shechem this corpus was updated by Joshua in order to make the Ten Commandments more applicable to the situation in Canaan (Josh. 24:25-26). This process continued in the period of the judges and carried over into the monarchy.

The later prophets, like their great predecessor Moses, often felt that their messages came directly from Yahweh. At times, however, the insights were triggered by events and objects of everyday life. Out of the despair and tragedy of his marriage, Hosea was given an insight into Yahweh's covenant love for his people Israel. Amos saw a mason building a wall with a plumb line and received Yahweh's word, "I am setting a plumb line in the midst of my people Israel" (Amos 7:8). A "boiling pot" being poured toward the south was the occasion for Yahweh's message to Jeremiah that evil would come over the people from the north (Jer. 1:14). While visiting the potter's house, Jeremiah learned of Yahweh's intent concerning Israel (Jer. 18:3-11). A basket of good figs in front of the temple became a symbol of the exiles to Babylonia, while the basket of bad figs characterized those who stayed on in Judah or would go to Egypt (Jer. 24:1-10).

After the destruction of the temple in 587/6 B.C., the

idea of God's immanence was dealt a severe blow. More and more God was envisioned as remote and otherworldly. In this excessive stress on transcendence the chasm between God and man became so great that some of the postexilic prophets believed that God communicated his message by means of heavenly messengers. Zechariah, for example, refers constantly to "the messenger [angel] who talked with me" (Zech. 1:1, 13, 14, 19; 2:3, etc.).

As noted above, the insights of the wise seldom claim to be the direct words of Yahweh, and yet the experience of living in covenant relationship with Yahweh is basic to receiving words of counsel. Thus even the understanding gained from the practical aspects of life is credited ultimately to the help of Yahweh.

The Biblical Concept of Revelation

In discussing the idea of revelation James Barr states, "In the Bible, however, the usage of the terms which roughly correspond to 'revelation' is both limited and specialized. . . . Thus there is little basis in the Bible for the use of 'revelation' as a general term for man's source of knowledge of God, or for all real communication from God to man."[2] His conclusion is possible because of his limited definition of revelation: "Previously I did not know God, but now (since this incident or speech) he is known or revealed to me."[3] "It is the absence of this kind of approach," according to Barr, "which makes the revelational model doubtful for application to the Old Testament; and, we may add, to the New Testament also, for even the coming of Christ does not produce the kind of statement which I have just cited. The coming of Christ, like the Old Testament incidents, is a further (and amazing) act of one who is known; it is not a first disclosure of one who is not known."[4]

On the other hand, Barr admits that "it is not easy to

2. *Old and New in Interpretation*, p. 88.
3. *Ibid.*, p. 82.
4. *Ibid.*

develop a different term which will say what used to be said by 'revelation' "; therefore he does not "strictly avoid the use of 'revelation,' " but he treats it in a loose way as an equivalent of communication.[5]

"My argument," Barr declares, "is not against the word 'revelation', but against the way in which the use of this word has grouped together a number of different things in a way that does not suit them and so distorts them."[6] Yet this is precisely the problem posed by the biblical evidence. The solution is not to discount the data by an arbitrary definition of revelation. Rather, the inductive method demands that we analyze and distinguish as carefully as we can the various ways by which, according to the biblical writers, God made himself known and communicated his message to man. Admittedly there are the difficulties of evaluation of the claims and of classification of the various levels of revelation, but these will be considered in the next chapter. For the moment, however, it is absolutely clear that practically all theological insights in Scripture are attributed to God or his Spirit. The claim is explicit in the case of the prophets, where the message is perceived directly by means of their ears, eyes, and lips, or delivered to them by messengers, and it is implicit in wisdom where the insight comes in the context of a life in covenant relation with Yahweh.

5. *Ibid.*, p. 86.
6. *Ibid.*

Chapter Two

Scripture as Revelation

While it is evident that the idea of revelation pervades the Bible, it is necessary to examine various aspects of the concept and to understand how these relate to Scripture.

Revelation and Discovery

The basic biblical claim is that man did not think his way to the solution of his problem. On the contrary, God made it known to him. For the secular scholar, the idea of a personal God who created mankind and made his will known to his creatures is beyond his present capacity to believe, and the thought of fellowship with such a God is outside his realm of experience. In his judgment, therefore, the biblical claim is not in accord with reality. Rather, man *discovers* what is already in the nature of things.

There are differences within Christian churches, and some more conservative groups interpret these differences as irreconcilable, but the really unabridgeable chasm is that between the theistic claims of Christianity and the non-theistic or atheistic views of secular humanism. The "God-is-dead" movement went so far as to proclaim a doctrine of "Christian atheism," yet the mental juggling involved in trying to harmonize these contradictory terms resulted in a redefinition of the appropriated term "Christian."

Notwithstanding the opinions of Nietzsche, Marx, and their successors, this writer shares the conviction of Donald G. Miller, "An examination of the history of the race would seem to suggest that the outcomes have been better when men lived on the assumption of the existence of God than when they assumed the opposite."[1] While neither side of this crucial dispute can claim rational proof for its position, there are some indications that secularism has not disposed of theism.

Even in the realm of science, supposedly the most perfectly objective aspect of modern life, the "discovery" of reality has a nonrational element. Concerning the scientic revolution, Edwin A. Burtt comments, "One of the most curious and exasperating features of this whole magnificent movement is that none of its great representatives appears to have known with satisfying clarity just what he was doing or how he was doing it."[2] In a very instructive book, *The Sleepwalkers*, Arthur Koestler wrestles with "the psychological process of discovery" and finds that both faith and reason are involved. His study counteracts "the legend that Science is a purely rational pursuit, that the Scientist is a more 'level-headed' and 'dispassionate' type than others (and should therefore be given a leading part in world affairs); or that he is able to provide for himself and his contemporaries, a rational substitute for ethical insights derived from other sources."[3] Koestler elaborates:

> The progress of Science is generally regarded as a kind of clean, rational advance along a straight ascending line; in fact it has followed a zig-zag course, at times almost more bewildering than the evolution of political thought. The history of cosmic theories, in particular, may without exaggeration be called a history of collective obsessions and controlled schizophrenias; and the

1. *The Authority of the Bible*, p. 18.
2. *The Metaphysical Foundations of Modern Physical Science*, p. 203.
3. *The Sleepwalkers*, p. 15.

manner in which some of the most important individual discoveries were arrived at reminds one more of a sleepwalker's performance than an electronic brain's.[4]

A prime example is Johannes Kepler (1571-1630), the famous astronomer-mathematician. On July 9, 1595, while conducting a class in mathematics, he was suddenly struck with the idea that the universe was built around symmetrical figures such as triangles, squares, pentagons, etc. He was delighted beyond words with his "discovery," and the next year, when he was twenty-five, he published it in *Mysterium Cosmographicum*, his first book on astronomy. Inasmuch as he had been reared and trained in theological circles, he attributed this "chance" insight to divine Providence, and he spent the rest of his life trying to prove his idea. When he was fifty, he published a second edition of *Mysterium Cosmographicum*. In the dedication he expressed the feeling that the original manuscript had come as though dictated to him by "a heavenly oracle." The irony is that Kepler's "discovery" was completely false, and yet his strange blend of religion and science led eventually, as Koestler notes, "to Kepler's Laws, the demolition of the antique universe on wheels, and the birth of modern cosmology."[5]

Unlike Kepler, Isaac Newton (1642-1727) did not record for posterity the various steps that led to his law of gravity, but somehow he arrived at a new synthesis in which the scientific insights of his predecessors were seen as parts of a more comprehensive whole. Building on the work of Newton, Albert Einstein (1879-1955) developed the theory of relativity to account for his insights into the complexity of the universe. His famous formula $E=mc^2$ led to the development of nuclear power, but his claim to have found the key to a unified field theory has not proven true. The next synthesis is of such immense complexity that no scientist has yet been able to comprehend its vast sweep. When this insight comes, as it will, the secularist will give sole credit for the discovery to the genius quality

4. *Ibid.*
5. *Ibid.*, p. 247.

of the human mind. But is it not equally possible that the Creator of this awesome universe and its geniuses is playing a part in the intuitions of truths about our physical world?

In the arts the intuitive aspect plays an even more conspicuous role. At times compositions sprang full-blown into the consciousness of Beethoven, and they came with such rapidity that he could hardly copy the notes fast enough. How does one account for such a phenomenon? Beethoven did not attribute it to the inspiration of God as Handel had done after the composition of his oratorio *Messiah*, but this does not rule out the possibility that the Creator who endowed Beethoven with his enormous gifts used him as a channel for contributing to the totality of truth and beauty.

The secularist denies this possibility, yet his dogma cannot claim authority because he does not comprehend the totality of ultimate reality. Inasmuch as those associated with the most far-reaching insights of mankind have been at a loss to explain their findings in completely rational terms, it is evident that there is a "plus" in such moments of intuition. Working from the assumption that ultimate reality is of one piece, that all facets of truth when seen in proper perspective are complementary, this author frankly attributes this "plus" to a personal God communicating with his creatures.

The Uniqueness of Biblical Revelation

However meaningful the general revelations of God through nature and his creatures may be, they do not speak to man's crucial condition—his sin, guilt, and need of forgiveness. Thoughtful men of all cultures have dealt with mankind's problems and various solutions have been proposed. It is the conviction of Christianity, however, that God made himself and his will known in a special way through ancient Israel and finally through Jesus Christ. In the present context of congeniality any reference to uniqueness is likely to be viewed as an impropriety stemming from pride. But regardless of how one accounts for the fact, it is indisputable that Israel came to a level of moral, ethical insight that none of her neighbors achieved.

In a period of inspiration at Mt. Sinai, Moses realized that the treaty form used by the Hittite suzerains with their vassal kings was an analogy of Yahweh's sovereign care for his people Israel. Accordingly, a covenant between Yahweh and Israel was confirmed with the Ten Commandments as the stipulations of obedience. The first commandment, with its demand of exclusive worship and implicit prohibition of apostasy, was unique in the realm of religion in that, as the other commandments show, it went beyond the solar monotheism of Amenophis IV (Akhenaton). The next two commandments (prohibition against images of Yahweh and the stricture against the misuse of his name) were equally unique. The idea of a sabbath was known centuries before Moses, but his insight was distinctive in that every seventh day was Yahweh's day and to be devoted to him. The remaining six commandments have similarity with ideas of earlier periods in Mesopotamia and Egypt, but they were raised to a new level of moral insight when they were stated in the context of Yahweh's covenant with Israel.

Discoveries are often made independently by persons within groups at the same level of intellectual and spiritual development. Since the components for most of the Ten Commandments were at hand, theoretically the other peoples of the ancient Near East could have come to the same insights as Moses, but in fact they did not! The crucial difference was Yahweh's revelation of himself. Moses was a brilliant person, yet were it not for his understanding of Yahweh as the holy, moral sovereign over all the earth and all the nations, there would have been no Decalogue and the subsequent history of Yahweh's covenant with Israel.

In its conviction that Jesus represented the hopes of Israel, Christianity goes beyond the claim of Judaism. Again, the present trend is to soft-pedal this affirmation, but the experience of the church has authenticated the claims of Jesus, "I am the way, and the truth, and the life. No one comes to the Father, but by me" (John 14:6) and

"He who has seen me has seen the Father" (John 14:9). Many in the church push these claims with an arrogance that belies the very spirit of the Christ they profess to serve, but such excesses do not discount the necessity of proclaiming the uniqueness of Jesus with love and humility. In essence, biblical revelation deals with man's relation to God and its main concern is redemptive—to make new creatures and a new world. Those who discount the biblical claims (on the grounds that they are either too chauvinistic or not relevant) do so at their own peril. "As the Scriptures recede," James D. Smart correctly observes, "the unique nature and reality of God as Father, Son, and Holy Spirit, is forgotten and is replaced by some other conception of God that is only vaguely Christian."[6]

Søren Kierkegaard and Existentialism

In order to understand more fully the complexity of the term "revelation," it will be instructive to survey the rise of existentialism and its interaction with Orthodoxy. The spearhead of this new approach was Søren Kierkegaard (1813-1855) of Copenhagen, Denmark. When at seventeen he entered the University of Copenhagen, one of the towering figures of the intellectual world was Georg Hegel (1770-1831). But the pantheism and rationalism of this German philosopher only frustrated Søren's quest for a warm, dynamic relationship with God. Abstract speculation or reason could never find God, Kierkegaard affirmed, because there is an "infinite qualitative difference" between time (man's realm) and eternity (God's realm). Finite mankind is incapable of knowing the divine, infinite, utterly transcendent God unless the latter breaks in upon him by spanning the gulf.

According to Kierkegaard, God, in taking the initiative, reveals himself through a continuous series of crises. At each "encounter" or "confrontation" man is faced with an *either-or:* either he yields his whole being to God or he bears the responsibility of rejecting God's claim on him.

6. *The Interpretation of Scripture,* p. 228.

Knowledge comes at this moment of confrontation—it can never come through human reason. It is readily apparent why Kierkegaard rejected the cold ritualism and intellectual stress on doctrine that characterized the National Church in Denmark at this time. Its impersonal nature, he discerned, was due to the idea that God, Christ, and the Scriptures were *objects* to be examined, pondered over, and finally assented to. Christianity for Kierkegaard meant something within his being. Faith was a subjective leap made against anything human reason could furnish.

This contrast between objectivity and subjectivity was basic to all of Kierkegaard's thought. Because, according to him, no person could do both at the same time, the situation was an eternal *either-or*. His definition of essential truth (the truth that is essentially related to existence) is as follows: "When the question of truth is raised in an objective manner, reflection is directed objectively to the truth, as an object to which the knower is related. Reflection is not focused upon the relationship, however, but upon the question of whether it is the truth to which the knower is related. If only the object to which he is related is the truth, the subject is accounted to be in the truth. When the question of the truth is raised subjectively, reflection is directed subjectively to the nature of the individual's relationship; if only the mode of this relationship is in the truth, the individual is in the truth even if he should happen to be thus related to what is not true."[7] He expresses his theme in the summary statement, *"The objective accent falls on WHAT is said, the subjective accent on HOW it is said."*[8]

In discussing the relative merits of the two approaches to truth, he writes: "Now when the problem is to reckon up on which side there is most truth, whether on the side of one who seeks the true God objectively, and pursues the approximate truth of the God-idea; or on the side of one who, driven by the infinite passion of his need of God, feels an infinite concern for his own relationship to God in

7. *Concluding Unscientific Postscript*, p. 178.
8. *Ibid.*, p. 181. Italics his.

truth (and to be at one and the same time on both sides equally, is as we have noted not possible for an existing individual, but is merely the happy delusion of an imaginary I-am-I): the answer cannot be in doubt for anyone who has not been demoralized with the aid of science. If one who lives in the midst of Christendom goes up to the house of God, the house of the true God, with the true conception of God in his knowledge, and prays, but prays in a false spirit; and one who lives in an idolatrous community prays with the entire passion of the infinite, although his eyes rest upon the image of an idol: where is there most truth? The one prays in truth to God though he worships an idol; the other prays falsely to the true God, and hence worships in fact an idol."[9] The references to "Christendom," "house of God," and praying "in a false spirit" are scars of the bitter disappointment he experienced in the church. A heathen praying passionately to an idol, "what is not true," is actually "in the truth." This is the extreme to which the stagnant Danish Church drove the warmhearted Kierkegaard. There is certainly some truth in this reaction, for "man looks on the outward appearance, but the LORD looks on the heart" (1 Sam. 16:7). God will have more mercy on heathen with sincerity of heart than on hypocrites who frequent churches on Sunday for reasons of business or status.

However, Kierkegaard's views did not take hold in any great way during the nineteenth and early twentieth centuries. The liberalism of Schleiermacher, Ritschl, and Harnack, with its naive optimism in the innate goodness and moral perfectibility of man, was too appealing. But when this fantasy was shattered by the shells of World War I, the mood began to change—the time was ripe for the insights of Søren Kierkegaard. While existentialism became the new frontier of thought, it took on many diverse interpretations: the Russian Orthodox Nicholas Berdyaev (1874-1948); the Jew Martin Buber (1878-1965); the German philosopher Martin Heidegger (1889-   ), whose non-Christian approach found full atheistic expression in his

9. *Ibid.*, pp. 179-180.

student, the Frenchman Jean-Paul Sartre (1905-   ); the German Lutheran Rudolf Bultmann (1884-   ), who, although indebted to Heidegger, remained within the Christian context; the Swiss Reformed theologian Karl Barth (1886-1969); and his Swiss colleague Emil Brunner (1889-1966).

Barth and Brunner were the most orthodox of the existentialists, and until the 1960's they had the greatest influence on the thinking of the church. Their interpretation of existentialism has been known as "the New Reformation Theology," or more popularly "Neo-orthodoxy," because of its return to some traditional themes. The emphasis on crisis and decision gave rise to the designation "Crisis Theology." The method of expressing truths by a series of paradoxes or apparently contradictory statements evoked the title "Dialectical Theology."

Orthodoxy and Doctrine

"Orthodoxy," a term derived from the Greek word *orthodoxos* (*orthos*, "straight, upright" plus *doxa*, "opinion, thinking"), has been used to designate that portion of the church which has defined revelation primarily in terms of teaching or doctrine. Orthodoxy has not been ignorant of God's historical acts, but correct doctrine has been considered to be the ultimate criterion of a Christian.

This emphasis on teaching has some basis in the Old Testament, especially with respect to the law. Moses is commanded to teach Israel commandments, statutes, and ordinances (Ex. 24:12; Deut. 6:1), and this teaching ministry is in turn assigned to the priests (Lev. 10:11; Deut. 33:10). The primary purpose of this teaching is obedience and correct practice (orthopraxy) rather than correct doctrine (orthodoxy).

The clearest exhortations in behalf of correct doctrine come from the later books of the New Testament: "All scripture is inspired by God and profitable for teaching" (2 Tim. 3:16); "For the time is coming when people will not endure sound teaching" (2 Tim. 4:3); "Therefore rebuke them sharply, that they may be sound in the faith" (Titus

1:13); "But as for you, teach what befits sound doctrine" (Titus 2:1); "So that in everything they may adorn the doctrine of God our Savior" (Titus 2:10); "To contend for the faith which was once for all delivered to the saints" (Jude 3).

It is quite evident why this stress on doctrine, a package of truth called "the faith," became so prominent as the church expanded. While the Lord was still with the disciples, the outstanding feature was the vitality of his fellowship with them. This was also true of Saul in those first years after he yielded himself to the Lord on the way to Damascus. Later on, however, the apostles, with opposition on all sides, felt compelled to give greater attention to matters of content and doctrine. Many different ideas were afloat, both inside and outside the early church, and there were men with missionary zeal to promote them. Since Christ was gone, the next most authoritative source was the apostles, and in meeting the challenge of these new ideas they appealed to their experiences of fellowship and instruction with Jesus. As time widened the gap between the ascension and the expanding church, the essential core of teaching crystallized into "the faith." The early church fathers considered it their primary task to carry on the struggle against heresies, and so their writings consist largely of *apologia*, "defense" of the gospel.

Following the Reformation in 1517 and the accompanying spiritual awakening, the young Protestant Church, not unlike the early church, found itself confronted with antagonists on all sides—the Roman Catholic Church as well as the secular world of science and philosophy. In its desperate fight for existence, doctrine became the chief weapon. During the seventeenth century—a century filled with wars and characterized by hatred and unbridled attacks against any and all opponents—the Protestant theologians often fought viciously, trying to maintain the truth of God. What they failed to see was that *love*, the greatest and most powerful force in God's Kingdom, was itself a part of doctrine, and that no defense of doctrine, however sincere, could really please God unless it was done in love.

The Reaction to Doctrine

It seems to be a law of nature that extremes beget extremes, and so undue emphasis on doctrine brought forth a decided reaction that tended to repudiate all doctrine. According to this view, the early emphasis in the New Testament was "believe in," an expression of dynamic personal faith. This was also true of Paul, with his favorite expression "in Christ." Later on, the emphasis was "believe that"; for example, Hebrews 11:6, "For whoever would draw near to God must believe that he exists and that he rewards those who seek him." To "believe that," so it is affirmed, was spiritual degradation from the early fellowship, which said "believe in."

The classic expression of this viewpoint was made by Archbishop William Temple in his Gifford Lectures, *Nature, Man and God.* "The primary fact concerning revelation in its essence," writes Temple, "is that it is a personal self-disclosure to persons, and has authority as such." [10] The late Scottish theologian John Baillie explains further: "All revelation, then, is from subject to subject, and the revelation with which we are here concerned is from the divine Subject to the human. But there is a further distinction that must be drawn. We speak, as has been said, of a man's revealing himself, that is, his character and mind and will, to his fellow, but we also sometimes speak of a man's revealing to his fellow certain items of knowledge other than knowledge of himself. . . . According to the Bible, what is revealed to us is not a body of information concerning various things of which we might otherwise be ignorant. If it is information at all, it is information concerning the nature and mind and purpose of God—that and nothing else. Yet in the last resort it is not information about God that is revealed, but very God himself incarnate in Jesus Christ our Lord." [11]

10. *Nature, Man and God*, p. 354.
11. *The Idea of Revelation in Recent Thought*, pp. 27, 28. Quotations from this book are used by permission of the publisher, Columbia University Press.

In a similar vein, C. H. Dodd, the Cambridge University scholar, writes: "Jesus was primarily concerned not with delivering 'doctrine,' but with making men anew, so that they could receive the revelation of himself which God is always seeking to communicate. Similarly, the most important thing we find in the Bible is not 'doctrine' but something that helps us into a new attitude to God and to life."[12] Brunner expresses this point of view as follows: "In the time of the apostles, as in that of the Old Testament prophets, 'divine revelation' always meant the whole of the divine activity for the salvation of the world, the whole story of God's saving acts, of the 'acts of God' which reveal God's nature and his will, above all, him in whom the preceding revelation gains its meaning, and who therefore is its fulfillment: Jesus Christ. He himself is the Revelation. Divine revelation is not a book or a doctrine; the Revelation is God himself in his self-manifestation within history."[13] Baillie was certainly correct when he observed that this concept of revelation "is the first thing we notice as running broadly throughout all the recent discussions, marking them off from the formulations of earlier periods."[14]

Two Kinds of Truth

Basic to an understanding of this qualitative distinction between revelation and doctrine is the recognition that there are two different kinds of truth: objective and subjective. Objective truth is rational truth that has to do with "things" or "objects"—not only *concrete* things found in the material world all about us but also *abstract* things in the realm of ideas, values, laws, and culture. Since it is ascertained by means of reason, and thus impersonal in nature, objective truth is referred to as "it-truth."

Subjective truth, on the other hand, is personal because it involves the heart and happens only between persons. The difference between the two kinds of truth is quite

12. *The Authority of the Bible*, p. 294.
13. *Revelation and Reason*, p. 8.
14. Baillie, *op. cit.*, p. 29.

evident even on the level of human love. One can read love stories and understand the psychology of love, but this rational knowledge or "it-truth" can never be the "thou-truth" that two people in love experience.

The qualitative gap between objective and subjective truth is much clearer, however, when it comes to the realm of man's spiritual needs. Here the "thou" of true love between husband and wife, or the "thou" of true brotherly love, is ineffectual. As Brunner observes, "the 'thou' of my fellow man cannot give me what I need, because he is only my—equally poor—fellow self. He cannot give me the truth which is life, because he possesses only the truth that I also possess."[15]

A rational knowledge about God is not the answer either, because it is not the true "Thou" that makes me a new creature in Christ. With respect to thoughts about God, Brunner comments: "Even God is here part of *my* rational world, in which I am the center; even he is the *Object* of my knowledge. It is true that I think of him as Subject, as the absolute Subject; but I myself am the subject of this thought; it is *my* thought; I introduce God into the world of my thought. Nothing happens that breaks through the circle of my self-isolation. I am alone with my truth, even with my idea of God. The God whom I think, is not the one who really confronts me."[16] He explains this "it-truth" more fully as follows: "All the transcendence that I think out for myself is only transcendence within immanence; all that I describe as *thou* within this my world of immanence is only 'thou-within-the-world-of-the-self.' This world of immanence, in spite of all the variety that takes place within it, is at bottom a static system. No real communication takes place. God does not communicate himself because I simply think *about* God, and that is all."[17]

One should not imply, however, that "it-truth" is untrue. God as creator is responsible for all truth. There is objective truth because God is also concerned with the

15. Brunner, *op. cit.*, p. 367.
16. *Ibid.*, p. 366. Italics his.
17. *Ibid.*, p. 367. Italics his.

impersonal realm of things and objects, but to appropriate rational truth is not to experience newness of life. The distinctiveness of "Thou-truth" is clearly set forth by Brunner: "This truth cannot therefore be appropriated in one act of objective perception of truth, but only in an *act of personal surrender and decision.* In order to gain this truth, not only must we make room for it, but we must 'die' in order that we may be raised by Christ to a new way of life. We cannot 'possess' this truth as we can 'possess other truths,' but we must *be* in this truth, we must *live* this truth, we must *do* it."[18]

Revelation and Doctrine

Undoubtedly the uniqueness of the Christian life is the experience of being "in Christ." But if we are to continue in the truth and doing the truth, there must be repeated encounters in which God reveals more of his will to us by the aid of the Holy Spirit. The means for maintaining this dynamic experience with God is the Bible. As a record of redemptive history—both the events and the interpretation of the events—Scripture is "it-truth." Without the Bible there would be no special revelation and without doctrine there would be no true faith. In approaching man, God must begin at the point of contact, namely, man's ability to reason. Accordingly, a minimal amount of theological ideas or teaching is necessary as a prerequisite for true faith. Sound doctrine is also necessary during the maturing of Christian experience, both for the individual and for the church.

Notwithstanding the indispensability of correct doctrine, there is no assurance that this rational, objective truth will lead to or preserve genuine faith. On this point, Brunner declares: "Christian doctrine, it is true, springs from the Word of God; but the Word of God is different from Christian doctrine. Faith cannot exist apart from sound doctrine, it is true, but it is not itself the understanding of doctrines. It is possible to hold correct views of doctrine without faith—and, indeed, in the course of the

18. *Ibid.*, pp. 371-372. Italics his.

history of the church very many people have held correct doctrinal views without possessing genuine faith. Correct doctrine is something that can be learned, and indeed anyone who has a good brain and is able to study at a good college or university can learn it easily. But faith is not something that a man can 'learn'; it is the free gift of God. It is extremely bad for the church to confuse that which is the gift of the Holy Spirit alone with that which anyone with a good brain can learn at a good college."[19]

The futility of employing orthodox doctrine as the ultimate criterion for evaluating Christian experience is made explicit in the following statement from Brunner: "We would now add further that it is possible to understand the new message of the apostle Paul completely, intellectually and logically, and that means theologically, without having real faith. The believer, it is true, will reply, 'Then the message has not been rightly understood!' But the difference between an understanding based on genuine faith and the kind that can coexist with unbelief cannot be proved in intellectual terms. An unbeliever can pass the stiffest theological examination and prove that he understands 'Pauline theology' so well that no examiner could find any fault with his answers—and yet in the sense of spiritual understanding based on real faith he has understood nothing, but has remained a complete pagan. The Devil would pass the most rigorous examination in dogmatic and Biblical theology with distinction. Theology stands very close to the Word of God, but it is not itself the Word. Sound doctrine springs from the Word of God and from faith, but it is possible to understand it intellectually, to reproduce it theologically, and to make it part of one's intellectual equipment apart from faith. Faith, it is true, must pass through an understanding of theological ideas, even if they are very simple ones, but is not itself theological understanding."[20]

This insight has frightening implications for all those who handle the "sacred things" of Scripture. Regardless of one's location in the theological spectrum, there is the

19. *Ibid.*, p. 420.
20. *Ibid.*, pp. 419-420.

ever-present danger of knowing the truth objectively, but not being in it subjectively. It is imperative, therefore, that revelation and doctrine be distinguished. "Here, and here alone," says Brunner, "lies the gulf between this world and the world beyond, between reason and revelation. That is why a person who has long ago given up faith can still go on for a long time teaching correct theology. It is always at his disposal. But there is one thing that he can no longer do: he can no longer pray from his heart."[21]

Revelation and Propositional Truth

Just as traditional, conservative Christianity has endeavored to protect Scripture by equating revelation and doctrine, so it has contended that revelation is a series of eternal, timeless truths set in propositional form. Conversely, most of the recent theologians have affirmed that revelation is not a set of eternal truths. Here again, however, the points of view are not nearly so divergent as they would appear. The problem is really one of semantics— either the failure or unwillingness to understand one another. Contemporary theologies do not deny that there are timeless truths in the realm of objective truth. Their basic assertion is that eternal or propositional truths, like doctrine, cannot be considered as revelation because they cannot save. Even before existentialism took hold, P. T. Forsyth declared, "There are doctrines of salvation but no saving doctrines."[22]

Nevertheless, the Holy Spirit does not engender true faith apart from Scripture, a written record replete with teaching and objective truths. Notwithstanding the differences between John and the three other Gospels, all four depict the life of Christ primarily in terms of teaching (by parables and discourses), which is authenticated by miracles or signs. The concern with content is clearly stated in Mark 4:33-34: "With many such parables he spoke the word to them, as they were able to hear it; he did not speak to them without a parable, but privately to his own

21. *Ibid.*, p. 421.
22. *The Principle of Authority*, p. 452.

disciples he explained everything." In the Gospels one of the most common titles for Jesus is "teacher." When many of Jesus' larger group of disciples murmured at his comments about the bread of life, he declared to them, "The words that I have spoken to you are spirit and life" (John 6:63). After many of the disciples drew back and Jesus asked the Twelve whether they too would go away, Peter affirmed, "You have the words of eternal life" (John 6:68). In another discourse Jesus said to the Jews, "If you continue in my word, you are truly my disciples, and you will know the truth, and the truth will make you free" (John 8:31). In his high-priestly prayer Jesus said concerning his disciples, "I have given them the words which thou gavest me, and they have received them and know in truth that I came from thee" (John 17:8). But even all of this instruction was not sufficient; therefore Jesus informed the disciples, "I have yet many things to say to you, but you cannot bear them now. When the Spirit of truth comes, he will guide you into all the truth" (John 16:12-13).

Without this preparatory instruction and the combination of signs and words at the cross, Christ's death would have been an enigma to the disciples. As it was they saw only dimly the meaning of reconciliation, and so the resurrected Christ continued his ministry of teaching and interpretation; for example, he opened the meaning of the Old Testament to the two persons on the way to Emmaus. The apostles, especially Paul, had the conviction that through the aid of the Holy Spirit they had received further insight into the meaning of Christ's life, death, and resurrection. Thus, the church has traditionally accepted the whole New Testament as a witness to Christ.

When Jesus was challenged to select the great commandment in the law, he replied: "You shall love the Lord your God with all your heart, and with all your soul, and with all your mind. This is the great and first commandment. And a second is like it, You shall love your neighbor as yourself. On these two commandments depend all the law and the prophets" (Matt. 22:37-40). Thus Jesus distilled the whole Old Testament down to two eternal truths, love for God and love for man. These commandments are propositional in form, and certainly there has never been and never will be a time when these truths are not valid and applicable. Love, as Paul noted (1 Cor. 13:13), is greater than faith and hope because it will be appropriate when the need for faith and hope has passed.

In spite of this fact, these and other teachings of Jesus are nonetheless objective truth. The only way to experience subjective truth is to be "in Christ," who said, "I am ... the truth" (John 14:6). The words of Jesus are spirit and life, they are eternal, and they are indispensable for true faith, but they are mere words without the energizing and vitalizing influence of the Holy Spirit. Response can never become a reality by the sheer force of the written page. No doctrine, no matter how rationally and logically presented, can elicit true faith.

Scripture states, in clear propositional form, "God is love" (1 John 4:8), but this truth is not the same as the timeless truth $2 \times 2 = 4$. Since human reason cannot discover and demonstrate that "God is love," many people have read this passage without coming to a subjective knowledge of its truth. While such lack of faith eliminates neither God nor the fact of his love, revelation never becomes a reality for those who do not believe—truth does not happen for them.

As further explanation concerning this kind of truth, Brunner states: "For our rational understanding of truth, this is an absurdity. Truth has nothing to do with 'happening'; truth 'is.' Truth is the agreement of something thought with something that exists. Such truth we can discover, and thus introduce it into time; but when it is known already this introduction into time becomes meaningless. A geometrical theorem was once discovered by someone for the first time; but since then this fact is of no interest so far as truth itself is concerned. The moment that it was perceived it became timeless. The truth of revelation is totally different, 'Grace and truth came by Jesus Christ.' This does not mean that they were discovered, so that all this now 'is' because it has been discovered. Rather, the knowledge of the truth remains permanently united with the historical process in which it came to us for the first time. The truth, the eternal Being and the eternal will of God, 'the mystery which hath been hid from ages and from generations now is made manifest to his saints.' But because it has been made manifest it has not become a 'static' truth. It is, and it remains, truth only for him who enters into that Event which is Jesus Christ, and remains there. It is always true only as something that 'happens,' as grace. Therefore 'grace and truth' belong indissolubly to one another."[23]

Although human reason can do its best to understand the statement "Jesus is Lord," the entire activity is within the realm of objective truth. This claim, which is propositional in form, remains a static truth until something "happens" in the realm of subjective truth. As Paul declares, "No one can say 'Jesus is Lord' except by the Holy Spirit" (1 Cor. 12:3). On the other hand, this fact does not eliminate the objective phase that is preparatory to the Spirit's activity. Inasmuch as the Holy Spirit does not demand credulity, the leap of faith necessarily involves some consideration of the Lord to whom commitment is contemplated. As Brunner has stated, "Faith . . . must pass through an understanding of theological ideas, even if they are very simple ones."

Scripture, the objective record of revelation, sets forth its elemental ideas of God and Christ. If these are classified (in line with traditional categories) as doctrine, then a minimal core of doctrine is basic to genuine faith. But if, with Barth, Dodd, Baillie, and Brunner, "doctrine" is defined as a more or less elaborate, systematic body of teaching, then doctrine is the outgrowth, not the prerequisite, of faith. Herein, of course, lies some of the breakdown in communication between the two points of view. The essential point is that the objective truth of Scripture, whether defined in terms of doctrine or not, is the means by which the Holy Spirit leads to subjective truth.

While the means are necessary, God's ultimate purpose is that all men should enter the realm where grace, love, and truth become subjective realities. Paul depicts this

23. Brunner, *op. cit.*, pp. 369-370.

process of re-creation as follows: "And we all, with un-veiled face, beholding [or, reflecting] the glory of the Lord, are being changed into his likeness from one degree of glory to another; for this comes from the Lord who is the Spirit" (2 Cor. 3:18). Paul recognized that teaching had a part to play, but his highest desire for his spiritual children was that they share in the revelation that occurs in subjective truth. Thus, in his prayer recorded in Ephesians 3:14-19 he yearns that his readers may: (1) be strengthened in the inner man by the Holy Spirit; (2) have Christ dwelling in their hearts; (3) have power to comprehend the dimensions of love; (4) know the love of Christ, which surpasses knowledge; and (5) be filled with the fullness of God.

Revelation as Communication

Putting the matter simply, revelation (like communication) has three essential factors: (1) a communicator or source; (2) his message; and (3) the response of the receiver. If any one of these three is missing, there is no revelation or communication. As has been noted previously, the fact of God as Communicator is a biblical claim that must be taken seriously.

The message (involving both feelings and ideas) was expressed in a variety of ways (noted in Ch. 1), but language was the most effective means of all. In general, speech is more basic than writing because all human beings can speak. Moreover, the tone of voice and gestures communicate more directly and completely the intention of the speaker. Accordingly, speech played the major role in the original revelatory events. Many ancient persons had trained memories that could transmit orally with great accuracy long poems and stories, overtones and all. This fact explains the amazing accuracy of many of the early biblical traditions. But by the time of Moses there was an appreciation for the permanence and objectivity of written records, and so the Decalogue was inscribed on stone tablets, which were then housed for safekeeping in the ark. Moses recorded a log of the wilderness camp sites, and he most certainly started the listing of case laws, decisions reached during trials attempting to clarify the interpretation of the Ten Commandments. Later on, Jeremiah and Ezekiel were instructed to record their oracles after twenty years or so of prophetic activity.

The indispensability of the message is illustrated by the old argument as to whether there would be a sound if a tree fell in the woods and there was no animal or human being to hear it. We know now that hearing takes place in the mind. The ear is simply an organ for converting air waves into electrical impulses. In reality, therefore, sound is dependent on the organs of receptivity and response. This concession, however, does not eliminate the necessity of the falling tree and the resultant air waves. Without these the ear and mind would wait in vain—there would be no sound.

Most of the Israelites and the Jews were dependent on reports and records to learn what Yahweh had revealed to the patriarchs, Moses, and the prophets. Aside from the earliest Christians, the same has been true of the church with respect to the life and teachings of Jesus. Without the Bible, the Written Word, there would be no dependable message today. Long before now, as the history of the church in the second and third centuries A.D. indicates, the basic messages of the Old and New Testaments would have been skewed and garbled beyond recognition by an oral tradition that had lost the ancient ability to transmit with fidelity. Inasmuch as the vast majority of God's creatures have not been favored with such extraordinary self-disclosures as depicted in Scripture, the Written Word is and will continue to be indispensable.

It should be pointed out, furthermore, that God's special disclosure of himself involved more than what is recorded in the Bible. Not all of the revelatory deeds and sayings of God and Jesus have been recorded and preserved for us. In the Old Testament, for example, there is no reference in the historical narrative to the devastation of Shiloh cited by Jeremiah as Yahweh's judgment on his wicked people (7:12). The fact of selectivity is made explicit in the New Testament: "Now Jesus did many other signs in the presence of the disciples, which are not written in this book" (John 20:30). Scripture is that portion of redemptive history which was recorded and transmitted to us. It is implicit that the record is sufficiently complete to lead to belief in Jesus Christ, the fullness of revelation, and thereby to eternal life.

Finally, a response to the message is necessary if revelation is to become an experiential reality. An excellent example is the account in John 20:24-29. Thomas, called the Twin, was not with the disciples when Jesus appeared to them, and so he refused to believe their story. Eight days later Jesus appeared to the disciples again and specifically confronted Thomas with his nail-scarred hands and his wounded side. This encounter was revelation to Thomas and he exclaimed, "My Lord and my God!" Jesus is then reported to have said: "Have you believed because you have seen me? Blessed are those who have not seen and yet believe." The precise act of Jesus' appearing to Thomas cannot be experiential revelation for us—we were not there. But the record of Jesus' disclosure to Thomas becomes the *means of revelation* to us. Even though we cannot see as Thomas saw, nevertheless, if we take the account seriously, the Holy Spirit confronts us with his witness. In that moment of encounter and faith, revelation becomes a reality for us and we exclaim with Thomas, "My Lord and my God!"

From the foregoing discussion it is evident that the term "revelation" has a dual meaning when understood as communication. Even current dictionaries recognize this when they list the basic definitions as: (1) God's disclosure of himself; and (2) that which is disclosed. In other words, revelation has a subjective side as well as an objective side. This duality is expressed with crystal clarity in the biblical understanding of "knowledge" as experiential (life in fellowship with God) and factual (the deposit of teachings and doctrine associated with that fellowship). In short, the Written Word is objective revelation and the response of faith is subjective revelation. The latter is not possible without the former, and the former without the latter is incomplete.

Chapter Three

Revelation, History, and Interpretation

Since the rise of critical study of the Bible one of the most hotly debated issues has been the accuracy and historicity of the biblical narratives. Can the experience of revelation as subjective truth become a reality if some of the key events of the objective record, the Written Word, are in fact untrue? To what extent is history important as a means of revelation? These and related issues are crucial; therefore it is imperative that they be discussed.

Facts and Faith

The Old Testament writers never wearied of repeating the facts concerning God's gracious acts in behalf of Israel. Neither could they get away from the conviction that their God was back of so-called "human history." It is impossible to explain Israel's unique faith without acknowledging first that God did break into history and make himself known. In the Old Testament, therefore, it is beyond question that faith is rooted in fact.

This point of view is held with equal conviction in the

New Testament. When the gnostic doctrine of the inherent sinfulness of matter and flesh began to creep into the early church, the incarnation had to be reinterpreted. Since Jesus of Nazareth was human, he could never be the Christ, the Son of God. Jesus appeared to be the Christ, but there was never any union of the two. Christ came down as a dove and clothed Jesus at his baptism. The New Testament writers were quick to recognize the fatal nature of this docetic view of Jesus. Accordingly, anyone who denied that Jesus Christ had come in the flesh had the "spirit of antichrist" (1 John 4:2-3). Docetism not only necessitated a reinterpretation of the incarnation, it also had to deny the fact of the resurrection. Therefore, Paul is so bold as to affirm, "If Christ has not been raised, your faith is futile and you are still in your sins" (1 Cor. 15:17).

Here, then, is the taproot of our faith, and here evangelical Christianity must take its stand. Docetism is still the enemy of the church—only its form has changed. Older liberalism thought in terms of objective history, and so in order to get around the historical problems in Scripture it separated facts and faith. Robert H. Pfeiffer (1892-1958), Old Testament scholar at Harvard, championed this view in all seriousness. He cited a number of interpretive sections in the historical books (e.g., Chronicles) and then showed how impossible it was to square the point of view expressed with the facts as learned from other portions of the Old Testament or from sources outside the Bible. Pfeiffer considered the attempt to combine faith with facts as "a snare and a delusion."[1] He justified his statement as follows: "Half measures, however, will not place Biblical research on a solid basis, on a par with research in other fields of the humanities, enjoying the full respect of competent scholars. The unhappy marriage of history and theology, owing to the prevalence of one over the other or else to mutual incompatibility, was never a true union and only divorce will result in the fruitful development of each of the two disciplines."[2] Near the close of his article

1. "Facts and Faith in Biblical History," *Journal of Biblical Literature*, Vol. LXX, Part I (March, 1951).
2. *Ibid.*, p. 13.

Pfeiffer makes the sweeping statement, "Not only scholars, but even the humble untutored believers of all faiths intuitively know that facts and faith do not mix."[3]

History and Fact

Since the idea and meaning of the term "history" have exercised scholars and theologians greatly in the past few decades, these issues must be considered in our discussion of biblical facts. It was popular at one time to speak of history as being objective, a simple reporting of the facts, while interpretation was thought of as being subjective, a matter of one's opinion or value judgment of an event. In time it was seen that no complex event or situation in life could be reported with *absolute* historical objectivity. In the first place, no historian ever had all the facts relating to his subject. Moreover, even from the available facts historians have been under the necessity of choosing which items to employ. It is evident that subjectivity is involved in such a process because the choice is determined by the mental and spiritual elements that characterize the historian. Thus, all history writing is a combination of subjective factors entwined with objective data.

This fact is equally true of Scripture. The biblical writers mixed their faith and their history because their faith was a factor in recording the history. Herein lies the problem and the reason why varying forms of docetism have continued to this day. Pfeiffer took a more traditional view of history; therefore he interpreted the plain meaning of the text as the intent of the Old Testament writers. Thus, while frankly declaring that the writers were mistaken in many instances, he contended for the faith that Israel had.

On the other hand, the New Reformation Theology and similar contemporary theological developments have tended to solve the problem with a dual definition of history. Some find the key to the problem in Kierkegaard's "infinite qualitative difference" between time (man on

3. *Ibid.*, p. 14.

earth) and eternity (God in heaven). This tremendous gap between the Creator and his creatures means that revelation must come as God's vertical thrust into the historical realm of man. Revelation, therefore, can take place at only one point—the point of tangency being Jesus Christ. The claim in John 1:14, "the Word became flesh," must be maintained, accordingly, at all costs. God entered, in a very objective manner, the space-time categories of man's existence, but this act was not essentially a part of the running stream of history. Rather, it was "primal history" (*Urgeschichte*) breaking into human history. This concept of a history above history, a "superhistory," involves some neat juggling of *time* and *eternity* in which the two are related "dialectically."

Rudolf Bultmann approaches the historical problem with two different sets of German words: (1) *historisch*, "historical"—an event *(Historie)* that lies wholly in the past, and (2) *geschichtlich*, "historic"—an event *(Geschichte)* that has existential meaning for the present and possibly lies in the past as well. We come to know these differing events in two quite different ways—the "historical" by the common methods of research into human history and the "historic" by means of personal encounter. *Historie* gives meaningless acts; only *Geschichte* can give meaning.

H. P. Owen in *Revelation and Existence,* a study of Bultmann's theology, explains the subtle difference as follows: "The nerve of the distinction is the difference between two views of history's relationship to time. An 'historical' event is wholly temporal. Its nature and significance are exhausted by the stretch of time that it occupies. An 'historic' event, *the* historic event of Jesus Christ, is not wholly temporal; it is both temporal and eternal; it is the point at which eternity crosses time. Christ was a temporal figure, as much a temporal figure as Socrates or Julius Caesar; but the Word that God spoke through him was an eternal Word; therefore this Word can be renewed in each encounter."[4] Because the Bible is written in "historical"

4. *Revelation and Existence*, pp. 25-26. Italics his.

terms, Bultmann considers it obsolete and incapable of revealing the personal God in any effective, personal way. It has many passages which (while intelligible and capable of being understood) have no significance or application to modern life. These "meaningless" elements Bultmann calls "myth," and the process of reinterpretation he calls "demythologization."

John's doctrine of "the Word" as a being "with God" Bultmann reinterprets to mean "the Word of address" that the Father speaks. Christ as the incarnation of God becomes Jesus the human figure through whom the Word is spoken. Jesus' death on the cross is God speaking his Word of forgiveness.

One of the chief categories to be demythologized is miracles. Miracle stories are "myth" because they picture God's act as an object that draws the attention of the reader. When God reveals himself in personal encounter with man the act of disclosure must be concealed. It can never be demonstrated or proved by objective evidence. Therefore, the reinterpretation of Scripture must do away with all objective, historical elements. Faith must come from an inner revelation, person to person, not an appeal to external facts of past history.

What, then, does Bultmann do with the resurrection? Owen observes: "Bultmann is here faced with a difficulty. In the Incarnation and the Cross he had two indubitable historical events (a man and the death of a man) which he could demythologize, but, in his view, the Resurrection was not an historical event at all. His presuppositions are such that he is bound to assert that it could never have happened. Yet surely something happened, on the basis of which the New Testament accounts of the Resurrection-appearances were composed. Bultmann is prepared to admit that there was something—perhaps 'a series of subjective visions'—but he regards anything of this kind that may have happened as completely irrelevant to Christian faith. Nevertheless, a demythologized Resurrection must be connected with *some* historical event if it is to have the slightest credibility. This historical event is the Cross. To believe in the risen Christ is to believe that through the

Cross God forgives our sins and frees us for 'newness of life.' This is the only sense in which it can be said that God through Christ 'brought life and immortality to light.' 'The faith of Easter is just this—faith in the Word of preaching.' "[5]

In contrast to Bultmann's frank denial of the resurrection, Barth expressed the conviction that anyone who denies the resurrection of Christ is not a Christian. But Barth's belief in the resurrection must be understood in the light of his view of history. He, like Bultmann, distinguished between *Historie* and *Geschichte*. The fact that he did not define these terms precisely, and that he considered the resurrection as *Geschichte*, not *Historie*, has raised doubts as to whether he really believed that the resurrection occurred as an actual historical event in chronological time. Richard R. Niebuhr contends that Barth's concept of history forces him "to extrude the resurrection event from the sequence that anchors it in the New Testament."[6]

The Cruciality of Facts

In apparent contradiction to Bultmann and Barth, Brunner states: "Biblical theology is not only a theology of the Word, but also of facts, and it is true of such facts which are at the same time the object of historical research. The article of the Creed, 'Crucified under Pontius Pilate,' reminds us of this. It forms part of the 'offense' of the Christian faith that, in contrast to mysticism or to rational moralistic theism, it is connected with historic facts, which are the object of historical research."[7] He also expresses a fear that Bultmann and Barth are in danger of making Christianity into a form of docetism with timeless ideas; therefore he comments: "Another effort to evade this difficulty has been to depreciate the fact, in comparison with the 'given Word.' The Word has been given to us; the facts that lie behind it do not concern us; all we have

5. *Ibid.*, pp. 27-28. Italics his.
6. *Resurrection and Historical Reason*, p. 48.
7. *Revelation and Reason*, p. 281.

to inquire into is the meaning of the Word, not whether the facts actually took place. This position, however, contains a docetic tendency which is just as dangerous, and indeed at bottom still more dangerous, than docetism in the usual Christological sense. Only if Jesus Christ actually, in the sense of a historical fact which took place within time and space, was crucified upon the hill of Calvary, can he be our Redeemer. The question, What is told us? cannot be separated from that other question, What has happened? for what we are told is precisely that this event has actually happened."[8]

The Importance of the Resurrection

But Brunner's concern for facts is conditioned by the critical question with which he examines each concrete event recorded in the Bible: "Are there any results or truths of historical science that contradict the statements of the Christian faith? Thus, does the faith assert 'facts' whose actual historicity can be denied or contested by historical research?"[9] As R. R. Niebuhr declares: "Consequently, when he comes to the interpretation of the resurrection of Jesus—the central and crucial element in the whole 'fact' of Jesus Christ, according to Brunner—he is not in a position to give it any more of a footing in history than did his predecessors. The resurrection cannot be called a fact, he believes; rather it is a superhistorical or eschatological happening and 'no longer historical at all.' The resurrection is a 'hole' in history, of which only the edges are historical. Shining through that hole, faith sees ineffable eternity. The assumption of Brunner's thought, here and elsewhere, is that history is the facade or mask behind which true meaning is concealed."[10]

Brunner is careful to protect the historicity of Jesus and his death on the cross because there is no redemption apart from this event. Paul, however, goes farther and affirms

8. *Ibid.*, pp. 281-282.
9. *Ibid.*, p. 282.
10. Niebuhr, *op. cit.*, p. 27.

that if Christ has not been raised, then all of us are still in our sins (1 Cor. 15:17). Evidently the offense and scandal of the gospel includes the resurrection as well as the death on the cross. Brunner is certainly correct in his concern over those who "depreciate the fact," but does he not indict himself when he depreciates the most difficult fact for faith?

Of the more recent participants in the debate about the resurrection, one of the most embroiled has been Willi Marxsen, Professor of New Testament, University of Münster, West Germany. As a result of charges of heresy brought by the Evangelical Church of Westphalia, he published his views in 1968. "There is no doubt," Marxsen declares, "that the authors of the New Testament (or, to be accurate, the authors of some of them) were convinced that the resurrection of Jesus actually took place on the third day after the crucifixion. Anyone who says that this was not a real event is therefore saying something different from what these writers thought."[11]

But Marxsen cannot accept *their* view literally because of the numerous contradictions of details in the various accounts.[12] His form-critical study of the New Testament sources finds one unshakable fact: the faith that Peter held after the death of Jesus. It is no longer possible, according to Marxsen, to determine how Peter discovered this faith. "Later, people said that Peter discovered it by seeing Jesus. This may be the case. I do not know. But anyone who claims to know better must be able to produce his evidence."[13]

The Gospel writers, especially Luke, "set people on the wrong track."[14] The various stories of the appearances, ascension, and exaltation of Jesus are not a literal sequence of events. "At the beginning," Marxsen claims, "the fact was that each one of these stories was an expression of one and the same reality: the one who had been crucified did not remain among the dead; he is Lord; he sends out his

11. *The Resurrection of Jesus of Nazareth*, p. 121.
12. *Ibid.*, pp. 45, 156.
13. *Ibid.*, p. 126.
14. *Ibid.*, p. 172.

followers to call others to faith."[15] This faith was expressed in a number of ways, but "the idea of resurrection eventually won the ascendancy, towing the other ideas in its wake."[16]

According to Marxsen, this biblical interpretation cannot be the basis of faith today, however. "Commitment to the promise of the *earthly* Jesus demanded a trusting faith; and that was a venture. . . . This commitment to what Jesus demanded had no guarantee behind it. Jesus rejected the demand for signs as a preliminary legitimation. He wanted a daring faith."[17] "A theology," therefore, "which makes the possibility of contemporary faith dependent on the 'reality' of the interpretation can only be called a theology of fear. I do not hold out much hope for it; nor could I advise anyone to commit himself to such a theology."[18] Accordingly, "faith in the resurrection of Jesus is not a barrier which has to be overcome first—or even at a later stage. In my view, it is the man who fights for the preservation of this barrier today who is standing in the way of the Christian faith."[19]

Marxsen's sincerity is evident throughout his book. He is absolutely convinced that Jesus of Nazareth is living and calling him to faithful service, but he is equally certain that belief in the physical resurrection of Jesus is unfounded. Accordingly, he feels compelled to express his conviction honestly and openly. There are alternative ways of interpreting the biblical evidence, however, and thus Marxsen has not necessarily said the last word. This writer concurs with him in acknowledging that the biblical passages dealing with the resurrection swarm with difficulties, some details of which cannot be harmonized, but such contradictions do not cancel out the historical core back of the accounts.

Somehow, Marxsen is convinced of the historicity of Peter's faith, and yet from psychological and historical

15. *Ibid.*, p. 161.
16. *Ibid.*, p. 147.
17. *Ibid.*, p. 150.
18. *Ibid.*, p. 143.
19. *Ibid.*, p. 153.

perspectives it is no more firmly attested than the themes of "the empty tomb" and "the appearances of Jesus." Wolfhart Pannenberg contends that "the only method of achieving at least approximate certainty with regard to the events of a past time is historical research."[20] Accordingly, "the historian still remains obligated to reconstruct the historical correlation of the events that led to the emergence of primitive Christianity."[21] "How," Pannenberg asks, "could Jesus' disciples in Jerusalem have proclaimed his resurrection if they could be constantly refuted merely by viewing the grave in which his body was interred?"[22] Then, with commendation, he quotes Paul Althaus: "In Jerusalem, the place of Jesus' execution and grave, it was proclaimed not long after his death that he had been raised. The situation *demands* that within the circle of the first community one had a reliable testimony for the fact that the grave had been found empty. . . . (The claim) could not have been maintained in Jerusalem for a single day, for a single hour, if the emptiness of the tomb had not been established as a fact for all concerned." [23] Moreover, Pannenberg declares, "The Easter appearances are not to be explained from the Easter faith of the disciples; rather, conversely, the Easter faith of the disciples is to be explained from the appearances."[24]

Marxsen's "daring faith" is offended at any attempts at "legitimation" of faith. It is true that most Christians have exercised faith before certifying all the data leading them to trust in Jesus the Christ, but it is equally true that in the maturing process thoughtful Christians have made a place for examination and reaffirmation of their faith. Although Kierkegaard's "subjective leap" of faith seems to be made against all "human reason," faith is not being blindfolded, spun around a number of times, and challenged to leap. Human reason is a God-given capacity to lead a person to the springboard of faith, but reason cannot compel one to

20. *Jesus—God and Man*, p. 99.
21. *Ibid.*, p. 97.
22. *Ibid.*, p. 100.
23. *Ibid.*
24. *Ibid.*, p. 96.

make the leap of faith. Only the Holy Spirit can aid the human will to make the daring plunge into the pool of living water. On the other hand, with no external pointers or indicators faith becomes a credulous leap with the probability that the "believer" will find himself on the hard earth instead of being in the pool. Without criteria for differentiation, faith in the Golden Tablets of Joseph Smith is just as valid as trust in the New Testament accounts about Jesus Christ. Fortunately, the primitive church knew the difference between the extraordinary appearances of the risen Jesus and ordinary visions stemming from experiences with the earthly Jesus. Yet difficulties in the biblical accounts do not compel faith, and so Pannenberg's sole reliance on history as revelation is the opposite extreme of Marxsen's refusal to recognize any aids to faith. Neither this writer nor any other Christian has the authority to declare that Marxsen cannot possibly have genuine faith because he cannot bring himself to believe in the bodily resurrection of Jesus. But when this recognition is acknowledged, those Christians who share the witness of the primitive church do not constitute a "barrier" to faith.

The Importance of the Virgin Birth

Another area of disagreement among scholars is the doctrine of the virgin birth of Christ. Some who believe in the historical life of Jesus draw the line with this doctrine. They point out, quite accurately, that aside from Matthew 1:18-25 and Luke 1:28-35 no other portion of the New Testament makes reference to this doctrine. Paul, Peter, and John had numerous occasions to refer to it, but they pass it by. Obviously, the doctrine was not an issue in the beginnings of Christianity, and most important of all, it was not an essential element of the gospel as preached from Pentecost on. Accordingly, they reject the doctrine as nonessential to their salvation.

It is interesting that Barth, whom Brunner questions in other issues, takes Brunner to task for his negative attitude toward the virgin birth of Christ. Commenting on Brunner's *The Mediator*, Barth quotes Berdyaev as expressing his own views: "I read Brunner's book with tremendous interest, because I felt in him tenseness and acuity of thought, religious sensibility. But when I reached the passage in which Brunner confesses that he does not believe in Jesus Christ's birth of the Virgin, or at least confronts it with indifference, my mood became sad and the matter grew tedious. For it seemed to me as though everything had now been canceled, as though everything else was now pointless."[25]

With respect to this doctrine, C. S. Lewis (1898-1963) states: "I can understand the man who denies miracles altogether: but what is one to make of people who will believe other miracles and 'draw the line' at the Virgin Birth? . . . In reality the Miracle is no less, and no more, surprising than any others."[26]

The concern of Barth, Berdyaev, and Lewis raises the question as to the cruciality of this doctrine. In his book *The Virgin Birth of Christ*, J. Gresham Machen (1881-1937) comments as follows on this issue:

> Is belief in the virgin birth necessary to every man if he is to be a believer in the Lord Jesus Christ? The question is wrongly put when it is put in that way. Who can tell exactly how much knowledge of the facts about Christ is necessary if a man is to have saving faith? None but God can tell. Some knowledge is certainly required, but exactly how much is required we cannot say. "Lord, I believe; help thou mine unbelief," said a man in the Gospels who was saved. So today there are many men of little faith, many who are troubled by the voices that are heard on all sides. It is very hard to be a Christian in these times; and there is One who knows that it is hard. What right have we to say that full knowledge and full conviction are necessary before a man can put his trust in the crucified and risen Lord? What right have we to say that no man can be saved before he has come to full

25. *Church Dogmatics*, Vol. I, Part 2, p. 184. Quotations from this book are used by permission of Charles Scribner's Sons and T. & T. Clark.

26. *Miracles*, p. 165.

conviction regarding the stupendous miracle narrated in the first chapters of Matthew and Luke?[27]

Lest he be misunderstood, however, Machen adds, "We do not mean by what we have just said that denial of the virgin birth is to be treated as a matter of indifference by the wise pastor of souls."[28] Then he concludes, "One thing at least is clear: even if the belief in the virgin birth is not necessary to every Christian, it is certainly necessary to Christianity. And it is necessary to the corporate witness of the church."[29] Machen has shown the impossibility of prescribing a minimal core of biblical events to which assent must be given before saving faith is possible. God recognizes the sincere doubts of men and he undoubtedly saves men who do not have enough faith to believe certain teachings of Scripture.

Revelation and Salvation History

In addition to the issue of the cruciality of facts for faith there is the question of history's role in revelation. The dominant view of the last twenty-five years has been the theory designated *Heilsgeschichte* ("Salvation History"). Proponents have differed in a number of details, but in general the concept has been associated with the type of history involving *Geschichte.* As noted earlier, however, this split-level definition of history cannot stand the test of close scrutiny. There is *only one history* and this is as accessible to the secularist as to the theist. The truth of the "Salvation History" concept is that history can be approached in two different ways. If the story of mankind's experience is viewed without empathy and involvement, then the data remain as objective truth. If, on the other hand, the story is taken up into the experience of the hearer or reader, then history becomes subjective truth. This reality is well expressed by G. Ernest Wright: "Biblical theology is first and foremost a theology of recital. The

27. *The Virgin Birth of Christ*, p. 395.
28. *Ibid.*, pp. 395-396.
29. *Ibid.*, p. 396.

worshipper listens to the recital and by means of historical memory and identification he participates, so to speak, in the original events."[30] But the one who appropriates the past and makes it meaningful for the present does so in the stream of human history, not on the level of superhistory. Most likely the secularist does not share in the experience of subjective truth, but he can observe what happens to his fellow human and he can report objectively the latter's testimony concerning the experience.

As a general rule the advocates of "Salvation History" have stressed the uniqueness of Israel's view of history in contrast to the supposedly cyclical view of its neighbors. Yet, in the inscription of the Moabite Stone, for example, Mesha, King of Moab, declares that Omri, king of Israel, humbled Moab many years, "for Chemosh was angry at his land."[31] Mesha notes, further on, "And the king of Israel had built Jahaz, and he dwelt there while he was fighting against me, but Chemosh drove him out before me." [32] Thus, as James Barr comments, the inscription displays Chemosh, the chief god of Moab, "'acting in history' in a manner remarkably similar to that of the God of Israel." [33]

After a careful comparison of Near Eastern and biblical texts, Bertil Albrektson concludes that "historical events as a *medium* [italics his] of revelation is a general Near Eastern conception."[34] While Albrektson shows that Israel's view of history was not unique, he states "with some confidence" that "the idea of historical events as divine manifestations has marked the Israelite cult in a way that lacks real parallels among Israel's neighbors."[35] In short, Israel's worship made far more use of memory in re-creating God's redemptive acts of the past. Yet, this emphasis roots in the moral, ethical insights that Israel received from Yahweh. Here, as noted in Chapter 2, and here only, can one speak of uniqueness.

30. *God Who Acts*, p. 28.
31. *Ancient Near Eastern Texts*, p. 320.
32. *Ibid.*
33. *Old and New in Interpretation*, p. 72.
34. *History and the Gods*, p. 114.
35. *Ibid.*, p. 115.

Some criticisms of "Salvation History" have stemmed from an almost literalistic interpretation of "the acts of God." But Wright has always understood God's "acts" or "events" in a broader sense. In a more recent publication he explains, "A Biblical event is not simply a happening in time and space, but one in which the word of God is present (the 'speaking' of God), interpreting it and giving it special significance."[36] For Wright, therefore, biblical revelation is both act and explanatory word. This fact is indisputable in the biblical narrative. Without the verbal exchange between Yahweh and Moses, the act of God at the burning bush would have been a charade with a puzzled Moses vainly attempting to ascertain Yahweh's disclosure of himself and his name.

The one point at which Wright seems to have overstated his case is his tendency to give the Act primacy over the Word. In the preface to *God Who Acts*, Wright explains, "'God Who Acts' was chosen to point up the contrast with the more customary expression 'God Who Speaks'. Christian theology has tended to think of the Bible chiefly as 'the Word of God', though in point of fact a more accurate title would be 'the Acts of God'. The Word is certainly present in the Scripture, but it is rarely, if ever, dissociated from the Act; instead it is the accompaniment of the Act."[37] Wright is clearly thinking in terms of such great acts as the Exodus from Egypt, and some important traditions of the Old Testament support him in his claim. On the other hand, there are instances in which the situation is reversed. The call of Abraham (Gen. 12:1-3) was a spoken word of revelation with no reference whatsoever to a previous act of God. Two baskets of figs in the temple area were the occasion for Yahweh's word to Jeremiah (24:1-10). This commonplace event is certainly the context for revelation, but unless it is understood as "an act of God" Wright's claim goes too far.

Barr is convinced that God's acts do not fully explain Israel's historical situation. "Rather than use terms like

36. *The Old Testament and Theology*, p. 48.
37. *God Who Acts*, p. 12.

'acts of God in history','' he declares, "we might do well to talk of something like 'situations'. It is in situations that God moves to call for a response, a response which in turn moves the tradition in some new direction."[38] Barr elaborates:

> The situation may indeed be an act of God in history, or it may be an event in the consciousness of a prophet. It may be a social situation, in which the call for adjustment brings into existence a new turn in the tradition. It may be a crisis in thought, in which it is realized that existing traditions are no longer adequate, or no longer compatible, and that new directions have to be taken. It may be a cultic situation, in which questions arise about which elements in general customary law will be accepted as part of the sacred law of Israel. It may be the development of questioning and answering in the circles of the wise.[39]

Barr's intention is to make room in his theory for the wide variety of situations found in the Bible. Yet Wright, notwithstanding his apparent emphasis on the act, has been aware of the range of historical situations. In claiming that "history is the chief medium of revelation," he explains:

> The term 'history' in this connection is used in a broad sense to include not only events of seeming impersonal significance, but also the lives of the individuals who compose it. The experience, the acts and the words of individuals are media of revelation, but individual personality and experience are not the centre of attention in and by themselves alone. They are the mediate means whereby God accomplishes his historical purposes, and the latter are more inclusive and comprehensive than the words, works and inner life of any one personality.[40]

The dispute over the term "history" is largely one of semantics. What is a series of situations if it is not the story or history of the persons involved? The basic point, both for Wright and Barr, is that God works through people to

38. *Old and New in Interpretation*, p. 26.
39. *Ibid.*
40. *God Who Acts*, p. 13.

effect his will. The Exodus from Egypt was a historical event for the persons involved. When, later on, the Israelites in Canaan re-created the event in their lives, that experience was equally a historical event. In the course of history, therefore, revelation occurs at the original event or situation and also at any experience of it in worship.

Types of Revelation

It is important to recognize that there is a correlation between various types of insight and various types of human intellect. In the intuitive mind of the genius ideas seem to pop full-flown without conscious rational effort. Beethoven's enormous talent expressed itself in the spontaneity of hundreds of compositions, but his one attempt at writing opera was a long, frustrating experience because the libretto restricted the exercise of his intuitive powers.

Wagner and Verdi, however, exhibited another type of genius. Librettos did not frustrate them. On the contrary, they delighted in the challenge of matching music to words and created compositions that seem so integral to the text that the combination gives the impression of having been destined. Such is the case with the best hymns. Other musicians have the gift of arrangement and orchestration. They delight in making variations of themes from other composers. There is also the simple, fervent expression of the folk tune and the gospel song.

The same range of mental capacity is evident in the Bible. There are the overarching insights given Moses, Jesus, and Paul, the soaring beauty of the poetry in Isaiah, the searching relevance of the prophets, and the painstaking devotion to the law of Yahweh as expressed in Psalm 119, the long acrostic. The problem, however, is that all of these are considered the revelation of Yahweh. Accordingly, it is necessary to discuss in greater depth some of the types and levels of revelation if a proper understanding of the concept is to be achieved. For centuries it was customary to designate the Bible as "special" or "supernatural" revelation, whereas any theological insights found outside the Book were called "general" or "natural" revelation.

While there is a good deal of truth in these distinctions, they do not reckon with all the data of Scripture and the experience of God's people. A more helpful distinction is that expressed by the terms "primary" and "secondary."

Primary Revelation

In various ways the biblical narratives witness to the brilliant intellect of Moses. At the burning bush, Yahweh communicated knowledge of his person, name, and will to his gifted servant. Later on at Mt. Sinai, in the same geographical context, Moses came to the insight that the Hittite suzerainty treaty was the best analogy of the relationship between Yahweh and his people. The uniqueness of the Ten Commandments, especially the first three, is made crystal clear in one biblical tradition where the stipulations are attributed to "the finger of God" (Ex. 31:18).

The basic claim of the Israelite prophets was that their oracles came from Yahweh. In some instances this claim is described as "the word of Yahweh which came" to the prophet (Jer. 1:2; Hos. 1:1; Mic. 1:1; Jon. 1:1; etc.). At other times revelation is pictured as the "vision" (Isa. 1:1) or the "burden" (Hab. 1:1) that the prophet saw. In general, therefore, the prophets disclaim any credit for their declarations.

The Gospel accounts stress the authority of Jesus' deeds and teachings. In the Gospel of John the source of this authority is made explicit: "I do not speak on my own authority, but the Father who dwells in me does his works" (14:10). It is interesting that Paul, in turn, attributes his authority to a revelation by Jesus Christ. He describes as a "mystery" his insight that through the gospel the Gentiles are fellow heirs with the Jews, and he declares that it had not been made known to previous generations (Eph. 3:4-6). In Galatians 1:12 he is even more explicit concerning the uniqueness of his insight: "I did not receive it from man, nor was I taught it, but it came through a revelation of Jesus Christ." It is evident from Paul's writings that many of the details about the life and teachings of Jesus were received from the early church, including the apostles. Yet in the case of the mystery concerning the place of the Gentiles in God's plan of redemption, Paul claimed direct revelation from Christ.

There is an original quality about the disclosures noted above that merits the designation "primary revelation." It is no accident that all the recipients (Moses, the greatest prophets, Jesus, and Paul) were men endowed with great mental capacity.

Secondary Revelation

In contrast to "primary revelation" there are biblical insights that are secondary or derivative in nature and involve more of the rational activity of the channel of revelation. It is recognized at the outset, however, that the human mind is very complex, and in the continuum of its subtle activity the two types of revelation seem to merge at times. It is virtually impossible to classify some of the biblical revelation with certainty, and no such attempt will be made. On the other hand, if the categories "primary" and "secondary" are understood in their basic sense, the distinction will prove useful later on.

As noted in Chapter 1, case law developed as a result of the need for interpreting the Ten Commandments for daily life. Many of these biblical guidelines were related to the corpus of case law common to the Near East centuries before Moses, and in some instances the regulations are almost a literal quotation. In other words, these laws were not the direct revelation of Yahweh to Moses, Joshua, and their successors. Rather, revelation involved the process of selecting and applying some of these case laws to Israel's life under Yahweh. In the case of Moses, such disclosures probably came in the tent of meeting (Ex. 33:11), as did some of the priestly regulations (Lev. 1:1). Joshua continued the interpretive process by decreeing some new guidelines at the covenant service held at Shechem (Josh. 24:25-26), and undoubtedly the chief priests did the same for succeeding generations. In any case, although reason plays an important role in evaluation and application, there is a "plus" in the whole process because it occurs in the context of the covenant experience with Yahweh, and the case laws are raised to a new level of ethical insight.

The same can be said for many of the insights of the prophets. In general, their task was to lead sinful Israel and Judah to a renewal of the covenant relationship. Although innovative aspects appear in their oracles, most of the prophets were essentially reformers. Their authority and insights derived from the primary revelation given Moses.

The wise man, the third channel of biblical revelation, seldom claims that his insights come directly from Yahweh, but, as noted previously, the assumption is made explicit in Proverbs 2:6: "For Yahweh gives wisdom. Knowledge and understanding come from his mouth." In some instances, it is claimed that the experience of the covenant relationship with Yahweh adds a depth of insight not plumbed in the wisdom of neighboring cultures: "Awe [reverence] of Yahweh is the beginning of knowledge [wisdom]" (Prov. 1:7; 9:10).

In the New Testament the situation is no different. While Jesus' demand that his disciples show redemptive love *(agape)* toward their enemies is qualitatively in the realm of primary revelation, most of what he taught can be paralleled from Old Testament and Judaistic sources. What he did was to fill these ideas with their potential fullness.

Like Moses, the great prophets, and Jesus, Paul was a channel both for primary and secondary revelation. Many problems arose in the churches he organized and some of them involved situations concerning which Jesus had not expressed himself. In one such instance he admitted, "I have no command of the Lord," yet he added with conviction, "but I give my opinion as one who by the Lord's mercy is trustworthy" (1 Cor. 7:25). In connection with a related issue Paul expressed his "judgment," and then he declared, "I think that I have the Spirit of God" (1 Cor. 7:40). Paul is claiming apostolic authority for these Christian guidelines whether they came through tradition or his own interpretation. They are qualitatively different, however, from the revelation of the mystery of the gospel.

Revelation and Implications

The qualitative difference between primary and secondary insights is just as obvious outside the Bible. From the intuition of Einstein's formula $E = mc^2$ less gifted, but still superior, intellects have been able to work out implications and applications for science that never would have been possible without the formula. One result was the development of nuclear energy, but the use of this power to devastate Hiroshima was a nightmare that Einstein had not anticipated and he rued the day that he made his disclosure.

Thus, basic to the principle of primary insights is the corollary that the recipients do not completely understand all the implications of what they are declaring. This is true in all areas of human endeavor. In the concepts and compositions of musical geniuses, sensitive arrangers and interpreters have discovered facets and nuances that the originators did not realize were there. In the realm of poetry, Dorothy Sayers comments:

> A poet creates a character, a situation, a phrase for a particular purpose and, *after* having done so, realizes that he has created a universal symbol, applicable in a far wider sense than that which he immediately intended. Thenceforth he uses it, with or without "bothering to explain all its relevance," in the wider context to which he has found it applicable. But it sometimes happens that it is not the poet himself, but another, who discovers the wider relevance. If so, he is justified in so interpreting it in the place where he finds it; for the relevance was always potentially there, and once seen and recognized it is actually there for ever. This does not, of course, mean that we can "read into" poets anything that we jolly well like; any significance that contradicts the whole tenor of their work is obviously suspect. But it means that in a very real sense poets do sometimes write more greatly than they know.[41]

41. *Christian Letters to a Post-Christian World*, p. 169.

The same can be said for biblical revelation. In wrestling with the problem of how a Christian should interpret the Old Testament, Donald G. Miller suggests, "The clue to understanding here may lie in a distinction between what the ancient prophet said and what *God* [italics his] was saying through him. It may well be that God had more to say through the prophets than they themselves were aware."[42] Most certainly this is the claim of Paul when he states that the prophetic writings held the secret of God's purpose, but that Christ's revelation of the mystery to him was the key that unlocked the secret for all mankind (Rom. 16:25-26).

Revelation and Interpretation

In summary, the purpose of the designation "primary revelation" is to highlight the fact that God made known to a few gifted people the basic insights concerning his redemptive purposes for his creation and his creatures. In the words, deeds, and death of Jesus, the Living Word, God made the ultimate disclosure of himself. With the interpretation of Jesus' life, death, resurrection, and ascension by his disciples and some of their associates the determinative history of God's redemptive activity came to a close. Conservatives, both Roman Catholic and Protestant, have claimed that revelation closed in the twilight zone after the death of the apostles, and this author concurs if revelation is understood as "primary revelation."

On the other hand, God worked through the rational capacity of his servants to draw out from the major insights such references and implications as were appropriate for the covenant community. Although secondary in development, some of these insights preserve the permanent quality and relevance of primary revelation. When Yahweh, the sovereign God of the Israelites, brought his people into the land of Canaan, secondary revelation came in the form of the clear-cut inference "the land is mine"

42. *The Authority of the Bible*, pp. 64-65.

(Lev. 25:23). Some Israelites failed to live by this principle, and not yet has Christianity taken seriously the implications of this timeless claim. In a culture with its glorification of big money made by wheeling and dealing in real estate there is a desperate need for a new understanding of the truth that God owns our property—we are his stewards.

In the experience of primary revelation Paul realized that Jesus had "broken down the wall of hostility" (Eph. 2:14) between Jews and Gentiles and made them joint heirs. In Christ, therefore, "there is neither Jew nor Greek" (Gal. 3:28). The implication of this insight was that other separatistic categories were dissolved as well. Accordingly, Paul went on to say, "there is neither slave nor free, there is neither male nor female." Yet Paul did not see all the practical implications of his declaration. In fact, some of his statements about women contributed to centuries of male dominance on the grounds of biblical authority. Only recently has the full meaning of Paul's claim been recognized. In Christ, male and female are fully persons and all artificial, stereotyped definitions of roles are broken down along with all the other walls.

Not all the insights of secondary revelation had permanent relevance, however. Some interpretations were evoked by a particular need, and when the situation changed the regulation's validity ceased. The important fact is that at every stage of development within Israel and the church, the people of God were aided in making primary revelation relevant to their new context. This process of examination and reinterpretation is quite evident in the Bible, as will be shown in the next chapter, and it has continued down to the present. But this fact poses a genuine problem for the conservative Protestant. His tradition has taught that everything within the covers of the Bible is "special revelation" and, therefore, qualitatively different from Christian literature since the close of the New Testament. The solution to this one-sided theory is the recognition that the redemptive revelation of the Bible is of two basic kinds: "primary," which ceases with the close of the canon; and "secondary," a never-ending process of reinterpretation in which the implications of primary revelation are deduced and applied to life.

Many Christians today believe that the early creedal statements about the Trinity and the person of Christ are true. In doing so they are affirming that Christian theologians at Nicaea and Chalcedon spoke with greater clarity than the New Testament writers. Theologians have clarified many other points since then and they will continue to do so, but all of this involves a fuller understanding of primary revelation and not some new addition to it.

In conclusion, revelation in the broadest sense is the disclosure of God, the Creator, to all his creatures concerning the total range of truth and beauty. The Bible is God's self-disclosure of his redemptive purposes. Its chief themes are theological (God's nature and will), anthropological (man's nature and need), and christological (the provision for man's healing). Primary revelation ceased with Christ and the New Testament interpretation of him, but inasmuch as God was saying more through the biblical writers than they realized, the secondary process of reinterpretation and application will continue as long as man exists.

Chapter Four

Traditions of the Biblical Period

The fact of secondary revelation needs a good deal of elaboration, however, because the interpretive process is a variable and different points of view emerge, some more accurate and valid than others. In time, these partial truths develop into traditions or schools of thought where the respective supporters feel compelled to carry on their aspect of truth.

Tradition in the Old Testament

There is very little technical language in the Old Testament dealing with the concept of "tradition." The verb *qibbel* ("to receive, accept") does occur in Proverbs 19:20, "Listen to advice and receive instruction, that you may gain wisdom for the future," but the technical use of the verb and the derived noun *qabbalah* ("tradition") is a later development of Judaism. The same is true of *masar* ("to deliver, hand on") and the noun *masorah* ("tradition"). Notwithstanding the lack of technical vocabulary, the Old Testament is actually a compilation of traditions. The traditions of Abraham were carried on at Shechem, Hebron, and Beersheba, and those of Jacob at Bethel and Shechem.

The Mosaic and Prophetic Traditions

Before the rise of the monarchy, the dominant tradition in Israel was Mosaic. As noted earlier, Moses started the process of interpretation, Joshua continued it, and then the elders carried it on (Josh. 24:31). The commandment about the sabbath prohibited "any work," but then came the necessity of defining work. Ploughing and harvesting came under the ban (Ex. 34:21), and so did the lighting of a fire (Ex. 35:3). Numbers 15:32-36 is the story of a man caught gathering sticks on the sabbath. Since there was no regulation covering this incident, he was put into custody until a ruling could be obtained. Moses received orders from Yahweh to stone the man, and the congregation carried it out. During the monarchy, when commercial activities increased, bearing of burdens was prohibited (Jer. 17:21), and apparently the city gates were guarded to stop business (Amos 8:5). Obviously, someone had to work to keep others from working, but evidently such activity was exempted. After the exile, Nehemiah resorted to the same restriction (Neh. 13:19), but he had the Levites purify themselves and stand watch "to keep the sabbath day holy" (13:22).

Inasmuch as the covenant applied to all of life, this same interpretive process occurred throughout the spectrum of Israelite experience under Yahweh. Later on, in Judaism, students of the law probed every verse of the Pentateuch for general legal principles that could be more relevant. This "probing" was called *midrash*, from the verb *darash* ("to probe, search"). In Exodus 18:20 Jethro instructs Moses, "You shall teach them the statutes and decisions, and make them know the way in which they must walk [Heb. *halak*] and what they must do." On the basis of this verse, apparently, Judaism described the collection of moral and ritual teaching as *halakah* ("guidelines to walk by"). The use of a story to give instruction (the man picking up sticks, for example) was termed *haggadah* ("narration").

In spite of the law of Moses and serious attempts on the part of some to carry out its intent, life was hard and precarious for many Israelites. Over the years more and more people began to express their hopes that Yahweh would do some new thing to bring about peace and justice. The main tradition in Israel, the northern kingdom, was Mosaic. Hopes for the future were expressed in terms of Moses and Yahweh's covenant with Israel. The idea is expressed quite clearly as a promise of Yahweh to Moses, "I will raise up for them a prophet like you from their fellows, and I will put my words in his mouth, and he shall tell them all that I command him" (Deut. 18:18). Later on, some of those within the prophetic tradition expressed the belief that Elijah, the great prophet of the northern kingdom, who was taken up in a chariot of fire, would return as Yahweh's messenger: "I will send you Elijah the prophet before the great and terrible day of Yahweh comes" (Mal. 4:5).

Although there is no record of Moses and Elijah being anointed to serve as prophets, there are indications within the prophetic tradition that anointing was necessary to consecrate a prophet for his task. Elijah is told to anoint Elisha as his successor (1 Kings 19:16). Psalm 105:15 commands, "Touch not my anointed ones, do my prophets no harm." In Isaiah 61:1 the prophet states, "The Spirit of the Lord Yahweh is upon me, because Yahweh has anointed me to bring good tidings to the afflicted [poor]." Since the Hebrew word for "anointed" is *meshiah* (commonly transliterated *messiah* and translated *christos* in the Greek), the anticipated prophet was a messiah.

Still another interpretation within the prophetic tradition is the "suffering servant" theme (Isa. 52:13-53:12). Unfortunately, we know little about the precise historical characters and context involved in this remarkable passage, but the insight concerning vicarious suffering is found nowhere else in the Old Testament.

The Davidic Tradition

Because of the gifted David and his military successes, there arose a tradition that Yahweh had chosen to work his will through David's lineage and his city Jerusalem: "Your house and your kingdom shall be made sure forever before me; your throne shall be established forever" (2 Sam. 7:16). Saul was anointed (1 Sam. 10:1), David was anointed (1 Sam. 16:13), and a favorite designation of a king was "anointed one" (Ps. 2:2). It was even applied to Cyrus, the Persian (Isa. 45:1). Thus, any expectation of a greater David was messianic.

The Priestly Tradition

The third major tradition in the Old Testament is that of the priests. Inasmuch as the dominant priestly tradition was in Jerusalem, it existed side-by-side with the Davidic tradition, and there was anticipation of cooperation between the kingly and priestly roles. Ezekiel, for example, looks for another David, but this messiah is not pictured as lordly king with crushing military power. Instead, he would be a "prince" who reigns as a kindly shepherd and as an agent of peace (Ezek. 34:23-25). But the real leadership and action would come from the priests and be centered in the temple (Ezek. 40-48). This dual relationship was followed, in the case of Zerubbabel and Jeshua, after the return from exile (Ezra 3:2; Hag. 1:1). Since Aaron and his sons were anointed (Ex. 29:7, 21; Lev. 8:12), the future priest would be a messiah as well.

The Confrontation of Traditions

All of these traditions yearned for the day that Yahweh would restore righteousness and peace, and undoubtedly these longings arose as a result of a vital relationship with Yahweh. In each instance, therefore, the claim was supported by the authority of "the word of Yahweh." While there was truth in all of these hopes, the variant claims led to confusion and conflict. Isaiah, the city prophet, was steeped in the Davidic tradition. His whole theology revolved around Yahweh's choice of David and his city Zion (Jerusalem). During the siege of Sennacherib (701 B.C.) Isaiah delivered Yahweh's assuring word to King Hezekiah,

"I will defend this city to save it, for my own sake and for the sake of my servant David" (Isa. 37:35).

Not many years prior to this, Isaiah's contemporary Micah, the country prophet from Moresheth, declared that Jerusalem was a wicked city, and on the basis of the Mosaic covenant he predicted in the name of Yahweh, "Zion shall be plowed as a field; Jerusalem shall become a heap of ruins" (Mic. 3:12). Imagine the confusion of those who heard of both predictions! "Which one," they must have asked, "is really speaking the word of Yahweh?" Also imagine how Micah and his followers must have felt when Jerusalem was spared. They must have thought that Yahweh had failed in his promise to punish the wicked.

Although Micah was eventually right, and twice at that (587/6 B.C. and A.D. 70), the remarkable fulfilment of Isaiah's prophecy was interpreted as something Yahweh owed Jerusalem, not that it was an act of his mercy to give them another chance. This Jerusalem tradition became more arrogant as time went on, and during the period of Jeremiah they declared that there was no danger from enemies because the temple, where Yahweh was enthroned, was in the city. In a sermon, delivered in 609 B.C. at the temple gate, Jeremiah declared, "Do not trust in these deceptive words, 'This is the temple of Yahweh, the temple of Yahweh, the temple of Yahweh' " (Jer. 7:4). The courageous prophet suffered for years and almost perished because the proponents of the Davidic tradition forgot that, long before David, Yahweh had made with Moses and Israel a covenant based on obedience.

The Wisdom Tradition

As a channel of revelation, wisdom represented still another tradition. Many issues arose in ancient Israel and, in general, interpretation was influenced by the guidelines of the tradition in which the discussion occurred. As a result, the Old Testament has a number of variant points of view. While there is remarkable continuity of certain areas, it is not possible to weave all of the ideas into one coherent pattern. Even in Scripture, therefore, it is neces-

sary to determine which "word of Yahweh" is the most
authentic. The essential point is that tradition (both as
content received and the process of handing it on) is
doubled-edged: sometimes it preserves and reinterprets
correctly; at other times it distorts.

The Sadducee Tradition

The major Judaistic groups prior to and during the rise
of Christianity were the Sadducees, the Pharisees, and the
Essenes. The Sadducees, who claimed to be the descendants of the Davidic priest Zadok, were the priestly group
in control of the temple. Originally they were supported
by the Hasmonean priest-kings. Gradually they acquired
wealth and their outlook became quite secular. In spite of
this, they were the official interpreters of Moses. In theory
they claimed to be literalists, relying solely on the Written
Law. They rejected the doctrine of resurrection, for example, because they claimed that it was not clearly taught in
the books of the Hebrew Bible. The same concern for the
written text was missing, however, when it came to the
priestly regulations prohibiting the acquisition of wealth.
In practice, the Sadducees had to interpret the text to
make the Law relevant for their day. Obviously, their
theory was intended to endow their interpretations with
the authority of Moses.

The Essene Tradition

A competing priestly group, also claiming to be descendants from Zadok, were the Essenes, centered at Qumran
near the Dead Sea. In reaction to the Hasmonean kings and
the dissolute priests at the temple they went out into the
wilderness, sometime early in the reign of John Hyrcanus I
(134-104 B.C.), "to prepare the way of the LORD" (Isa.
40:3). Those who desired joining the community had to
contribute all their possessions to the common fund. The
founder, the Righteous Teacher, claimed to possess the
key to unlock the secrets of the prophetic writings. Accordingly, much time was devoted to interpreting the

sacred scrolls. Their daily routine included a purifying bath (baptism) and a common meal with bread, wine, and a blessing. Here, as in Ezekiel, the priests played the dominant role. They believed that they were living in the *eschaton*, the end of the age, and they anticipated a priestly messiah (of Aaron), a Davidic messiah (of Israel), and a prophet (Elijah?).

The Pharisee Tradition

The Pharisees ("Separatists") probably originated with those Hasidim ("Pious Ones") who, having obtained their religious freedom by 163 B.C., refused to follow Judas Maccabeus toward his dream of becoming another David. These common people, with no status or wealth, thought that by keeping the law of Moses perfectly the Messiah would come. Accordingly, they were zealous students of Scripture. Since the Written Law did not deal specifically with many issues of their time, the Pharisees developed guidelines for living from suggestions they found there. These interpretations, which proved more authentic for the common people, constituted the core of a growing corpus known as the Oral Law. Specialists, known as scribes, made interpreting the Law a vocation.

To counter the teachings of the Sadducees, who disdained the Oral Law, the Pharisees developed the doctrine that the Oral Law had been delivered to Moses on Mt. Sinai along with the Written Law, thus making it equally valid. The Talmud incorporated this doctrine in the Mishnaic tractate *Pirqe Aboth:* "Moses received [*qibbel*] Torah from Sinai and delivered [*masar*] it to Joshua, and Joshua to the elders, and the elders to the prophets, and the prophets to the men of the great synagogue." The latter has traditionally been interpreted to refer to the time of Ezra and Nehemiah. Simon the Just, one of the last survivors of the great synagogue, passed the Torah down until it was received by Hillel and Shammai.

As the Pharisees increased in number and importance they outranked the Sadducees in the area of interpretation. It was quite natural that in spite of a common base this dominant group would eventually polarize into two schools of interpretation. Hillel (about 20 B.C.-A.D. 20), the brilliant Jew from Babylonia, was the great teacher of the liberal wing, while his contemporary Shammai presided over the conservative school. Whereas Hillel had thirty-nine rules defining banned activities on the sabbath, Shammai had many more. Apparently both made an exemption for helping an animal in distress (Luke 14:5), but the Essenes, the strictest regarding sabbath observance, prohibited helping an animal in labor or even to lift the newborn out of a pit or cistern should it fall there.

One of the most innovative interpretations, the *prosbul* (meaning "before the court"), was introduced by Hillel. Deuteronomy 15:1-16 provided for the remission of all debts at the end of every seven years. When this sabbatical year was near, loans were almost impossible to obtain because lenders feared that the debts would not be repaid before being cancelled. The *prosbul* exempted the specific loan from the Mosaic law and assigned the collection of the debt to the court, which was free to continue collecting after the sabbatical year because it was not mentioned in the law of Moses. "Thus," as F. F. Bruce remarks, "a regulation which was humanitarian in purpose in the context of a simple agricultural economy was replaced by another, equally humanitarian in purpose, which was more appropriate to a developed mercantile economy."[1]

The basic motivation back of the Oral Law was a sincere desire to make the law of Moses a live, vital factor in all of life. Rabbi Aqiba (about A.D. 55-137), from the school of Hillel, is reported to have taught, "Tradition is a fence around the Law." The various restrictions of the Oral Law were intended to prevent breaching the law of Moses. In the process, however, attention was diverted more to the legal instead of the human aspects. Competition was keen and the demand for creative insights pushed the legal experts to employ some very imaginative, but subjective, methods. For some it was a matter of pride that a whole mountain of truth could be deduced from the law of

1. *Tradition: Old and New*, pp. 23-24.

Moses, even though suspended only by a hair. Some of the scribes recognized that this practice was stretching the claim of Mosaic authority. The story is told in the Talmud about the time Moses incognito visited the classroom of Aqiba. The implications that the great Rabbi claimed to derive from Moses puzzled the great lawgiver because he failed to recognize any of the teachings as related to his own.

The Criterion of Authenticity

Other traditions, such as the Samaritan and Hellenistic groups, and combinations of these various views made Palestine in the first century A.D. a very complicated religious scene. In this context John the Baptist and Jesus ministered and the church was born. Many of the early Christians were converts from these various groups. It is little wonder, therefore, that from the beginning there were competing factions. Although apostolic teaching developed a consensus on the major issues, a variety of former views persisted and strands of some of these can be found woven into the New Testament. All of these cannot be fitted into one scheme and so in the New Testament, as in the Old, there are various traditions, some more authentic than others.

The most accurate criterion for making the judgment is surely the claim of primary revelation. In this regard Jesus, Peter, and Paul are clearly the authentic voices in Christianity. Notwithstanding many similarities between Christianity and its religious context, there is a qualitative difference, namely, Jesus. His authority was evident in his encounter with the dominant tradition of the scribes and Pharisees. Since both sides believed in the authority of the Hebrew Bible, the *crucial difference* was one of *interpretation*.

The Tradition of Jesus

In dealing with the claims of the Oral Law, Jesus said, "You have heard that it was said to the men of old, 'You shall not kill, and whoever kills shall be liable to the judgment' " (Matt. 5:21). The "men of old" is clearly a reference to the tradition of the elders. The difficulty with the interpretation of the scribes was its external nature: he who had not committed the overt act had kept the law. Jesus countered, "But I say to you that everyone who is angry with his brother shall be liable to judgment" (Matt. 5:22). The law interpreted externally could restrain the end result, but it was helpless to deal with the beginning of transgression. Jesus realized, with incisive clarity, that to stop wrong actions it is imperative to stop wrong thoughts. The Oral Law thought in terms of *suppression*, but by going to motivation, the heart of the matter, Jesus was urging *elimination*. In short, Jesus contended that the *Law of God*, from the Ten Commandments on, *involved both the inner and outer aspects of life*. To fail internally, therefore, was to be guilty because such action breached the intent of God.

This conflict of interpretations is made quite explicit in Matthew 15:1-6 and Mark 7:1-13, where Jesus accuses the scribes and Pharisees of using "the tradition [Gk. *paradosis*] of the elders" to "make void the word of God." In unequivocal terms, therefore, Jesus is claiming that his interpretation, not the tradition of the elders, is the authentic voice of Moses. Even his hearers recognized the authority of his teaching over that of the scribes (Matt. 7:28).

The Tradition of Peter

When Jesus was in the region of Caesarea Philippi he asked his disciples concerning his identity. Peter, the natural leader of the disciples, replied, "You are the Christ [Messiah], the Son of the living God" (Matt. 16:16). Jesus claimed that his answer was a revelation from the Father. While form-critical scholars doubt the authenticity of the confession in this early context, it does indicate a tradition that Peter had been favored by a revelation. Jesus appeared to him personally after the resurrection (Luke 24:34; 1 Cor. 15:5), and certainly the vision at Joppa was another revelation (Acts 10:9-16). All of these events qualified Peter to be a special witness of the Jesus tradition.

The Tradition of Paul

Paul's whole theology was built on the revelation that he received from Jesus Christ. His insights ran counter to some of the dominant views in the early church, and the first part of his ministry was spent trying to authenticate his authority as an apostle. It is little wonder that many of the early Christians doubted his claims. He had never been one of the disciples during the earthly ministry of Jesus. How could the word of this late-comer outweigh that of Peter?

Recognition of Paul's authority was more rapid because of Peter's support. In the vision at Joppa, God made known to Peter the essence of the mystery that had been revealed to Paul. Yet when he associated with Gentiles he was severely criticized by the "circumcision party" in Jerusalem (Acts 11:2) because they believed that one had to become a Jew before one could become a Christian. This issue came to a showdown in the council at Jerusalem (Acts 15:1-21). After much debate, Peter reviewed his experience with the Gentiles and then Barnabas and Paul related what had been happening at Antioch. In his first trip to Jerusalem after his conversion, Paul visited with Peter and with James, the brother of Jesus (Gal. 1:18-19). Since the risen Lord had appeared to James personally (1 Cor. 15:7), he was recognized as an apostle. As the leader of the Jerusalem church, he settled the issue officially at the council by siding with Peter, Barnabas, and Paul.

But dominant members of the mother church in Jerusalem refused to accept the new point of view, and when James sent some of them to Antioch on a fact-finding mission, their presence made Peter fearful. When alone at Antioch he had mingled freely with the Gentiles and eaten whatever was served, regardless of levitical purity. But when the inspection party came around, Peter had nothing to do with the Gentiles because of his fear of the old guard. Even saintly Barnabas yielded to the psychological pressure of the commission; thus Paul had to act or the decision of the council would have been nullified. Accordingly, he rebuked Peter publicly for his duplicity (Gal. 2:11-14).

Paul studied with Gamaliel I (about A.D. 20-50), the successor of Hillel; therefore he was trained in the tradition of the elders and he knew all the technical language related to the idea of tradition (*midrash, halakah, haggadah, masorah* = Gk. *paradosis*, and especially the verbs *gibbel* = Gk. *paralambanō* ["to receive"] and *masar* = Gk. *paradidōmi* ["to deliver"]). In spite of his dramatic conversion, Paul continued to use some of these terms because they applied to the Jesus tradition that he had received.

In summarizing his life, Paul notes that for his age he was advanced in Judaism. Then he states, "I was extremely zealous for the traditions [*paradosis*] of my fathers" (Gal. 1:14). On the other hand, Paul writes to the Corinthian Christians, "I commend you because you remember me in everything and maintain the traditions [*paradosis*] even as I have delivered [*paradidōmi*] them to you" (1 Cor. 11:2). As a follower of Jesus' tradition, Paul is an imitator of Christ; therefore he dares to urge the Corinthians to imitate him (1 Cor. 11:1) by keeping the tradition he has delivered.

The Origin and Content of Paul's Tradition

Paul certainly learned some details about Jesus and "the way" during the stoning of Stephen and the persecution of the young church. Probably he received more from Ananias and the Christians at Damascus. Undoubtedly he learned still more from Peter and James on his visit to Jerusalem, especially about Christ's personal appearance to them. It is evident, therefore, that there was a sharing of details about the tradition relating to Jesus. This apostolic witness involved: (1) a summary of the gospel—a statement of faith consisting of the theological interpretation of facts from the life of Jesus; (2) Christian *halakah*—guidelines for faithful living; and (3) specific incidents from the life of Jesus.

A prime example of the first category is Peter's sermon on Pentecost (Acts 2:14-36). Although more brief, Paul has a summary of the essentials in 1 Corinthians 15:1-4. Concerning this tradition, Paul states, "I delivered [*paradidōmi*] to you as of first importance what I also received [*paralambanō*]" (15:3). After recounting the various appearances of the risen Christ to the apostles, including himself, Paul declares, "Whether then it was I or they, so we preach and so you believed" (15:11). He acknowledges, therefore, that at the point of the resurrection, all the apostles have the same testimony. Another expression of the Jesus tradition, without the technical language, is 1 John 1:1-3, "That which was from the beginning, . . . which we have seen and heard, we proclaim also to you. . . ."

The category of Christian *halakah* is well illustrated by 1 Corinthians 7. Paul is answering a number of questions that the church at Corinth has put to him. With regard to the married, Paul states, "I give the ruling, not I but the Lord, that the wife should not separate from her husband . . . and that the husband should not divorce his wife" (vv. 10-11). Evidently Paul had learned about Jesus' teaching on divorce such as appeared later in Mark 10:2-12. In related issues he comments, "I say, not the Lord" (v. 12) or "I have no command of the Lord" (v. 25). Thus, Paul goes beyond the regular tradition of the apostles and supplements it with a tradition of his own. He is very careful to distinguish between the two, but he is convinced that his judgments are authentic because he has "the Spirit of God" (v. 40).

Paul states this claim more emphatically in 1 Corinthians 11. After commending the Corinthians for maintaining the traditions just as he had delivered them, Paul chides them for improper customs in worship. Reasoning on the basis of God as the head of Christ, Christ the head of man, and man the head of woman, Paul declares dogmatically, "Any man who prays or prophesies with his head covered dishonors his head, but any woman who prays or prophesies with her head unveiled dishonors her head" (vv. 4-5). With the play on the word "head," Paul claims that any man worshipping with covered head dishonors Christ and God, and any woman with uncovered head dishonors her husband, Christ, and God. The principle applies even to the length of hair: "Does not nature itself teach you that for a man to wear long hair is degrading to him?" (v. 14). Evidently Paul had some apostolic backing because he concludes, "If anyone is disposed to be contentious, we recognize no other practice, nor do the churches of God" (v. 16).

Later on in 1 Corinthians 11 there is an example of the category of tradition pertaining to a specific incident or narrative about Jesus. The Lord's supper also has been abused at Corinth; accordingly Paul confronts them with what happened on the night that Jesus was betrayed. To strengthen his criticism he states, "For I received from the Lord what I also delivered to you" (v. 23). At first glance it would appear that Paul claims to have received by revelation from Christ the instructions for keeping the Lord's supper. Yet the two verbs indicate that he is thinking in terms of tradition. While some scholars still interpret Paul to mean a vision from Christ, most think he was referring to tradition, that is, a chain of tradition that began with the Lord. Oscar Cullmann (1902-   ) makes a good case for the following explanation of this anomaly: "The Lord himself is at work in the transmission of his words and deeds by the Church; he works through the Church."[2] Since the exalted Christ, not the historical Jesus, is at work in this process, Cullmann elaborates, "*It is the exalted Lord who now proclaims to the Corinthians, through the tradition, what he had taught his disciples during his incarnation on earth* [italics his]."[3]

In summary, Paul's tradition is the Jesus tradition (delivered to Paul by the apostles) interpreted in the light of the revelation the exalted Christ made known to him. Just as the Jesus tradition replaces the Jewish tradition, so Christ becomes the new Law. Paul, thereby, becomes the minister of the new covenant just as Moses was of the old (2 Cor. 3:6).

2. *The Early Church*, p. 62.
3. *Ibid.*, p. 68.

Chapter Five

Scripture and Noncanonical Traditions

Inasmuch as no apostles were commissioned after the twelve, Matthias, James, and Paul, their death was the setting sun of primary revelation. Twilight was short, as it is in Palestine. Literature of the late first and second centuries A.D., sources both outside and inside the church, indicate that in certain circles there was a swift deterioration of Christian understanding of the gospel. In addition to the need for the authentic witness of the apostles, these churches required more clarity and order in the areas of daily living, worship, and polity. Just as the Jews had been confronted with the problem of the valid interpretation of Moses, so the church fathers had to wrestle with the question of the authentic interpretation of the apostolic teachings.

The Problem of Defining Tradition

Before surveying the history of noncanonical traditions it will be helpful to consider some of the ways tradition has been defined. A helpful book in this regard is *Scripture and Tradition*, by the Christian Brother, Gabriel Moran. One classification describes tradition as: (1) *dogmatic*—revealed truths made known by God before the death of the last apostle; and (2) *disciplinary*—practices and liturgical rites of the church (either apostolic or postapostolic, but not part of divine revelation).[1] These categories are essentially those of "primary revelation" and "secondary revelation" as defined in Chapter 3.

Another classification defines tradition as: (1) *objective (passive)*—the content (beliefs and practices) of tradition; and (2) *subjective (active)*—the act of "handing over," or the organ of transmission.[2] The general truth of this distinction is evident—there was a deposit of tradition as well as a group of people who passed it on. But genuine understanding of tradition necessitates some questions: "Precisely what was handed over?" "In what way was it passed on?" "Was anything added in the process?" "Who did the handing over?"

The crux of the problem lies in the relation between Scripture and the truths of tradition. Normative Roman Catholic doctrine claims that there are three relationships: (1) *inherent tradition*—explicit truths in Scripture; (2) *declarative tradition*—implicit truths in Scripture; and (3) *constitutive tradition*—revealed truths not even implicitly found in Scripture.[3] The first two categories are beyond dispute from a theistic point of view. But constitutive tradition affirms that God has revealed himself in a *primary* way through *two parallel sources:* Scripture and tradition. This is the real point at issue, both inside and outside the Roman Catholic Church, and it will require a good deal of careful attention.

Postapostolic Tradition

The greatest of the early fathers was undoubtedly Irenaeus (about A.D. 125-202). He was reared at Smyrna in

1. *Scripture and Tradition*, p. 20.
2. *Ibid.*, p. 19.
3. *Ibid.*, p. 21.

Asia Minor. In 177, while a missionary in Gaul, he was appointed Bishop of Lyons. Considering it his greatest task to be an opponent of gnostic rationalism, he wrote *Five Books Against Heresies*, throughout which are scattered numerous statements expressing his views about Scripture and tradition. Irenaeus stresses the supreme importance of the written sources, but in order to refute the heretics who twist Scripture, he appeals to "the tradition derived from the apostles" and transmitted "through the successions of the bishops." Irenaeus summarizes this tradition in terms of the apostolic teaching about the Father, the Son, and the Holy Spirit. This threefold division is found in the early baptismal confession and in the Apostles' Creed, but tradition has expanded the discussion so that it becomes "the rule of faith."

Irenaeus has no question, therefore, that the churches founded by the apostles had handed on the tradition faithfully. The most authoritative church was Rome, in Irenaeus' opinion, because it had the authority of Peter and Paul as its founders. There was no practical distinction between Scripture and the tradition of the apostles, as far as Irenaeus was concerned. Tradition was the valid, plain teaching contained in Scripture. Had the apostles left no Scripture, the church would still abide by the tradition of the apostles. It is quite evident, therefore, that for Irenaeus the tradition of the apostles was the key to unlock the meaning of Scripture.

Tertullian (about A.D. 150-230), the fiery, devout Christian from Carthage, North Africa, shared the sentiments of Irenaeus on Scripture and tradition. So did Origen (about A.D. 185-254), the most scholarly of the fathers. As the battle with heresy became more intense, increasing stress was put on the church and its authority to safeguard the truth. Tertullian wanted to prohibit any heretic from using Scripture, and Cyprian (about A.D. 200-258), his disciple, went all the way to declare that not only was there no understanding of Scripture outside of the church—there was no salvation either. In order to strengthen the authority of the church, especially in the larger churches, Cyprian pressed for the superiority of the bishop over the local presbyters, and before long the episcopal form of government ruled the church. Thus, by A.D. 250 the basic pattern and direction of the church had been set.

In his *Holy Writ or Holy Church*, George Tavard, the French Roman Catholic, presents a very detailed survey of the Scripture-tradition issue from the postapostolic period down to the Council of Trent and its aftermath. Throughout the study the recurring theme of this ecumenically minded priest is that true blessedness consists in holding the two aspects as a unity. "Scripture cannot be the Word of God once it has been severed from the Church which is the Bride and the Body of Christ. And the Church could not be the Bride and the Body, had she not received the gift of understanding the Word. These two phases of God's visitation of man are aspects of one mystery. They are ultimately one, though one in two. The Church implies the Scripture as the Scripture implies the Church."[4]

Tavard states that this was the view of Irenaeus and other early fathers. He concludes, "As the whole life of the Church is read in Scripture by the Fathers, so the whole Scripture lives for them in the Church. We may call this a dialectic. We may invoke the category of sacrament. Whichever formula we prefer, we are led by patristic theology to consider that there is a sense in which 'Scripture alone' is an authentic expression of Catholic Christianity."[5] But "Scripture alone" does not mean just the books of the canon. Postapostolic writings were read and cherished, and gradually these were put alongside Scripture. "Tradition, then," Tavard notes, "was the overflow of the Word outside Sacred Scripture. It was neither separate from nor identical with Holy Writ. Its contents were the 'other scriptures' through which the Word made himself known."[6]

4. *Holy Writ or Holy Church*, p. 246.
5. *Ibid.*, p. 11.
6. *Ibid.*, p. 8.

Tradition in the Medieval Period

The union of Scripture and tradition was maintained in the medieval period, according to Tavard, but here again there is an extension of Scripture outside the canon. He cites Hugo of St. Victor, the great twelfth-century theologian, in his claim that since the Old Testament has three parts, "the Law, the Prophets, the Historians," so the New Testament contains "the Gospel, the Apostles, the Fathers."[7] For Hugo, "the Fathers" meant the Decretals, the Decrees of the Popes, as regular or canonical in authority, and the writings of Jerome, Augustine, Ambrose, Gregory, Isidore, Origen, Bede, and the other doctors. Yet the patristic writings are not considered canonical, just as some of the Old Testament books (Wisdom of Solomon, etc.) were not part of the canon. Then Tavard comments, "The trend is clear. Whereas the Canon proper is considered as closed, its limits are still fluid, and some writings, outside the Canon as such, share in the inspirational power of Holy Scripture. Hugo himself calls the whole, 'divine Scripture'."[8]

Similarly, Thomas Aquinas (1225-1274), the most renowned theologian of Roman Catholic scholasticism, states in the first question of his *Summa Theologica* that Sacred Scripture consists of the biblical text and the theology of the fathers and doctors. This union can be approached by two methods: as the object of faith or the object of investigation. Ultimately Sacred Scripture is Sacred Doctrine. Tavard concurs in this development: "This inclusion of the Fathers within the body, if not the Canon, of Scripture, is consistent with the above-noted correlation of Scripture and the Church."[9] It is this broadened definition of Scripture that becomes the basis for the union of canon and tradition throughout the medieval period.

7. *Ibid.*, p. 16.
8. *Ibid.*, p. 17.
9. *Ibid.*, p. 16.

Tradition During the Renaissance

It was in the fourteenth century, according to Tavard, that the rupture occurred between Scripture and tradition. The seeds of discord were sown by Henry of Ghent, a secular theologian, who wrote his *Commentary on the Sentences* between 1276 and 1292. He set the authority of Scripture over against that of the church or tradition. William of Ockham (1300-1359), an English Franciscan, abetted the idea. In reaction, Guido Terreni (d. 1342) "made Scripture entirely dependent on the authority of the Church."[10] In so doing he argued strongly for the infallible authority of the popes. This trend continued until canon lawyers ran amuck trying to outdo one another in praise of the pope. The period of the papal court in Avignon, France (1305-1376), was a time of power-politics. The sycophants went so far as to liken the pope to God. Since the pope had all power, priestly and kingly, heavenly and earthly, he could say with Jesus, "All power has been given to me in heaven and on earth" (Matt. 28:18).[11] It was such extravagant talk that incensed John Huss (1369-1415) and led finally to his being burned at the stake for heresy.

The papal schism (1378-1429), with popes at Rome and Avignon excommunicating and anathematizing each other, gave theologians some second thoughts about the infallibility of the papacy. In an attempt to reunite the church, officials from both popes met in Pisa in 1409. This gave rise to the Conciliar Movement (1409-1443), which believed that the church assembled as a general council was more authoritative than a pope. One of the most influential priests in the councils was Peter d'Ailly (1350-1420). He allowed for postapostolic revelation and, moreover, he believed that, separate from the canon, an authentic tradition about Jesus had been transmitted orally through the apostles and the church.[12] The Englishman Thomas Netter

10. *Ibid.*, p. 31.
11. *Ibid.*, pp. 47-48.
12. *Ibid.*, p. 55.

Waldensis (d. 1430) elaborated the idea of "oral tradition," and it persisted for some time.

In Tavard's opinion, "Conciliarism presented a subtle danger to the doctrine of the primacy of Scripture. For though Councils are deemed supreme, they do not all belong to the same level. Some Councils have been evidently mistaken."[13] The danger was that councils were "becoming the official recipients of post-apostolic revelations."[14] In evaluating the fifteenth-century dilemma, Tavard elaborates on his favorite theme, "In her essence, the Church is not a power of interpretation: she is a power of reception. She receives the Word which God speaks to her in the Scriptures. It is this Word as by her received which is authoritative for her members. Thus Scripture and Church are mutually inherent. To Scripture is attached an ontological primacy; and to the Church a historical one because it is only in her receptivity that men are made aware of the Word."[15]

The dispute between the conciliarists and papists carried over into the sixteenth century. Jacques Almain (1450-1514) contended that the pope himself had no authority other than that of the church. Moreover, his doctrine needed to be checked by that of the church at large. Sylvester Prierias Mazzolini (1456-1523) took the opposite extreme. The church had no authority except through the Roman pontiff. His judgments even superseded the authority of the gospel. Whoever did not accept his rulings as the infallible rule of faith was a heretic. Whereas Pope Leo X (1513-1521) praised Prierias, the scholar Desideratus Erasmus (1464-1536) quipped, "Everybody laughs at Prierias."[16]

A moderate view was taken by the Dominican Thomas de Vio, Cardinal Cajetan (1468-1534). Although he claimed that the pope's authority came directly from God, yet the excesses of the canon lawyers had shown that the pope must still be subject to Scripture. For Cajetan, this

13. *Ibid.*, p. 52.
14. *Ibid.*, p. 56.
15. *Ibid.*, p. 66.
16. *Ibid.*, p. 117.

meant the plain sense of the biblical text as found in the consensus of the fathers. At the beginning of the sixteenth century, therefore, there were three basic views of authority: Almain favored councils, Prierias the popes, and Cajetan the fathers.

It was in such a chaotic theological atmosphere that on October 31, 1517, Martin Luther (1483-1546) posted his ninety-five theses. The fathers, councils, and popes would have to bow to Scripture. Cajetan met Luther at Augsburg in 1518, but he was unable to move him from his stand on Scripture alone. In 1519 at Leipzig, Johann Eck (1486-1543) represented the Roman Church in its disputation with Luther. Eck was a fighter by nature, and he penned many articles against Luther and the Reformation. At first he had a moderate view like Cajetan. Since Christ had empowered the apostles, not the popes, to publish the gospel, Sacred Scripture was to have first place. He did not agree with Luther, however, because he held to the traditional Roman view that the fathers gave the true sense of Scripture.

When Luther took "justification by faith" as his standard of the gospel, he was ready to ignore James as a "very strawy epistle." This canon within the canon disturbed Eck a great deal and he began to change his views in order to counter Luther. God had revealed the gospel through Jesus Christ, who in turn passed it on to the apostles. The gospel was written in the hearts of the church; as a result the church had authority over written sources, both Scripture and tradition. Finally, in order to keep from misinterpreting Scripture, which was a sin against the Spirit, Eck concluded that Christians must yield to the church because it was the only true interpreter of the gospel. Tavard comments, "Eck had started with the superiority of Scripture over the Church. He ends at the opposite pole: superiority of the Church over Scripture."[17]

Tavard does not think too kindly of Luther, however: "The justified man" not only "judges Scripture itself," he "judges the Fathers and Doctors."[18] Both the church and

17. *Ibid.*, p. 119.
18. *Ibid.*, pp. 82-83.

the Bible are reduced to an ancillary status because they are "subject to a given doctrine, to 'my Gospel.' "[19] For Tavard, Luther was a rank individualist who saw nothing in Scripture except what he wanted to see. One might add that Luther did not have a monopoly on following his presuppositions. Many in the church did the same. The question is, "Whose partial insight was nearer to the essential message of the Gospel?" Tavard's answer is that Luther's doctrine of "justification by faith" did not account for all of Scripture or the church's tradition; therefore it was "neither scriptural nor traditional."[20] "The Lutheran Reformation," declares Tavard, "laid the basis for a novel tradition. In it, 'pure doctrine', understood as a reduced set of propositions, lorded it over the Scriptures and the fellowship of believers."[21] In this judgment Tavard is nearer the truth, as we shall see later.

Tavard has some affinity for John Calvin (1509-1564), but he cannot understand how such a first-rate thinker would leave the Church on his own (as he did in 1533). He appreciates Calvin's stress on the Word, yet when the Word is tied to the Holy Spirit instead of the visible church, he feels that Calvin introduced a vicious polarity of "the realm of the invisible" and "the level of personal experience," with his theology moving around in a circle. The problem is not the circle because "all thinking based on faith evolves in a circle."[22] "The trouble is," Tavard notes, "that now the circle has been entirely hammered out in the thought of Calvin. Along a former cycle, Scripture and Church had explained and justified each other; and because both were held to be equally dependent on Christ and the Spirit, a vertical dimension had kept their sum total intrinsically faithful to God's intent. Calvin's passage has erected another theological cycle. The reciprocity of Scripture and Spirit in the believer's experience has been substituted for the former proportions of analogy."[23] A

19. *Ibid.*, p. 83.
20. *Ibid.*, p. 95.
21. *Ibid.*
22. *Ibid.*, p. 109.
23. *Ibid.*

major consequence, of course, was Calvin's denial of the
traditional doctrine of apostolic succession. Apostolic
authority rested with all who were governed by Christ and
Scripture. If any were unfaithful, then authority would
forsake them because it was not bestowed on them personally. Scripture, for Calvin, excluded the "human traditions" tacked onto the biblical canon, the pure Word of
God.

The strict "Scripture alone" of Luther and Calvin
evoked the opposite claim "the Church alone" (*sola
ecclesia*) by Albert Pigge (1490-1542), a strong apologist
for Roman orthodoxy. Scripture is limited to the canonical books, but it needs to be supplemented by tradition,
"the apostolic message of the primitive Church, handed
down through the succession of Fathers and Bishops,
whether that message has been written or not in the Holy
Scriptures."[24] Recognition of this all-important body of
tradition raised the question as to how Christ had assisted
the church in defining, conserving, and passing it on. Some
apologists took the additional step of claiming the inspiration of the Holy Spirit for the extracanonical tradition.
Kaspar Schatzgeyer (1463-1527), arguing on the scriptural
ground of his Lutheran adversaries, held that inasmuch as
Christ had not unveiled all, "An 'intimate revelation from
the Holy Spirit' is an everyday possibility. Once known
beyond doubt, it is as binding as the teaching that came
from Christ's own mouth."[25] Nikolaus Ellenbog (d. 1543)
was more cautious in positing holiness as a criterion. Only
the holy, like the saintly fathers and doctors, were channels of inspiration.

The Council of Trent

While the various answers of Roman apologists to the
Reformation critique had a common base, there was still
no agreement on the precise relation of Scripture to tradition. Accordingly, the fourth session of the Council of

24. *Ibid.*, p. 150.
25. *Ibid.*, p. 164.

Trent was assigned the task of bringing some order out of confusion. The discussion began on February 8, 1546, and it did not finish until April 8. The bishops debated long and hard, and the first draft of the decree did not appear until a special meeting on March 23. In summary it stated:

> The "purity of the Gospel of God" promised by the prophets was promulgated by Christ. It was preached by the Apostles as the *"rule* of all saving truth and of all moral discipline"*. This "truth is contained partly (*partim*) in written books, partly (*partim*) in unwritten traditions." These traditions are ascribed to Christ himself or to the Apostles to whom the Holy Ghost dictated them. They have "reached down to us transmitted as though by hand". The Council therefore acknowledges the books of the Old and the New Testament, and these traditions "as dictated orally by Christ himself or the Holy Ghost and kept in the Catholic Church in continuous succession". *Equal adhesion of faith is due to both.* The Council receives them as "sacred and canonical". It will use both "to *constitute* dogmas and restore the morals in the Church".[26]

By the time the general assembly took up the discussion of the draft on March 27 there were three basic points of view. The dominant group thought highly of traditions and wanted them ranked equally with Scripture, if possible. The minority group included the learned General of the Servites, Bonuti (Bonucci), and the Dominican, Gianbattista Nacchianti, Bishop of Chioggia. Although the latter did not deny the value of traditions, he felt strongly that no traditions, either apostolic or ecclesiastical, should be mentioned in a decree on Scripture. The third group mediated between the extremes by claiming that revelation lay partly (*partim*) in the Scriptures and partly (*partim*) in the traditions.[27]

The draft met immediate opposition. Another member of the minority party, Pietro Bertano, Bishop of Fano, started the debate, and it continued off and on through

26. *Ibid.*, p. 202. Italics his.
27. *Ibid.*, pp. 198-200.

April 7. Then without warning a revised draft was submitted on April 8. The "partly"-"partly" had disappeared, and in its place was "and" (*et*): The gospel "truth and discipline is contained in the written books and in the unwritten traditions."[28] The minority group was able, finally, to accept the revision, and Bonuti himself pronounced the sermon at the solemn Mass that closed the fourth session of the Council.

Tavard interprets the decree as follows: "The dynamic element which constitutes the source (*fons*) of all saving truth and all Christian behavior, is the Gospel of Christ, the Word spoken by Christ and communicated to the Church through the Apostles. It is a living Word. It carries the power of the Holy Spirit. This dynamic element uses two sets of vessels: Holy Scripture and traditions. In as far as they convey the same Gospel of Christ, in as far as they channel the original impetus whereby the Spirit moved the Apostles, both Scriptures and traditions are entitled to the same adhesion of faith. For faith reaches Christ and the Spirit whatever the medium used to contact us."[29] "This would logically imply," comments Tavard, "that the whole Gospel is contained in Scripture as it is also contained in the traditions. Yet this was not made explicit at Trent." [30]

Another specialist concerning the Council of Trent is Josef Rupert Geiselmann, the German scholar. Concerning what was actually decided at Trent, Geiselmann declares, "We may now answer: neither the sufficiency of content of Holy Scripture was proclaimed, nor was the relation of Scripture and Tradition decided in the sense of 'partly-partly'. One cannot emphasize enough that nothing, absolutely nothing, was decided at the Council of Trent concerning the relation of Scripture and Tradition."[31] "With this *et*," Geiselmann states, "the Council avoided a decision about the relation of Scripture and Tradition; for, in view of the two conflicting theological positions repre-

28. *Ibid.*, pp. 207-208.
29. *Ibid.*, p. 208.
30. *Ibid.*
31. "Scripture, Tradition, and the Church: An Ecumenical Problem," *Christianity Divided*, pp. 47-48.

sented at the Council, the question was deemed not yet ripe for decision."[32]

Tradition in the Post-Tridentine Period

Tavard's and Geiselmann's restrained, balanced interpretations of the fourth session of the Council of Trent are in marked contrast to the views of the Roman theologians in the post-Tridentine period. Geiselmann places primary responsibility for this unfortunate retrogression on the influential twelve-volume work *Loci theologici* by Melchior Cano (1509-1560). In the third volume, probably written in 1546, Cano declares the *partim-partim* view. He quotes tradition to prove that "the apostles passed on the teachings of the gospel partly in writing and partly also orally."[33] Then he quotes, in abridged form, the decision of the Council as proof that the saving truth and moral teaching of the gospel "is continued in written books and unwritten traditions of Christ himself."[34] In short, the transmission of the gospel was divided between two sources of revelation: Scripture and tradition. Through the catechisms and theological writings of the irenic Peter Canisius (1521-1597) and the *Controversies* of the polemical Bellarmine (1542-1621) the two-source theory of Cano became the normative view for Roman Catholicism.

Geiselmann is incensed with the doctrine and its popularity. "To put it more clearly," he declares, "the latter view is un-Catholic. God is no plumber who, so to speak, provides the Church with running water, letting the word of God flow out of two sources of faith, Scripture and Tradition, as out of two water taps marked hot and cold."[35] As the basis for his own solution to the problem, Geiselmann quotes Johann Adam Möhler (1796-1838), one of the venerable professors in the founding years of the Tübingen School, "Church, gospel and tradition always

32. *Ibid.*, p. 48.
33. *Ibid.*, p. 41.
34. *Ibid.*, p. 42.
35. *Ibid.*, pp. 48-49.

stand or fall together."[36] The Council of Trent pointed the way. Scripture *and* tradition are thus two modes of existence of the gospel of Jesus Christ embraced within the church.[37]

Roman Catholic Tradition Today

In the aftermath of the Council of Trent the forces of the Reformation and the Counter-Reformation wore themselves down to a stalemate with neither side threatened seriously by the other or the secular world. But during the middle of the nineteenth century, three hundred years after the Council, the dark clouds of deism, atheism, rationalism, science, and nationalism moved in to threaten the Roman Church. Pope Pius IX (1792-1878) was elected to the office on June 16, 1846, and continued for thirty-two years, the longest pontificate on record. In the encyclical *Quanta cura*, written eighteen years after his elevation, he describes conditions at the time of his election: "Scarcely had We ... been called to this Chair of Peter, when We, to the extreme grief of Our soul, beheld a horrible tempest stirred up by so many erroneous opinions, and the dreadful and never enough to be lamented mischiefs which redound to Christian people from such errors."[38]

Also at the time of his elevation as Pope, Pius IX recalled that during the pontificate of Gregory XVI (1831-1846), his predecessor, there was a desire throughout the Church that the Virgin Mary finally be declared by Church decree as having been conceived without the stain of original sin. In an encyclical letter *Ubi primum*, February 2, 1849, Pius noted that there was no lack of "eminent theologians—men of intellectual brilliance, of virtue, of holiness and sound doctrine—who have so effectively explained this doctrine and so impressively expounded this

36. *Ibid.*, p. 50.
37. *Ibid.*
38. *The Papal Encyclicals in Their Historical Context*, ed. by Anne Fremantle, p. 136.

proposition."[39] Finally, he appealed to the bishops for their support and prayers "that the most merciful Father of all knowledge will deign to enlighten Us with the heavenly light of His Holy Spirit, so that in a matter of such moment We may proceed to do what will redound to the greater glory of His Holy Name, to the honor of the most Blessed Virgin, and to the profit of the Church Militant."[40]

The response was unanimous, and so on December 8, 1854, the bull *Ineffabilis Deus* proclaimed the dogma of the Immaculate Conception:

> We declare, pronounce, and define that the doctrine which holds that the most blessed Virgin Mary, in the first instant of her conception, by a singular grace and privilege granted by almighty God, in view of the merits of Jesus Christ, the Saviour of the human race, was preserved free from all stain of original sin, is a doctrine revealed by God and therefore to be believed firmly and constantly by all the faithful.[41]

To counter the threat of heresy, Pius instructed his officials to compile a list of the dangerous teachings. They finally defined eighty errors. On December 8, 1864, the tenth anniversary of the dogma of the Immaculate Conception, the *Syllabus of Errors* was sent out accompanied by the encyclical *Quanta cura*, which denounced the errors and urged the bishops to exercise great care in guarding the flock. Since the threat of the Reformation had led to the Council of Trent, Pius felt that the threat of heresy necessitated another council. Accordingly, on December 8, 1869, just five years after the promulgation of the *Syllabus*, Pius convened Vatican Council I. The doctrine of infallibility had been commonly accepted for centuries, but now Pius pressed for a decree to help him wage his war with error. The Constitution *Pastor aeternus* became a dogma on July 18, 1870, the vote being 451 yea, 62 yea subject to amendments, and 88 nay. Inasmuch as the idea

39. *Ibid.*, p. 133.
40. *Ibid.*, p. 134.
41. *Ibid.*

of infallibility rested on that of papal primacy, chapter 1 dealt with the origin of the primacy of Peter, chapter 2 argued for the continuity of the Roman papacy from Peter, and chapter 3 defined the nature of the Roman primacy. Chapter 4 defined infallibility as follows:

> The Roman pontiff when he speaks *ex cathedra*, that is, when exercising the office of pastor and teacher of all Christians, he defines with his supreme apostolic authority a doctrine concerning faith or morals to be held by the universal Church, through the divine assistance promised to him in blessed Peter, is possessed of that infallibility with which the divine Redeemer willed his Church to be endowed in defining faith and morals: and therefore such definitions of the Roman pontiff are irreformable of themselves (and not from the consent of the Church).[42]

The modernist threat came to a crisis under Pius X (1835-1914), who was elected pope on August 4, 1903. France's break with the Vatican in 1904 and its confiscation of church property led Pius to confront head-on the philosophical and political ideas endangering the church. On July 3, 1907, *Lamentabili sane*, a syllabus of sixty-five errors of the modernists, was issued by the pope's officials. The next day Pius confirmed the decree and ordered that each and every one of the errors be "condemned and proscribed." The explanation of his action came in the long encyclical *Pascendi Dominici Gregis*, issued on September 8, 1907. The inquisition was very thoroughgoing, and many sincere, open-minded priests were caught in the backlash.

The next major developments occurred under Pope Pius XII (1876-1958), who was elected in 1939. The most far-reaching decree of his term of office was the encyclical *Divino afflante spiritu* ("On Promotion of Biblical Studies"), dated September 30, 1945. Pius, following the counsel of the late Augustin Cardinal Bea (1881-1968), urged scholars to carry out a thoroughgoing interpretation of the text so that the plain meaning could be understood by the

42. Hans Küng, *Infallible? An Inquiry*, p. 99.

faithful. Knowledge of textual criticism and biblical languages was encouraged because the fathers had encouraged these tools. "However," it was acknowledged, "such was the state of letters in those times, that not many,—and these few but imperfectly—knew the Hebrew language. In the middle ages, when Scholastic Theology was at the height of its vigor, the knowledge of even the Greek language had long since become so rare in the West, that even the greatest Doctors of that time, in their exposition of the Sacred Text, had recourse only to the Latin version, known as the Vulgate."[43] This whole new approach to biblical study carried one restriction, "The commentators of the Sacred Letters . . . should no less diligently take into account the explanations and declarations of the teaching authority of the Church."[44]

In response to widespread desire, the Constitution *Munificentissimus Deus* defined on November 2, 1950, the dogma of the Assumption of the Virgin Mary: "We pronounce, declare and define it to be a divinely revealed dogma: that the Immaculate Mother of God, the ever Virgin Mary, having completed the course of her earthly life, was assumed body and soul into heavenly glory."[45] A warning followed: "Hence if anyone, which God forbid, should dare wilfully to deny or to call into doubt that which we have defined, let him know that he has fallen away completely from the divine and Catholic Faith." [46]

The references to "divinely revealed dogma," "doctrine revealed by God," and "teaching authority of the Church" clearly root in the concept of infallibility of the Roman Church and the pope. The origin and development of the concepts of inerrancy and infallibility will be discussed later on; therefore the implications of these relatively recent traditions will be more fruitfully examined in that context.

A most amazing development was the election of Pope John XXIII (1881-1963) to succeed Pius XII, who died

43. *The Papal Encyclicals in Their Historical Context*, p. 278.
44. *Ibid.*, p. 280.
45. *Ibid.*, p. 299.
46. *Ibid.*

October 8, 1958. "John XXIII, by his whole attitude, by his words and deeds," Hans Küng comments, "exercised the ecclesiastical 'teaching office' in a new, Christian way—or perhaps in reality in a more original way, a way therefore more potent for the future. People listened to him, both inside and outside the Catholic Church."[47] In hopes of renewing the church and expanding its influence, Pope John convened Vatican Council II in October, 1962. The agenda included a series of schemas or statements prepared ahead of time to deal with current issues concerning the teaching and life of the Roman Church. One of the most crucial schemas was *De Fontibus Revelationis* ("On the Sources of Revelation"). There was much discussion of the statement because it favored the two-source theory of revelation, and Pope John intervened by appointing a special commission to rewrite the schema.

The revised text, entitled *De Divina Revelatione* ("On Divine Revelation") was submitted at the second session of Vatican II, September-November, 1963. It was never discussed openly, however, and in closing the session Pope Paul VI urged that it be considered seriously in the third session. On the basis of comments received during and after the second session, the Doctrinal Commission revised the text. This third version, presented to the third session, September-November, 1964, had the following outline:

> Prologue
> I. Revelation Itself
> II. The Transmission of Divine Revelation
> III. The Divine Inspiration and the Interpretation of Holy Scripture
> IV. The Old Testament
> V. The New Testament
> VI. Holy Scripture in the Church's Life

After more debate and letters of comment, some slight revisions resulted in the fourth version of the text. This was submitted to the fourth and final session of Vatican II,

47. *Infallible? An Inquiry*, pp. 14-15.

September-December, 1965. It was approved overwhelmingly, and on November 18, 1965, Pope Paul promulgated "The Dogmatic Constitution on Divine Revelation." While it ruled out the two-source theory of revelation, Vatican II, like the Council of Trent, failed to make explicit the relationship between Scripture and tradition. This issue was left to the theologians.

Protestant Tradition Today

Because of the extremely individualistic attitudes found within Protestantism a thorough treatment of tradition would require a whole book. Accordingly, only a few aspects will be highlighted to indicate the situation. An important development came out of the Fourth World Conference on Faith and Order, held in Montreal, Canada, in 1963. In presenting its report on Scripture and tradition, the Second Section set forth some working definitions of tradition: (1) *tradition*, as a continuous activity of the church to relate the past to the present and future, involves both the process of transmission and the content of what is transmitted; (2) *traditions* are the distinctive features of life and doctrine that develop within congregations and denominations or associations of churches; and (3) *the Tradition*, the history of God's people, starting with Israel, highlighted by Jesus Christ, and continuing in the church. The norm of *the Tradition* is Scripture, and by it *traditions* are reformed and renewed.

For many Protestants, however, the insights of these helpful definitions are completely lost. The amazing fact is that some of the Protestants who are most horrified at the Roman Catholic understanding of tradition as the Spirit-guided interpretation of Scripture actually believe the same. An excellent case in point is the widespread scheme of interpretation known as dispensationalism. Although the major force in developing the teaching was the Irish clergyman John Nelson Darby (1800-1882), the popularity of the movement came through the notes and commentary of the Scofield Reference Bible, which appeared in 1909. The editor, Cyrus Ingerson Scofield (1843-1921), claimed no originality on his part. He compiled and systematized the opinions of biblical scholars within the tradition.

The Bible met with such success that it was revised and set in new type in 1917. When from the standpoint of format and type style the Bible societies were publishing shamefully shabby editions of Scripture, the attractive format of the Scofield Bible, with its section headings and parallel passages, sold millions of copies worldwide. As a result, dispensational teachings made inroads into churches with no historical connection to the movement. The influence of the Scofield notes became so dominant within evangelical circles that many adherents considered the commentary as *the true interpretation* of the Bible, thus implicitly granting the commentary equal authority with the biblical text. The average reader did not have enough training or insight to see that in many instances the distinctive features of dispensationalism represented only one of two or more alternative explanations of the text.

In 1967 appeared the New Scofield Reference Bible. The members of the Editorial Committee consisted mainly of presidents and deans of schools associated with the movement. A number of erroneous features, such as Ussher's chronology, have been dropped, but in essence the dispensational view has been maintained. Clearly, the Committee was convinced that its interpretation was the teaching of Scripture. It had not departed from the conviction of Darby, whom Francis William Newman (1805-1897), a former disciple, eloquently described as follows: "He only wanted men 'to submit their understanding *to God*', that is, to the Bible, that is, to his interpretation!"[48] In this respect dispensationalism and the Roman Church share the same view. The different results are due to varying criteria and methods of interpretation. Of course, the same could be said of all the mainline Protestant denominations where they anchor their distinctive insights to the teaching of Scripture. In short, the problem of tradition confronts every Christian regardless of label.

While certain conservative church groups may agree doc-

---

48. *Phases of Faith*, p. 34.

trinally, they will differ widely in mores or customs of life style. Some groups with European background have no qualms about smoking and drinking beer or wine, but they protect the pulpit zealously from all laymen or clergy ordained outside the denomination in question. Other groups open the pulpit to any and all conservatives, but are aghast to see any so-called Christian smoking or drinking. Hardly any item of clothing (including ties) and accessories (especially jewelry and cosmetics) has been overlooked in the category of sins, and there has never been a lack of people with conviction to propagate their views as the biblical standard for living. Traditions that were formed during the early days of the movies tended to ban all motion pictures, whether in or out of the theater. In most instances opera was not a threat or a viable option; thus no dictum was laid down. Accordingly, people who would not be caught dead in a theater attended operas that, from the biblical point of view, were more inappropriate than some good movies.

The whole history of the conservative Protestant movement indicates how many convictions about life style are conditioned by environment. The Bible says different things when read from different traditions, and not all of the numerous claims to have the aid of the Holy Spirit can be equally correct. The ultimate problem for all Christians, whether Roman Catholics, Greek Orthodox, or Protestants, is how to reform and renew teaching, thereby producing more mature followers of Christ.

The Definition of "the Gospel"

Any attempt to break out of one's circle of tradition necessitates a reexamination of the gospel. Tavard defines tradition as "the art of passing on the Gospel."[49] What is this gospel? It certainly includes the first-century records of the deeds and sayings of Jesus, who claimed that the revelation back of these came from God, his Father (John 14:10). The content of Jesus' earthly ministry came to

49. *Holy Writ or Holy Church*, p. 1.

Paul prior to his conversion through reports about the Jesus "way" and afterwards through the tradition of those who had been with him. But it was the revelation of the risen Christ (Gal. 1:12) that formed the basis of his theological understanding. At first, this gospel of primary revelation was preached orally, but later on, due to doubts concerning the authority of his message and also as a result of variant teachings among his converts, he reiterated his understanding of the gospel in letters to the various churches. These were read, copied, and handed on (traditioned, one might say). Much of this was in process before the Gospels were written. Some scribal errors and marginal notes crept into these copies, but the essence was there, even in the most poorly copied text. Although there was undoubtedly some oral tradition of Paul's teachings, the written tradition gradually assumed a primary role, especially after Paul's death when memories faded with the receding years of his ministry.

From the objective side of the issue, therefore, the gospel consisted of that collection of books and letters which were written (for various reasons) by the apostles and their associates as witnesses of the incarnate Christ. On the subjective side, the gospel was the experience of the presence of Jesus Christ made possible by the aid of the Holy Spirit at the hearing or reading of the gospel content.

The Definition of "Apostle"

The term "apostle" is derived from the Greek verb *apostellō* ("to send out"). In the Septuagint, the Greek Old Testament, the verb translates Hebrew *shalah* in Exodus 3:10 where Yahweh says to Moses, "I will send you to Pharaoh." Clearly, Moses was sent with the authority of Yahweh. Time and time again the prophets claim that they were sent by Yahweh, and he says the same. Although Jesus is never called an apostle, the Gospel of John, using the same verb, declares, "For God sent the Son into the world, not to condemn the world, but that the world might be saved through him" (3:17). Jesus himself makes the claim that he was sent (Matt. 15:24). In fact, then,

Jesus was God's incarnate Apostle. In turn, Jesus gave authority to his twelve disciples (Matt. 10:1) and sent them out (10:5). The resurrected Christ gave authority to the remaining eleven and told them, "Go . . . make disciples . . . baptizing them . . . teaching them to observe all that I have commanded you . . . " (Matt. 28:19-20). The early church felt compelled to bring the number of apostles back to twelve. The criterion for candidates was their association with Jesus "from the baptism of John until the day when he was taken up" (Acts 1:22). Two candidates were put forward, Joseph and Matthias. "The lot fell on Matthias and he was listed with the eleven apostles" (Acts 1:26).

Matthias is never heard of again because God had his own man to succeed Judas. Jesus confronted Paul on the road to Damascus and later Ananias was assured that Paul was "a chosen instrument" to carry his name "before the Gentiles" (Acts 9:15). In most of Paul's letters he claims to be "an apostle of Jesus Christ." He also calls himself "a servant" or "a prisoner," clearly implying that he is under the authority of another. In the early church, therefore, the term "apostle" was reserved for those few persons whom Jesus had chosen, taught, and sent out with authority. In the total perspective of the Bible, however, the "sent ones" were additionally those commissioned persons like Moses, the prophets, and Jesus, who served as God's agents of primary revelation.

The Problem of Apostolic Succession

There is no indication anywhere in the Pentateuch that Moses planned or tried to hand over his apostleship to his assistant Joshua. He had received it from Yahweh and it was not his to pass on. As his time of ministry drew to a close, Yahweh instructed Moses, "Take Joshua the son of Nun, a man in whom is the spirit, and lay your hand upon him" (Num. 27:18). "You shall invest him," Yahweh continued, "with some of your authority, that all the congregation of the Israelites may obey" (27:20). In other words, Yahweh instructed Moses to lay his hands on

Joshua in the sight of all the people in order that they would respect him as their new leader. But Joshua did not receive, thereby, Moses' authority as Yahweh's channel of revelation. That was never really passed on. The priest Eleazer was to be the channel of Yahweh's word, but even that was limited to the use of Urim and Thummim, the priestly means of answering "Yes" or "No" to simple questions such as "Shall I do this?" or "Shall I take this road or this action?" Elijah commissioned Elisha as his successor, but it was due to Yahweh's instruction, not his own volition (1 Kings 19:16). The classical prophets as well realized that their apostleship was not theirs to hand over to another.

This recognition is equally true of the New Testament. In Matthew 16:19 Peter is promised "the keys of the kingdom of heaven." Peter's power as leader of the early church will be to "bind" and "loose," rabbinic terms meaning "prohibit" and "allow." Later on, the rest of the disciples are promised the same authority (Matt. 18:18). In no case did they pass this authority on to their successors. On Paul's second missionary journey he came in contact with Timothy, a disciple (follower of Jesus) who was greatly respected at Lystra (Acts 16:1-2). This young man, who apparently had been a convert during Paul's first visit to the area, became his closest associate. He is called "my true child in the faith" (1 Tim. 1:2) and "my beloved child" (2 Tim. 1:2). Regardless of one's critical judgment as to the authority of these two letters, in the mind of the author there is a clear-cut understanding of the qualitative distinction between Paul and his favorite associate. Paul is the apostle, and nowhere in the letters does he pass his authority on to Timothy. Rather, he charges him repeatedly to be a faithful preacher and teacher of the gospel that he has received from Paul. Nowhere else in the New Testament is there any indication that Paul transmitted his authority as an apostle. According to the Bible, therefore, the authority of a prophet and apostle was God-given and the receiver had no power to hand it over to another person, even the closest associate. It is equally clear from the New Testament that no more apostles were commis-

sioned after Paul. This is proof that God deliberately
eliminated the role of apostle at the close of the period
associated with Christ. Cullmann is biblically accurate,
therefore, when he makes a distinction between "apostolic
tradition" and "ecclesiastical tradition."[50] "The function
of bishop, which is transmitted," he explains, "is essentially different from that of apostle which cannot be transmitted. The apostles appoint bishops, but they cannot
delegate to them their function, which cannot be renewed.
The bishops succeed the apostles, but on a completely
different level. . . . This means that the apostolate does not
belong to the period of the Church but to that of the
incarnation."[51] For this reason the so-called "apostolic
succession" is a misleading term. *Only the ecclesiastical
authority to preach, teach, and perform the sacraments is
passed on.*

Scripture and Tradition

In attempts to give tradition equality with Scripture, a
rather popular theme is the idea that religious tradition
was responsible for the compilation of Scripture. There is
some truth in the theory in that tradition evoked some of
the biblical material as well as having a part in the process
of canonical selection, but the essential thrust of the claim
is an exaggeration. The oracles of Amos sprang from an
authentic Mosaic tradition, but the authority came from
the revelation to Moses, not Hebrew tradition in Egypt.
The religious tradition centered at the temple in Bethel did
not produce the message of Amos—it simply evoked it!
The same was true of the message of Jeremiah. It came
from Moses, not the dominant tradition of the temple and
court in Jerusalem. The church at Corinth had many gifted
people, but these theological mavericks swarmed with
problems. It is inane to claim that this congregation played
any creative role in the disclosure of new insights. The
Corinthians evoked the letters of Paul, but it was the agent

50. *The Early Church*, p. 79.
51. *Ibid.*, p. 78.

of revelation who set forward the authentic word. Where was the church in the showdown at Antioch? Peter and Barnabas, cowed by fear, separated themselves from the Gentiles. One man alone, Paul, spoke the truth, and had it not been for him, the church and the New Testament would be different entities today. The fact of revelation is the most important factor in the formation of Scripture. Tradition does not control Scripture. Rather, revelation breaks in on old traditions and reforms them.

The Definition of "Tradition"

The prophets and apostles were channels of primary revelation, but both the office and its function terminated with the death of the last apostle. It was at this point, somewhere around the end of the first century A.D., that the qualitative transition to bishops became complete. From that time on, all teachings and writings were on the level of secondary revelation because they derived from the apostolic witness of the gospel. From the standpoint of content, therefore, tradition is best defined as the body of teaching that has been produced by the long chain of ecclesiastical successors to the apostles. Tradition sees new implications of the gospel, clarifies it in some instances, and continually makes it relevant to the present. But in all of this, there is no primary revelation.

The Problem of the New Testament Canon

During the period of transition from the apostolic tradition to the ecclesiastical there were some fairly accurate lines of oral tradition. Irenaeus recalled vividly his youth in Smyrna, where he listened to the sainted Polycarp (about A.D. 70-156) tell of his conversations with the apostle John. Another strand of oral tradition came through Papias, the bishop of Hierapolis in Phrygia. Irenaeus claimed that Papias was a contemporary and companion of Polycarp; thus his dates would be about A.D. 70-155. Unlike Polycarp, he seems never to have talked with John or any of the other disciples of Jesus, but whenever he came in contact with the "elders," those who had known the apostles, he questioned them thoroughly to find out all he could.

Throughout the period of Polycarp and Papias there were numerous other persons involved in oral tradition, both inside and outside the church. Those with the largest store of information about Jesus were accorded great honor, and gradually the human factors of faulty hearing and one-up-manship led to the expansion of his deeds and sayings. Those outside the church, such as the Gnostics, participated in the same process but their reason was more theological—they wanted to present Jesus as favoring their views. The elaborated stories found ready hearers among the many naive persons with little or no historical sense. Even though Papias took great pride in his store of oral tradition and considered it more authentic than the written sources, he seems to have been taken in at times because critical examination of some of his accounts disproves his claim.

Books were expensive and few people had a collection of Paul's letters or the Gospels. Accordingly, the charm of oral tradition swept throughout the churches with a resultant deterioration of the apostolic gospel. This fact alarmed some of the leaders in the young church. Apparently each cluster of churches began to compile a collection of the books that seemed authentic to it. Although there were some differences in the collections, the writings of Irenaeus and the Muratorian Fragment, a list of canonical books approved at Rome, indicate that around A.D. 200 there was a fairly uniform consensus concerning the authentic books. The basic criterion for this selection was apostolic authorship or authority. But in cases of doubt, the correlative criterion was the role of the Spirit. As Tavard explains, "The Word spoke to them when they read or listened to some writings. He kept silent when others were read. The power of the Word imposed itself on the Christians."[52] It took the historical perspective of a few generations to make a final decision on the borderline

52. *Holy Writ or Holy Church*, p. 5.

books. The epistles of Clement and Barnabas, and the Shepherd of Hermas, among others, were read and considered canonical by some Christians, but eventually they were excluded because they did not have apostolic authority. On the other hand, the little book of Jude was questioned for some time, yet it finally authenticated itself as an apostolic witness and a channel of the Holy Spirit.

The Canon and Tradition

As recognized earlier, there is secondary revelation in the Old Testament, between the Testaments, and in the New Testament. On the basis of this fact there have always been some within the Roman Catholic Church who have contended for the canonicity of tradition. If secondary revelation is permitted within the Bible, so the argument goes, why is it not valid following it? Secondary revelation was not excluded from the Bible because it was woven in with primary revelation, and any attempt to extricate it would have decimated the story of God's preparation for his incarnate Son. Before the church ever got around to defining its New Testament canon it had accepted the Hebrew Bible as Scripture. It did so because Jesus had considered it authoritative, and in turn it understood the Old Testament in the light of the incarnation. Once primary revelation ceased, however, there was no justification for continuing secondary revelation as a canonical collection. Postapostolic tradition is helpful, but it is qualitatively different from the gospel of Jesus.

At this point there is no need to go into further detail about the precise books in the canon. Furthermore, the problem of nonapostolic authorship need not concern us. In general, the collection is apostolic in tone and message. The sensitive Christians of the second and third centuries A.D. made that decision and there is no reason to revise it. A shift of a book or two would make no appreciable difference in the overall effect. The important fact is that by setting the canon, the church set limits for its rule of faith and its teaching ministry. The restrictions imposed by the canon undoubtedly explain why the Christian understanding of the gospel was far nearer its pure form in the period 175-200 than it was 125-150. Although composed by the fathers, the Apostles' Creed is essentially a summary of the rule of faith found in the canon. In a sense, therefore, it is apostolic. This separates it from the later creeds of the church.

Finally, it cannot be stressed too much that the fact of the canon proves that the early church, sensing what God had done, drew a line between apostolic and ecclesiastical traditions. If the gospel had been in a pure, stable form carried on by oral tradition within the succession of bishops, there would have been no concern over a collection of books. That they did form a canon shows that they put their trust more in written sources and, moreover, that they wanted to separate the authentic reports of the gospel both from spurious accounts and from later interpretations. Robert McAfee Brown states the issue well: "The very fact that the canon was established is the best evidence that the early Church was determined to distinguish between the apostolic tradition and all later tradition, and to insist that the former be the norm for the latter."[53]

The Meaning of Sola Scriptura

It should be recognized at the outset that it is impossible to practice the use of "Scripture alone" in an absolute sense. Even Martin Luther did not understand it that way. Those who take Scripture seriously are hardly consciously dishonest, yet the prejudices of religious training and cultural environment often conspire to prevent clear understanding of the truth in the text. Moreover, since the biblical writers eliminated many details because their intended audience had the information, a simple reading of the Bible cannot bring out the nuances of the message as given in its original context. For this reason, a thorough comprehension of Scripture necessitates a knowledge of biblical languages, history, and background.

53. "Tradition as a Protestant Problem," *Theology Today*, XVII (Jan., 1961), 450.

On the other hand, the Holy Spirit can work through certain portions of the Bible so as to lead the simplest reader into fellowship with Christ. This is true because at the close of the apostolic age the role of the Holy Spirit was changed from that of revealer to that of interpreter. One of the long-standing convictions of the Roman Catholic Church is that Scripture cannot be understood outside the church. One biblical passage cited in support of this belief is Acts 8:26-40. When Philip heard the Ethiopian eunuch reading Isaiah 53:7-8, he asked him, "Do you understand what you are reading?" "How can I," the eunuch asked, "unless someone guides me?" But the implication of the question does not apply to the whole story in Acts because the Christian interpretation given by Philip is incorporated, and people have come to Christ simply by reading the passage themselves. It is understandable why persons who have spent their whole lives strictly within the Roman Catholic fellowship find it hard, if not impossible, to believe that with no human interpreter the written text of the Bible can lead to Christ. Yet the Bible societies around the world have thousands of witnesses to this very fact. Actually, this possibility has been authenticated in the lives of many Roman Catholics because of the marked increase in recent years of Bible reading for personal devotion. Even biblical scholars can gain new insights by letting the Holy Spirit speak through the text during meditation.

After the convert has come to Christ, however, the power of the new experience compels him to seek Christian fellowship and to minister to persons about him. Thus, even though one can come to Christ isolated from others, one cannot come to Christian maturity in isolation. It is necessary to have the shared insights of fellowship and corporate living. The Roman conviction is essentially sound, therefore, because the Holy Spirit seeks to work through the church, the body of Christ. But the conviction is wrong when it equates the work of the church completely with the work of the Holy Spirit.

The Jews of Jeremiah's time were convinced that the temple and Mt. Zion were inviolable. They had forgotten that God's permanent covenant with them rested on the condition of obedience. But in the exile, Ezekiel had a vision of the glory of Yahweh rising from the temple and moving east (11:23). Christ's covenant with his church is no less an obedience-based fellowship. Any disobedient group or individual within the institutional bounds of the church, whether Protestant, Orthodox, or Roman Catholic, and regardless of hierarchical rank, is subject to the judgment of God. Persistent disobedience may even result in the loss of the Spirit's presence. The Holy Spirit is no more a prisoner of the church than Yahweh was of the temple.

The core meaning of "Scripture alone" is that the canon is the only place where one can go to find the authoritative gospel of Christ. Notwithstanding all the difficulties of the Bible, it presents the clearest picture of Jesus and God his Father. The writings of the postapostolic fathers are valuable, and Protestants have not given them the reading and study they deserve. Certainly the biographies of Christian saints are inspiring and contribute to the fullness of Christian experience. But the vast majority of ecclesiastical tradition resulted from the Holy Spirit's working through the canonical books. For this reason, Calvin's doctrine associating the Holy Spirit directly with the Written Word is a more accurate assessment of biblical teaching. This is also why there can be no constitutive tradition outside of the biblical canon. Once the apostolic period was closed, ecclesiastical tradition could never be the criterion for the truth.

The Authority of the Church

Because of his burning desire to maintain the purity of the gospel of Jesus, Paul wrote the following to the churches of Galatia: "But even if we, or an angel from heaven, should preach to you a gospel contrary to that which we preached to you, let him be accursed" (Gal. 1:8). This is strong language. Concerning the possibility of distorting the gospel, Tavard remarks, "To preclude this happening, the Church, guided by the Holy Spirit, practices the principle of authority. The Gospel is passed on from bishop to bishop, from teacher to teacher. The list of the men through whose care it has been kept undefiled in each local Church is what the Fathers termed the *paradosis* or tradition of that Church. The sum total of these traditions forms *the* Tradition of the universal Church."[54]

Tavard believes that the church's exercise of authority has prevented distortion of the gospel and that the bishops and teachers have handed it on undefiled. Before attempting to examine the validity of these assumptions, let us assume for the moment the possibility of minute deviations through human frailty. If a novice, do-it-yourself carpenter cuts a number of two-by-four studs for his house using each new piece as the measure for the next, he soon learns that the multiplied width of a pencil mark can make a real difference. Bureaus of standards are maintained to prevent such creeping errors. The crucial point is that *once a standard of measure is adopted, no object measured by it can displace it as the standard.*

The ancients were just as astute as we at this point. In fact, the word "canon" means "rule, standard." The selection of the canon was precisely to have a basis for checking religious teaching from that moment on. Knowledgeable leaders of the church had seen too much distorted gospel making the rounds of the local churches and they determined to restore the purity of the gospel as much as possible. In the light of the historical evidence the assumption of "undefiled" transmission of tradition is wishful thinking. In fact, the selection of the canon was the responsible use of authority to correct previous failure to exercise authority.

A further difficulty is the problem of deciding which one of the fathers is most accurate when two or three of them disagree. Tavard gives the interesting answer of Rupert of Deutz, "When the holy Doctors, who are in agreement concerning faith, fail to agree on a point of doctrine, I will most willingly and trustfully listen, like a pupil to a teacher, to the one whose doctrine is more or better in keeping with the testimonies of canonical Scripture."[55] As

54. *Holy Writ or Holy Church*, p. 1.
55. *Holy Writ or Holy Church*, p. 21.

noted in the survey of Roman Catholic tradition, there have been varying points of view at every stage of the church's development. In fact, the most crucial issues have not been resolved yet. Alternative opinions have continued on in tension, one point of view in ascendancy for a while only to be suspended by another when conditions changed and a more charismatic exponent appeared on the scene. This is precisely the Achilles heel of the Roman definition of tradition. In practice there has seldom been a unified speaking of the Spirit through the church; therefore it has been necessary to resort to some authoritative voice, either the pope and his advisors or the councils. Pope Pius IX convinced the majority at Vatican I that there was only one answer to the plurality of voices in tradition—he and his successors would speak infallibly for God.

Chapter Six

Traditional Theories of Inspiration

Before discussing the implications of the previous chapters it is necessary to fill out the cluster of ideas associated with Scripture. Probably the most hotly contested concept has been that of inspiration, and so it must be treated in considerable detail. The various definitions of inspiration have been categorized under four general views, and as a frame of reference it will be helpful to note them before surveying the history of traditional theories.

General Views of Inspiration

One extreme example is the view that characterizes inspiration as *intuition*—an inspired person is the religious genius who has a talent for spiritual insight. Thus the biblical writers were merely gifted men who were distinguished from their contemporaries only by their keener natural insight into truth.

This definition may account for Luke's claim with respect to his historical investigations, but it discounts completely the claims of Moses and the prophets. True inductive reasoning must also account for the conviction of

Jeremiah, for example, that "the word of the LORD" became for him "a reproach and derision all day long" (20:8). When he resolved not to speak again the name of the LORD there arose within him "a burning fire," as it were, which made it impossible for him to be silent any longer. This kind of inspiration was far more than heightened natural insight. The God of Israel was at work here.

Another general view defines inspiration as *illumination*—the person who has a deep experience with God is inspired. On this theory the Spirit of God is active in the biblical writer, but it is essentially an intensification of that illumination which is common to all followers of God. A number of passages in Scripture can be explained by this view, but it too is an oversimplification that cannot account adequately for the very personal, dynamic experiences of Isaiah and Jeremiah, for example.

An opposite extreme from the intuition view defines inspiration in terms of *dictation*—the inspired person is one to whom the Holy Spirit dictates the precise words of God's message. This mechanical concept of inspiration was held by some of the ancients, both Jews and Christians. A few formulations of inspiration made since the Reformation have been criticized by others as teaching the dictation view, but in each instance the author (or his disciples) has denied the charge. Perhaps the clearest evidence in support of this view is found in Exodus 31:18; the two tables of testimony were written "with the finger of God." This implies that God aided Moses in a special way while formulating the Ten Commandments. But to conceive of this rare event as God's usual method of revelation is an unwarranted assumption. An inductive approach to the biblical data indicates clearly that as a general rule God's servants were alert and in control of all their faculties during the process of communication.

A fourth general definition is the so-called *dynamic* view of inspiration—the inspired person has the extraordinary help of the Holy Spirit without violating his individuality and personality.

The Prophetic Concept of Inspiration

It is clearly evident in the Old Testament that prior to the exile the Israelites had a dynamic view of revelation and inspiration. Yahweh was free to make himself known personally when and with whom he chose. Every new generation was an occasion for further insight inspired by the spirit of Yahweh. Yet the Old Testament prophets were not overpowered by the act of inspiration. They heard the word of Yahweh while exercising their rational powers. The truth came from God, yet the expression of that truth always involved the characteristics of the prophet and his time. In the truest sense the word of Yahweh was a divine-human word. Moreover, while the true Israelite remembered the past, there was always the expectancy of a new word from God. In other words, the record of Yahweh's deeds and words was open-ended.

During Jeremiah's ministry there were few with this understanding. Most of the people held to the inviolability of Mt. Zion and the temple, and they pointed to the deliverance from Sennacherib as historic proof. Jeremiah's warning against this fallacious view went unheeded, but in the traumatic aftermath of the destruction of Jerusalem and the temple the exiles were forced to acknowledge their error. Now Moses and the prophets came to have a new meaning and their oracles were cherished as the only real hope. Aside from a few minor prophets, the canon of the Torah and the Prophets, the first two parts of the Hebrew Bible, was fixed during the exile.

The third part, the Writings, was left open, but there was less and less prophetic activity. Attention was focused on the torah ("teaching, instruction") of Moses and the prophets as the basis for life in the covenant community. Yet with this emphasis the sense of expectancy faded. The postexilic struggles under Zerubbabel-Joshua and Ezra-Nehemiah led to a desperate expression of self-preservation that resulted in theological rigidity and extreme separatism. Mainstream Judaism was correct in its claim that the spirit of prophecy had ceased by this time.

The Greek Concept of Inspiration

In Greece, meanwhile, there were religious developments along different lines.[1] In both the *Iliad* and the
Odyssey, Homer, the great poet of the eighth century B.C.,
invokes the inspiration of the Muses, the nine Greek god-
desses who were patrons of the arts and sciences, to carry
out his poetic work. Without their help no mortal human
can compose such elevated works. About the same period
of Greek history, Hesiod describes a dream in which the
Muses come to him with a laurel wreath, the symbol of his
inspiration. Pindar (about 518-438 B.C.), probably the
greatest of the Greek lyric poets, repeatedly credits the
Muses with being the true authors of the form and content
of his odes. The philosopher Parmenides, a contemporary
of Pindar, outdoes Hesiod. Rather than wait for the Muses
to approach him, he journeys to the heavens to consult
them about the eternal existence of the gods. The philosopher Democritus (about 460-370 B.C.) held that the poet's
inspiration came from outside himself, while rational powers were suspended, as in sleep. Plato (427-347 B.C.)
believed similarly, except that later on he placed the inspiration of the philosopher far above that of the poet.
Notwithstanding some variation there was a deep-rooted
belief in ancient Greece that the highest insights of beauty
and truth were the gifts of the gods and true in every
detail.

Times changed, however, and not everything Homer and
Hesiod wrote made sense to Pythagoras (582-507 B.C.)
and Xenophanes (570-480 B.C.). Their critical assessment
of the poets and their claims elicited the process of alle-
gorization. The truth of the ancient poets, so it was said,
was hidden beneath the surface meaning of the words.
Zeno (about 336-264 B.C.), the founder of the Stoic
school of philosophy, employed the allegorical method
and his followers became experts at it. They could find in
the ancient writers all their own philosophical truths.

1. See Robert M. Grant, *The Letter and the Spirit*, pp. 1-30, and
James D. Smart, *The Interpretation of Scripture*, pp. 179-190.

This extremely appealing method of interpretation spread to Egypt along with the doctrine of the overpowering inspiration of the gods. Aristobulus, a Jewish priest in Alexandria during the second century B.C., believed in Greek philosophy as revealed truth, and he found these philosophical views in the Old Testament. Moreover, by the allegorical method he was able also to get around the offensive anthropomorphic references to God's hands, feet, eyes, etc. The tradition started by Aristobulus became the dominant view of Jews in Alexandria. The letter of Aristeas (probably first century B.C.) evidences this same understanding of inspiration when explaining the origin of the Septuagint.

One of the greatest Alexandrites was the Jewish philosopher Philo (about 20 B.C. to A.D. 50). Exclusive of books that may have been lost, and those which have been spuriously attributed to him, Philo wrote thirty-eight different works. Four deal with special problems of philosophy, while three tell of current Jewish events in Alexandria. The remaining thirty-one deal primarily with the Torah or Pentateuch, being either running commentary on the text or discussions of topics found therein.

Philo believed that there were three sources of prophecy or revelation: (1) the Voice of God, (2) the Divine Spirit, and (3) angels. All three means of revelation are divine, even though angels can reveal to a non-Jew. The Divine Spirit reveals in Scripture, but this same Spirit can also give prophecy to a non-Jew of moral character. The Voice of God, however, is direct prophecy that occurs only in the Scripture given to the Jews.

But Philo's doctrine of inspiration must be evaluated in the light of other views that he held. The basic text for his theological writings was the Septuagint. Concerning the translators of this version, Philo wrote, "Reflecting how great an undertaking it was to make a full version of the laws given by the Voice of God, where they could not add or take away or transfer anything, but must keep the original form and shape, they proceeded to look for the most open and unoccupied spot in the neighborhood outside the city."[2] Having decided upon the island of Pharos, in the harbor of Alexandria, Egypt, the translators began their task, which Philo describes as follows: "Sitting here in seclusion with none present save the elements of nature, earth, water, air, heaven, the genesis of which was to be the first theme of their sacred revelation, for the laws begin with the story of the world's creation, they became as it were possessed, and, under inspiration, wrote, not each several scribe something different, but the same word for word, as though dictated to each by an invisible prompter."[3]

This statement shows that for Philo the Septuagint was as divinely inspired and authoritative as the Hebrew Scriptures. The translators, being "prophets and priests" who had the "spirit of Moses," made an absolutely accurate translation, and the finished product of each of the seventy-two scribes agreed identically, word for word, "as though dictated to each by an invisible prompter." Here in its clearest terms is the dictation theory of inspiration applied to the translation of the Septuagint.

Another aspect of Philo's thinking that has some bearing on his doctrine of inspiration is his manner of interpreting the Old Testament. He assumes that Scripture has two meanings: (1) the literal, obvious meaning, and (2) the underlying meaning, described most often by the term "allegory." "To allegorize," therefore, was to interpret the Scriptures in accordance with the hidden meaning. Only talented people with training and moral character were qualified for instruction in this method. With regard to Philo's use of these two methods of interpretation Harry A. Wolfson notes: "Everything in Scripture, from names, dates, and numbers to the narration of historical events or the prescription of rules for human conduct, is to him subject to allegorical interpretation. But as for the literal method, it is to be used, according to him, with certain reservations. One general rule laid down by Philo is that no

2. Philo, *Life of Moses,* Book II, par. 34, as tr. by F. H. Colson, *Philo with an English Translation,* VI, 465.
3. *Ibid.,* par. 37, p. 467.

anthropomorphic expression about God is to be taken literally. As proof text for this general rule he quotes the verse 'God is not as man,' which is taken by him to contain the general principle that God is not to be likened to anything perceptible by the senses."[4] Thus, in the Genesis account "it is quite foolish to think that the world was created in six days or in a space of time at all," because *six* is "not a quantity of days, but a perfect number," indicating that creation took place in a certain plan and order.[5]

The only time the literal meaning of historical events must be rejected, according to Philo, is whenever such an interpretation compels the reader to admit anything base or unworthy of the inspired words of God. The story in Genesis 37:13-14 of Jacob sending Joseph to see how his brothers and the flocks were faring cannot be accepted literally by any sensible person, for "is it likely that Jacob, who had the wealth of a king, was so badly off for household servants or attendants as to send a son out abroad to bring word about his other children, whether they are in good health, and about the cattle to boot?"[6] Nevertheless, Philo would not doubt that Joseph, for some other reason, went to see his brothers and was sold by them. Wolfson comments: "All these statements merely show that by the allegorical method Philo found it possible to explain away any narration of incident in Scripture that seemed to him to run counter to reason or expectation or to have some similarity with Greek myths, without necessarily impugning the historicity of the essential basic fact of the story."[7] But concern for the essential facts of the Bible does not involve precision of *all* details, so is not Philo in *practice*, then, negating some aspects of his *theory* of inspiration?

The Concept of Inspiration in Judaism

With the loss of the prophetic spirit after the exile, the stress of Judaism was increasingly minute interpretation of

4. *Philo*, I, 116.
5. *Ibid.*, p. 120.
6. *Ibid.*, p. 124.
7. *Ibid.*, p. 125.

the law. Although the rabbis in Palestine were not interested in philosophy as such, their interpretation hinged on the precise wording of the text, so the need for a more authoritative doctrine of inspiration led them to accept the Greek concept of inerrancy. This view became the dominant one in Judaism, and it is found in the tractate Sanhedrin in the Talmud: "He who maintains that the Torah is not from Heaven shall utterly be cut off—even if he states that the whole Torah is from Heaven excepting a particular verse which was not uttered by God but by Moses himself" (99a). The Jewish historian Josephus (A.D. 37-95) held a similar view of inspiration by which he explained the accurate predictions of the prophets.

The Concept of Inspiration in the New Testament

From A.D. 1850 to 1950 many scholars, both conservative and liberal, concluded that Jesus and the New Testament writers shared the view of inspiration held by the rabbis. The difficulty, however, is that notwithstanding some similar expressions, the practices of Jesus and some of the writers indicate genuine differences. Detailed discussion will occur in later chapters, but for the moment only the broad outlines need be sketched. With respect to the authority of the Hebrew Bible, its inspiration, and its origin from God, Jesus and the New Testament writers were on the same ground as the rabbis. The real difference comes in the understanding of inspiration. It is quite clear, for example, that Matthew is close to the rabbinical concept of inspiration. On the other hand, Jesus and Paul spoke with a unique authority that confounded their opponents and convinced their followers. There is a genuine difference in their understanding of inspiration and in the way they use the Old Testament. In fact, there is every indication that they marked the return of the Old Testament spirit of prophecy. Whereas the Greek concept of inspiration tended to be impersonal, with some or all of the human faculties blocked off, Jesus and Paul had that prophetic sense of personal relation with God which gave them remarkable freedom in the use of the Old Testament.

The author of the Fourth Gospel, whether the apostle John or some disciple of his, is an outstanding example of this freedom with respect to the actual words of Jesus himself. If the sayings of Jesus in the Synoptic Gospels are accurate verbally, then the messages of Jesus in John are clearly elaborations of the ideas Jesus expressed. No writer under the conviction of the inerrancy of every word of Jesus would have dared take the liberty that the author of John did. With the close of the apostolic age, however, there were threats on every hand, and the need for safeguarding the Gospel record made the doctrine of inerrancy more attractive.

The Early Church Fathers

Justin Martyr (about A.D. 100-165), an early defender of Christianity, wrote a book that he entitled *Apology* (meaning "Defense"). In this work, as well as in his other writings, appear numerous statements indicating his view of inspiration. Concerning the prophets, he affirms: "But when you hear the utterances of the prophets spoken as it were personally, you must not suppose that they are spoken by the inspired themselves, but by the Divine Word who moves them.... For they do not present to you artful discourses ... but use with simplicity the words and expressions which offer themselves, and declare to you whatever the Holy Ghost, who descended upon them, chose to teach through them to those who are desirous to learn the true religion."[8] Thus, while stressing the activity of the Holy Spirit, Justin did not deny the part played by the human instrument.

Probably the most extreme view of inspiration held by any of the church fathers was that proposed by Athenagoras. He was unknown to the church fathers of the third and fourth centuries, and little is known of his life. Apparently Athenagoras, an Athenian philosopher, became a

8. Justin Martyr, *Apology I*, ch. 36, p. 38, and *Hortatory Address*, ch. 35, p. 323, *The Writings of Justin Martyr and Athenagoras*, Vol. II, Ante-Nicene Christian Library.

convert to Christianity while studying Scripture in an attempt to refute it. Later he wrote an apology for the Christians, addressing it (about A.D. 177) to the Roman emperor Marcus Aurelius and his son Commodus. He said that the prophets, "lifted in ecstasy above the natural operations of their minds by the impulses of the Divine Spirit, uttered the things with which they were inspired, the Spirit making use of them as a flute player breathes into a flute."[9] It is quite evident that Athenagoras accepted the old Greek concept of an impersonal dictation of the message of God.

The inspiration of the Scriptures, according to Irenaeus, involved both the inspired man and the inspiration of the Spirit, making the writings the words of God. In theory, therefore, he denied the dictation view of Scripture, yet at the same time he always considered the inspiration of the book as transcending that of the man. The book, however, was the Septuagint, since Irenaeus spoke Greek, and, like Philo, he considered the LXX just as inspired and authoritative as the Hebrew text.

There are indications that Irenaeus rebelled against the allegorical type of interpretation that was so popular with the Christians and Gnostics at Alexandria. He was still a child of his age, however, and though holding to the literal method in theory, he often took great liberties with his own rule. Balaam's ass was a type of Christ, the three (?) spies who came to Rahab represented the Trinity, Gideon's fleece was a type of Israel, the Last Supper and Gethsemane were types of the descent into hell, and the good Samaritan was a type of the work of the Holy Spirit. Notwithstanding these interpretive lapses, Irenaeus has been considered by some scholars as holding to the verbal plenary view of inspiration.[10] But how can this be when he believed in the inspiration of the Septuagint?

Tertullian (about A.D. 150-230), the fiery, devout Christian from Carthage, North Africa, expressed his view

---

9. Athenagoras, ch. IX, *ibid.*, p. 384.
10. See, e.g., J. Barton Payne, "The Biblical Interpretation of Irenaeus," *Inspiration and Interpretation*, p. 21.

of inspiration as follows: "From the beginning He sent into the world men who, because of their innocence and righteousness, were worthy to know God and to make Him known to others. These men He filled with the Holy Spirit, that they might teach that there is but one God who made the universe and formed man from the earth."[11] He did not hesitate, therefore, to call the Scriptures the "writings of God" or the "words of God." Yet this general use of language should not be pushed too far. Furthermore, since Scripture (as defined by Tertullian) meant a Latin translation of the Bible, one cannot actually attribute the present-day interpretation of verbal plenary inspiration to him either.

Origen studied under Clement of Alexandria, and later became the leading teacher of the Alexandrian School. Inasmuch as Clement and Origen were in Alexandria, the shadow of Philo was bound to fall across both of them. Clement claimed there was an allegorical meaning throughout the entire Bible, and Origen, in principle, followed in his teacher's footsteps. All of Scripture, according to Origen, came to be recorded through the power of the Holy Spirit, so he could declare: "Small wonder if every word spoken by the prophets produced the proper effect of a word. Nay, I hold that every wonderful letter written in the oracles of God has its effects. There is not one jot or one tittle written in Scripture which, for those who know how to use the power of the Scriptures, does not effect its proper work."[12]

As the first great scholar to deal with the problem of the New Testament text, Origen knew there were difficulties in the various wordings of the Greek manuscripts available to him, but he felt that all of them could be overcome eventually with the allegorical method. Where the Greek text was clear, he admitted problems in connection with the literal meaning. He confessed: "And in many other

11. Tertullian, *Apology*, ch. 18, par. 2, pp. 53-54, in *Tertullian, Apologetical Works*, Vol. 10, The Fathers of the Church.
12. Origen, Homily XXXIX, in Jeremiah, p. 50, *Selections from the Commentaries and Homilies of Origen*, tr. by R. B. Tollinton.

instances, if a man carefully examines the Gospels with discrepancies of the narrative in view, . . . bewilderment will fall upon him, and either, abandoning all attempt to give the Gospels their real authority, he will arbitrarily adhere to one of them, not having courage to reject entirely his faith in our Lord; or else he must accept the four with the admission that their truth lies not in their outward and visible features."[13] It is unlikely that this statement and Origen's allegorical method of defending the absolute truthfulness of Scripture conform precisely to the doctrine of verbal plenary inspiration as defined today.

In summarizing the views of inspiration held by the early church fathers, B. F. Westcott (1825-1901) comments: "The unanimity of the early fathers in their views on Holy Scripture is the more remarkable when it is taken in connexion with the great differences of character and training and circumstances by which they were distinguished. In the midst of errors of judgment and errors of detail they maintain firmly with one consent the great principles which invest the Bible with an interest most special and most universal, with the characteristics of the most vivid individuality and of the most varied application. They teach us that inspiration is an operation of the Holy Spirit acting *through* men, according to the laws of their constitution, which is not neutralized by his influence, but adopted as a vehicle for the full expression of the divine message."[14] Finally, Westcott affirms: "It is possible that objections, more or less serious, may be urged against various parts of the doctrine, but it cannot, I think, be denied that as a whole it lays open a view of the Bible which vindicates with the greatest clearness and consistency the claims which it makes to be considered as one harmonious message of GOD, spoken *in many parts and many manners* by men and to men—the distinct lessons of individual ages reaching from one time to all time."[15]

13. Origen, Commentary in John, X. 3, *ibid.*, p. 107.
14. Westcott, "Appendix B. On the Primitive Doctrine of Inspiration," p. 455, *An Introduction to the Study of the Gospels.* Italics his.
15. *Ibid.*, p. 456. Italics his.

Westcott was not explicit as to the meaning of "full expression," but it would appear that he was referring to Scripture as a statement of God's redemptive purpose and activity that is sufficiently complete to achieve the desired goal with respect to mankind. Since Westcott was not ignorant of the variation within Scripture, his reference to "one harmonious message of God" was most likely an allusion to the essential unity of God's redemptive message in both the Old and New Testaments.

Accordingly, Westcott was convinced that these early church fathers saw clearly the great principles that are in the Bible and that their doctrine "as a whole" vindicates the claims that Scripture makes for itself. At the same time, however, he makes it equally clear that beyond the general truths of their formulations there are errors of judgment and detail that are subject to more or less serious objection. This dual estimate evidences Westcott's insight and objectivity, and there is little reason to question the validity of his conclusions.

Later Church Fathers

Two fathers are worthy of note in the next period of church history: Jerome (347-420), the famous scholar who made the Latin translation of the Bible known later as the Latin Vulgate, and Augustine (354-430), the remarkable Bishop of Hippo in North Africa. The two were of extremely different temperaments and as a result they approached Scripture with exceedingly divergent points of view. At the risk of oversimplifying matters, E. Harris Harbison contrasts the two men as follows: "Jerome was a philologist, a lover of words and language; Augustine, a philosopher, a lover of ideas. . . . For over twenty years (394-416) the two argued over scriptural interpretation by correspondence across half the Mediterranean. Augustine believed that the *Septuagint* was an inspired translation of the Old Testament into Greek, of equal authority with the Hebrew, if not greater. Jerome based himself upon philological analysis of the Hebrew. Augustine was particularly troubled by Jerome's insinuation that St. Paul was, on one occasion at least, a liar. Jerome was not one to take such criticism lying down, of course, and the controversy was boiling merrily when Jerome finally decided that it was making a bad impression on heretics and called it off. 'I have decided to love you,' he wrote Augustine. Jerome was a great scholar who was a Christian; Augustine was a great Christian who left an indelible mark on scholarship."[16]

In a letter to Jerome dating from about A.D. 405, Augustine wrote, "For, I admit to your charity that it is from those books alone of the Scriptures, which are now called canonical, that I have learned to pay them such honor and respect as to believe most firmly that not one of their authors has erred in writing anything at all."[17] This quotation appears to be a clear reference to the inerrancy of the original writings, but such an interpretation fails to recognize that Augustine read Scripture in a Latin translation made from the Septuagint. This fact, in conjunction with Augustine's belief in the inspiration of the Septuagint, makes it difficult to read back into Augustine's declaration the modern interpretation of verbal plenary inspiration. This conclusion is supported by the fact that those who believe in the inerrancy of the original writings have sided with Jerome in rejecting Augustine's view of the Septuagint while at the same time holding to Augustine's formulation of inspiration.

In common with most of his predecessors, Augustine's doctrine of inspiration must also be viewed in the light of his use of the allegorical method. He admitted frankly that this was a means of solving the difficult problems of the Old Testament. The "sun which comes forth like a bridegroom leaving his chamber" (Ps. 19:4-5) was for Augustine a reference to Christ's emergence from the Virgin's womb. He prided himself in the belief that he had seen hidden meanings in the Old Testament that had not been observed by the New Testament writers.

One of Augustine's pet subjects was numerics or numer-

16. Harbison, *The Christian Scholar in the Age of the Reformation*, pp. 18-19. Italics his.

17. Augustine, Letter 82, p. 392, in *Augustine, Letters* (1-82), Vol. 12, The Fathers of the Church.

ology, and he was not to be outdone by any of his predecessors. An extreme illustration is his attempt to find a sacred meaning for the number 50, which was associated with Pentecost. He suggested taking 50 three times (for the Father, Son, and Holy Spirit) and adding three (the number in the Trinity), making a total of 153. Since this total is the same as the number of fish taken after the resurrection of the Lord, it indicates the special sanctity of the number 50. "And so," Augustine continues, "certain mysteries of comparison are expressed in the Sacred Books in many other numbers and arrangements of numbers, which are hidden from readers because of their ignorance of numbers."[18] This emphasis on numerics was actually a reversion, however, because Irenaeus had pointed out, two centuries earlier, the folly of such an approach to Scripture.

Of all the church fathers, Augustine's formulation comes the closest to expressing the doctrine of inerrancy, but his theory appears to be vitiated in practice both by dependence on allegorical and numerological interpretations of Scripture and by belief in the inspiration of the Septuagint.

The Reformation

For over a thousand years after Jerome and Augustine there was little change in the formulation of the doctrine of inspiration; we are justified, therefore, in moving on to the towering figures of the Reformation, Martin Luther (1483-1546) and John Calvin (1509-1564). Since both of these men wrote so much over such a long period of time and from so many different theological contexts, it is difficult to formulate clearly from their works their doctrines of inspiration.

In rejecting the authority of the pope, Luther was compelled to place great emphasis on the authority of Scripture. Since he assigned the entire Scriptures to the

18. Augustine, *Christian Instruction*, Book 2, ch. 16, p. 85 in Vol. 2, The Fathers of the Church.

Holy Spirit, he considered them the Word of the most exalted God, not the word of man. Luther said that the so-called trivial things in the Bible were divinely inspired, and in one context declared that the Scriptures had never erred.

On the basis of these and similar ideas expressed in Luther's writings, certain scholars are convinced of Luther's belief in the inerrancy of Scripture. On the contrary, other twentieth-century theologians are convinced that Luther broke with the traditional view of inspiration. The ground for this view is Luther's consistent appeal to Christ as the essence of the gospel. Using this criterion, Luther is bold enough to call the book of James, where Christ is seldom mentioned, a very "strawy epistle." With this facet of Luther's thinking as their basis, these scholars today affirm that whenever Luther uses the expression "Word of God" he is not thinking about the Scriptures, the Written Word, but Christ, the Living Word of God. If this is true, one is perplexed by Luther's explicit declaration in another context: "No other doctrine should be proclaimed in the church than the pure Word of God, that is, the Holy Scriptures."[19] Apparently this diversity of interpretation with respect to Luther's writings stems from his concern to protect both the divine and the human aspects of Scripture.

Whereas Luther was of a more practical turn of mind, his younger contemporary, John Calvin, possessed an amazingly systematic, orderly mind that produced at the early age of twenty-six the *Institutes of the Christian Religion*. In many respects his views on inspiration are more clear-cut than Luther's, yet he also wrote much that is ambiguous in nature. While some interpreters of Calvin contend that not a single word can be taken as favoring a literal inspiration, others affirm that Calvin held to a verbal, inerrant view of inspiration.

This extreme diversity of interpretation results from two sets of data relating to Scripture. When speaking of

19. Luther, *Sämmtliche Schriften*, ed. by Johann Georg Walch, St. Louis Edition, IX:87.

the Bible as a whole, Calvin stresses its divine origin and authority. He affirms in many places that the writings of Scripture were dictated to the prophets and apostles by the Holy Spirit. But he does not mean mechanical dictation, because in other contexts he is strongly opposed to the concept that conceived of the biblical writers as mere robots. The term "dictation" was for Calvin the means of declaring the divine aspect of Scripture.

Over against this general affirmation, however, must be placed the statements that Calvin made when dealing with the phenomena and teaching of the sacred text. After the Pharisees accused the disciples of desecrating the Sabbath, Jesus countered them with a reference to "the burnt offering of every sabbath" (Num. 28:10): "Or have you not read in the law how on the sabbath the priests in the temple profane the sabbath, and are guiltless?" (Matt. 12:5). At this point in his commentary Calvin claims that Jesus has accommodated himself to his hearers and so the statement is not "strictly accurate." In commenting on the disbelief of Thomas (John 20:25), Calvin notes again how human ignorance makes it necessary for God to accommodate himself to man's way of speaking. Calvin even suggests that at times God "stammers" in his attempt to communicate with his creatures.

The repetitions of 1 John 2:14 are "superfluous," according to Calvin. Although not doubting the meaning of the passage, he claims that "bitter jealousy and selfish ambition in your hearts" (James 3:14) is an "improper" way of speaking. Psalm 83:9 reads, "Do to them as thou didst to Midian, as to Sisera and Jabin at the river Kishon." Only the Canaanites Jabin and Sisera were defeated at the Kishon, and so Calvin acknowledges that the psalmist mingles two histories together. "Strict accuracy" would demand a revision of the sentence.

One of the most conspicuous examples of Calvin's paradoxical handling of Scripture is found in *The Book of Jeremiah*. He comments on 1:2 that even though verse 1 refers to "the words of Jeremiah," God is really the author of Jeremiah's words. Yet in commenting on Jeremiah's bitter complaint against God (20:14-18), Calvin contends that a blind, insane impulse caused Jeremiah to utter these ungrateful, inconsiderate words which are directed against man as well as God. Was God the author of these impious words?

The ambiguity in the writings of Luther and Calvin stems, of course, from the complex nature of Scripture and its inspiration. They claimed repeatedly, as had their predecessors, that Scripture derived from God; thus it was God's Written Word. But in their attempt to refute the dictation view, such as expressed by Athenagoras, they also contended for the reality of man's part in the process. Where man's part was in danger of being denied or over-looked, Luther and Calvin were quick to correct the error. Yet, in contexts where the divine aspects of the Bible were at stake, both of them rallied to the defense of God's part in the recording of Scripture.

Prior to the period of the Reformation, no doctrinal statement on inspiration was ever formulated at the great councils convened by the church. Among the earliest creedal statements was the Belgic Confession of Faith (1561). Article VII of this formulation, drafted by Guido de Brès, refers to Scripture as "this infallible rule." Scholars in the Reformed tradition are still trying to determine what the statement meant to those who framed and adopted this confession of faith. The clue, according to some, is the preceding sentence, which characterizes man's ways and words as false and vain. God's words, on the contrary, are neither false nor vain. They never deceive and they will never fail or return empty. God's words will always accomplish the purpose for which they were given (Isa. 55:11). It is interesting to note that a Latin translation done in London rendered the original French text as "this most certain rule." This translation, which met with approval at the Synod of Dordt, raises the question as to what extent the concept of inerrancy was actually intended. In any case it points up the ambiguity that existed in the minds of Luther, Calvin, and all religious leaders of the sixteenth century. The doctrine of inspiration had not yet developed to the point where God's part and man's part in Scripture were considered simultaneously. This refinement in doctrine was to come later with the rise of the scientific method and the critical mind.

The Counter-Reformation

Augustine's theory of inspiration was accepted right up through the middle ages, and it appears in the Council of Trent. The biblical books and the unwritten traditions were received "orally from Christ or dictated by the Holy Spirit." Although inerrancy is implicit, Trent never makes the claim that the inspiration of the Bible meant that it was free from error. Inasmuch as the Roman Church had placed more emphasis on tradition and the role of the church, the doctrine concerning Scripture was not as thoroughly thought out or expressed. Moreover, since the major thrust of the Reformation had been against the church, Trent was careful to authenticate the authority of the church. The bishops, as successors of the apostles in the roles of pastors and teachers, shared in that ecclesiastical infallibility which made it impossible for them to fall into error. Thus, the essential battle lines were drawn: the infallibility of the church vs. the inerrancy of Scripture.

As noted earlier, however, the proponents of the theory of inerrancy invariably deviated from their theory in the actual process of wrestling with the data of Scripture. They neither defined what they meant by error nor did they really think through the implications of their theory. This was equally true of the Roman decree of infallibility at Trent. It did not clarify whether this freedom from error rested in the universal church (as was normally the case during the middle ages), or in councils, or in the popes. It is extremely important to observe that in the history of the concepts of inerrancy or infallibility the use of the dogmas has invariably been in periods where the church group in question has been seriously threatened. In short, the theories have been the last bastion of defense, and as such they have strengthened the faithful. But it is equally clear that these propositions, hammered out in a time of emotional crisis, were not always thought through with enough objectivity. Their primary purpose was to eliminate a threat. No more perfect example of this fact can be found than the post-Reformation theologians of the seventeenth century.

The Post-Reformation

Whereas Luther and Calvin had some trying times in the sixteenth century, their troubles were not to be compared with those of the theologians in the seventeenth century. In this difficult period the Protestants had to defend themselves against the Counter-Reformation of the Roman Catholic Church as well as against the secularism and liberalism of the burgeoning scientific age. Moreover, from 1600 to 1700 Europe had only about seven years of peace, and the violent hatreds that were rampant throughout the Continent infested the Christian church as well.

One of the outstanding defenders of the faith in the seventeenth century was J. A. Quenstedt (1617-1688). The fame of his dogmatic theology won for him the nickname "Bookkeeper of Lutheran Orthodoxy." He formulated his doctrine of inspiration as follows: "The canonical Holy Scriptures in the original text are the infallible truth and are free from every error; in other words, in the canonical sacred Scriptures there is found no lie, no falsity, no error, not even the least, whether in subject matter or expressions, but in all things and all the details that are handed down in them, they are most certainly true, whether they pertain to doctrines or morals, to history or chronology, to topography or nomenclature. No ignorance, no thoughtlessness, no forgetfulness, no lapse of memory can and are to be ascribed to the amanuenses [scribes] of the Holy Ghost in their penning the Sacred Writings."[20] Although such exactitude of details would seem to approximate the mechanical dictation view of inspiration, the biblical writers, according to Quenstedt, were not in a trance when the Holy Spirit spoke to them. Rather, they wrote cheerfully, willingly, and intelligently. Thus, instead of alleviating the

20. Quenstedt, *Theologia Didactica-Polemica sive Systema Theologicum*, I, 112.

problem, the systematic refinements of Quenstedt only served to heighten the ambiguity that was inherent in his predecessors.

While Quenstedt represented the followers of Luther, the Westminster Confession (1647) represented Calvin's adherents. Chapter I sets forth the doctrine relating to Holy Scripture. After listing the Protestant canon, Article II affirms that all these books were "given by inspiration of God to be the rule of faith and life." Article V speaks of the "entire perfection" and "infallible truth" of the Word of God. This would appear to argue for the inerrancy of Scripture, and yet Article II seems to restrict these qualities specifically to the areas of faith and life. For this reason the Westminster Confession has been commonly interpreted to mean that Scripture is "the infallible rule for faith and practice." Since the Bible does not claim to speak authoritatively in the realms of science, for example, one can allow for errors of fact in such areas.

With respect to the autographs and manuscript transmission, Article VIII states that the Old Testament in Hebrew and the New Testament in Greek were "immediately inspired by God." Scripture in the original languages is "authentical" because God by his "singular care and providence" kept the manuscripts "pure in all ages." The stress is on the authenticity and purity of the extant manuscripts in Hebrew and Greek. The original writings were "inspired by God," but it does not say that this inspiration was characterized by an inerrancy that was lost during the process of transmission. Language that can refer to copies of Scripture as being "pure" is most certainly not precise enough to be interpreted as intending explicit reference to inerrant autographs.

The failure of the sixteenth- and seventeenth-century theologians to understand the precise implications of their formulations is illustrated by their belief in the accuracy of the vowel points in the extant Hebrew manuscripts of the Old Testament. The Hebrew alphabet was, and is, composed of consonants. While some of these consonants were also used to indicate certain long vowels, Hebrew manuscripts did not indicate *all* of the vowels prior to about

A.D. 600. It is impossible, of course, to speak without using vowels; so in learning to read the Hebrew Bible aloud, it was necessary to learn which vowels to supply. This *oral tradition,* passed on from generation to generation, was undoubtedly the primary means for determining the vowel signs to be added to the manuscripts.

By about 1600 the validity of the vowel signs (known as "vowel points") became a matter of dispute between the Jesuits and the Lutherans. The Jesuits denied their authenticity, while the Lutherans and almost all the other Protestant theologians contended for their accuracy. The battle raged even more furiously among the Reformed theologians, who carried on the ideas and work of John Calvin and Theodore Beza (1519-1605). During the years 1645-1653, Johann Buxtorf the younger carried on a violent dispute with Cappellus. Buxtorf's belief in the antiquity and divine authority of the vowel points was given public approval when the Swiss Reformed Churches incorporated his ideas into their new confession of faith, *Formula Consensus Helvetica,* and formally adopted it in 1675.

Although this extreme article of faith is rejected by the Reformed tradition today, it bears out the fact that all the creedal statements on inspiration formulated during the sixteenth and seventeenth centuries were precritical in nature and that they neither elaborated nor reconciled the divine and human elements of Scripture in any systematic way. This attitude was also true of John Wesley (1703-1791), the founder of Methodism. The Bible, for him, was God's Word, but it was mediated through human instrumentality. Thus, from Irenaeus in the second century up to the turn of the nineteenth century, the formulations of inspiration were essentially general affirmations of the divine and human aspects of Scripture. Nowhere were these two facets of the truth explicitly reconciled.

The Modern Period in Conservative Protestantism

The most influential advocates of the verbal plenary view of inspiration during the nineteenth century were Louis Gaussen (1790-1863) of Geneva, Switzerland, and

Benjamin B. Warfield (1851-1921) in the United States of America. Gaussen defined inspiration as "that inexplicable power which the Divine Spirit put forth of old on the authors of holy Scripture, in order to their guidance even in the employment of the words they used, and to preserve them alike from all error and from all omission."[21] To forestall any accusations of "mechanical dictation view" he discussed at great length the individuality of the sacred writers. Although admitting that he could not explain how the *full* activity of God and of man were possible at the same time in Scripture, Gaussen asserted, "There, all the words are man's; as there, too, all the words are God's."[22]

Here, as with all his predecessors, Gaussen is endeavoring to protect God's part in Scripture along with man's. Notwithstanding this sincere attempt, however, one can hardly refrain from asking, How, in the light of scientific data concerning Scripture and its origin, can the divine and human aspects of the Bible be pushed to the point where both function equally in every word?

Warfield's definition, still considered by many as the classic formulation, is as follows: "Inspiration is that extraordinary, supernatural influence (or, passively, the result of it), exerted by the Holy Ghost on the writers of our Sacred Books, by which their words were rendered also the words of God, and, therefore, perfectly infallible."[23]

Twentieth-century restatements of Warfield's view are numerous, but perhaps the most extended recent treatment is that of the late Edward J. Young (1907-1968). According to him, "Inspiration is a superintendence of God the Holy Spirit over the writers of the Scriptures, as a result of which these Scriptures possess Divine authority and trustworthiness and, possessing such Divine authority and trustworthiness, are free from error."[24]

---

21. Gaussen, *The Inspiration of the Holy Scriptures*, p. 34.
22. *Ibid.*, p. 29.
23. Warfield, *The Inspiration and Authority of the Bible*, p. 420. Quotations from this book are used by permission of Presbyterian & Reformed Publishing Company.
24. Young, *Thy Word Is Truth*, p. 27.

The Modern Period in Roman Catholicism

In an excellent survey of Roman Catholic theories of inspiration since 1810, James Tunstead Burtchaell begins his "Introduction" by adding two words to Isaac Newton's First Law of Motion, thereby raising it to a level of theological relevance: "Every body (of theologians) continues in its state of rest, or of uniform motion in a straight line, unless acted upon by an external force."[25]

Coming into the nineteenth century the Roman Church officially continued on a straight line from Trent with the same doctrine of inspiration and the same ambiguities. But in actuality many within the Church reacted against the extremes of the Lutheran definition of inspiration. In this period, Geiselmann notes, "the inspiration of Holy Scripture was abandoned; it was treated as a purely human, historic document."[26] During the last half of the century, however, an external force moved the Roman Church to the right. "Verbal inspiration," Hans Küng notes, "is asserted and thought out rigorously and systematically only in Protestantism. It was only toward the end of the nineteenth century under the pressure of a destructive critical exegesis, that the popes took over—with a remarkable switch of phases—the theory of verbal inspiration worked out by Protestant orthodoxy."[27] "Plenary inspiration and total inerrancy," Burtchaell states, "were repeatedly urged by a succession of pontifical acts: the *Syllabus Errorum* (Pius IX in 1864), *Providentissimus Deus* (Leo XIII in 1893), *Pascendi Dominici Gregis* (Pius X in 1907), *Spiritus Paraclitus* (Benedict XV in 1920), and *Divino Afflante Spiritu* (Pius XII in 1943)."[28]

Thus it was that a doctrine of biblical inerrancy locked arms with the dogma of papal infallibility. Vatican II raised hopes for many in the Roman Church, but these unyielding twins have dashed them temporarily. The situa-

---

25. *Catholic Theories of Biblical Inspiration Since 1810*, p. 1.
26. "Scripture, Tradition, and the Church: An Ecumenical Problem," p. 51, in *Christianity Divided*.
27. *Infallible? An Inquiry*, p. 212.
28. *Catholic Theories of Biblical Inspiration Since 1810*, p. 2.

tion is quite similar in some conservative circles of Protestantism. Although the ruling groups in the various hierarchical systems have not issued a dogma of infallibility in their own behalf, they still think and act with the same fears that motivate the papacy. Because of this similarity and the widespread dissemination of these ideas in Roman Catholicism and Protestantism, it is necessary to examine in some detail the implications of the theories. In this process various theories will be mentioned in an attempt to find a healthier, more complete approach to Scripture. Burtchaell is well aware that "papal and conciliar documents" do not represent all that happens in the Roman Church, and so his survey shows "that Catholic opinion in the last century was more progressive and competent than lately imagined."[29] Some of these theories add perspective, and where they are pertinent they will be noted along with Protestant views.

The Problem of Defining "Error"

The doctrine of inerrancy is a negative statement with the specific intent of protecting God and his Written Word. The early adherents had no idea how complex and multifaceted the term "error" was. They naively thought that the Bible had no deviation from absolute truth, and of course by Scripture they meant the copies in hand. When the recognition of errors in copies became a reality, then the defense of the doctrine was pushed back to the original biblical writings. Later on, when it was acknowledged that God had not given a science textbook, then the focus shifted to theological integrity and authenticity as the standard for defining error. Where biblical data raised problems even in the realm of theology, the standard of reference was sometimes shifted to the intention of the writer. In more recent years the study of linguistics has shown the enormous burden that the proponents of inerrancy have shouldered. It will be very helpful in the

29. *Ibid.*, p. 5.

following chapters to realize that the standard of reference for defining an error has been shifting over the generations and that even now the adherents to the doctrine of inerrancy do not have a full-blown, consistent definition by which their theory can be put to the test.

Chapter Seven

Autographs, Translations, and Inspiration

For more than a century now, the autographs, the original manuscripts of the various biblical books, have figured prominently in conservative discussions of inspiration. In line with the inductive method, our first task is to learn what Scripture itself has to say on this issue.

The Autograph of the Book of Jeremiah

The most detailed account of the origin of a biblical book is found in Jeremiah 36:1-32. In the fourth year of Jehoiakim (605 B.C.) the LORD told Jeremiah, "Take a scroll and write on it all the words that I have spoken to you against Israel and Judah and all the nations from the day I spoke to you, from the days of Josiah until today" (v. 2). Jeremiah called his scribe, or secretary (known technically as an "amanuensis"), Baruch, who "wrote upon a scroll at the dictation of Jeremiah all the words of the LORD which he had spoken to him" (v. 4).

Inasmuch as Jeremiah had been debarred from going to the temple, he ordered Baruch to read the scroll to the people on some fast day. This Baruch did (v. 10); whereupon a certain Micaiah, one of the officials, hearing the startling words of Jeremiah, reported what he heard to the princes who were sitting in the king's house. They sent for Baruch and had him read the scroll to them (vv. 14-15). In fear they reported to the king, who in turn asked to have the scroll read to him. Since it was winter, he happened to be warming himself before the fire in the brazier. Then "as Jehudi read three or four columns, the king would cut them off with a penknife and throw them into the fire in the brazier, until the entire scroll was consumed in the fire that was in the brazier" (v. 23).

The scroll must have been much shorter than our present text, because it was read three times, with intervals, apparently all on the same day. At any rate, after Jeremiah learned of the burning of the scroll, the LORD told him, "Take another scroll and write on it all the former words that were in the first scroll" (v. 28). Then "Jeremiah took another scroll and gave it to Baruch the scribe, . . . who wrote on it at the dictation of Jeremiah all the words of the scroll which Jehoiakim king of Judah had burned in the fire; and many similar words were added to them" (v. 32).

Some of the additional words were the oracle (included in our present book at 36:29-31) against King Jehoiakim for his shameless deed in burning the first scroll. However, the text says "many similar words were added," so the second scroll (written in 604) was quite a bit longer than the first. On the other hand, this second scroll was much shorter than our present book of Jeremiah, for it did not contain the material dating from 604 to the fall of Jerusalem, 587/6 B.C.; nor did it have the section, 43:8 to 44:30, which reports Jeremiah's activities in Egypt sometime after 586 B.C. When the latter unit was added, the preface of Jeremiah (1:1-3) was not brought up to date because it only purports to give the "words of Jeremiah . . . until the captivity of Jerusalem."

The differences between the text of Jeremiah in the Hebrew (known as the Masoretic text, or MT) and in the Greek translation of the Hebrew known as the Septuagint (meaning "seventy," and commonly designated LXX) indicate clearly that the book is a collection of materials, some of which circulated as separate units before being incorporated into the collection. An excellent example is the unit composed of chapters 46 to 51, a book of oracles against the nations, which appears in the Septuagint after 25:13a. In this process of an enlarging prophetic collection or anthology, what is the autograph? Inasmuch as the Hebrew text of Jeremiah available in Jesus' day was essentially the same in extent as our present Hebrew copies, it would seem advisable to define the autograph as the original scroll, which corresponded in *extent* to the traditional, canonical compilation. To do otherwise would necessitate deleting portions of the text as having no rightful place in the book, but from our vantage point it would be impossible to determine precisely what to omit.

If the average Christian today were asked to define an autograph, the most likely answer would be, "The book that came from the hand of the author." This definition springs from an assumption that the original text of each biblical book was written at a certain time by the author. While this may have been true in some cases, it is not even the general rule in the New Testament. Aside from Paul's closing greeting and signature, most (if not all) of his letters were given by dictation (2 Thess. 3:17; Gal. 6:11). Strictly speaking, then, the original letters of Paul involved the activity of various scribes. Here, as in the case of Jeremiah, the question is whether scribes, as well as authors, were preserved from error.

Scriptural Claims About the Autographs

In addition to the data of Scripture concerning the origin of biblical books it is also necessary to ascertain if there are any specific claims or clear implications by Jesus and the New Testament writers concerning the autographs.

An excellent starting point for this inductive study is the classic statement on inspiration found in 2 Timothy 3:16-17. The passage begins, "All Scripture *theopneustos*." The Greek word transliterated *theopneustos* occurs nowhere else in the New Testament and it never appears in the LXX. The term originated in classical Greek to describe the madness (*mania*) of the ecstatic prophet while under the control of a divine spirit, but this understanding has clearly been replaced by the biblical concept of God working dynamically with his channels of revelation. The King James Version translates, "All Scripture is given by inspiration of God." The Revised Standard Version and the Jerusalem Bible read, "All scripture is inspired by God," and the New American Bible renders similarly, "All Scripture is inspired of God." While the American Standard Version of 1901 has, "Every scripture inspired of God is . . . ," the New American Standard Bible follows the RSV, "All Scripture is inspired by God." The New English Bible translates, "Every inspired scripture has. . . ." Thus the major translations into English interpret *theopneustos* to mean "given by inspiration of God," or "inspired [by God]." The term has also been interpreted to mean "God-breathed."[1]

The word "scripture" (Gk. *graphē*) seems to refer back to the previous sentence in verses 14-15: "But as for you, continue in what you have learned and have firmly believed, knowing from whom you learned it and how from childhood you have been acquainted with the sacred writings which are able to instruct you for salvation through faith in Christ Jesus." Scripture, however, does more than prepare for salvation. It completes the man of God by teaching, reproof, correction, and training in righteousness. Therefore, the "sacred writings" that instructed Timothy in the past will continue to guide him as he matures in his Christian experience. It would appear, then, that for Paul the "scripture" and the "sacred writings" meant the extant Old Testament manuscripts.

The Greek text of verses 16-17 is verbless, but since English idiom demands a verb, all the translations into English supply "is" or "has." The clear implication of Paul's claim is that *theopneustos* is a permanent attribute

---

1. See Warfield, *The Inspiration and Authority of the Bible*, pp. 245-296.

of Scripture. The extant manuscripts were considered the same as the original writings because they were inspired by God and capable of accomplishing the purpose for which they were given. In all likelihood Paul never thought in terms of the technical distinction between the autographs and copies of Scripture. More important, however, is the fact that he never makes any claims nor proposes any definitions that would set the original writings apart as a special group to be clearly distinguished from copies of Scripture.

Another key passage on the doctrine of inspiration is the statement of Jesus as found in John 10:34-36: "Is it not written in your law, 'I said, you are gods'? If he called them gods to whom the word of God came (and scripture cannot be broken), do you say of him whom the Father consecrated and sent into the world, 'You are blaspheming,' because I said, 'I am the Son of God'?" Here Jesus is refuting his Jewish adversaries, and so he refers to their copies of the Old Testament as "your law." By quoting from their manuscripts of Psalm 82:6, Jesus is establishing a common ground for discussion.

The question as to what Jesus meant by "broken" will be considered in another context. The important question here is to ascertain which "scripture" Jesus had in mind as having this characteristic. Did he mean "the word of God" that came to the gods (apparently a reference to the judges of Israel), or did he have in mind the Old Testament writings common to himself and his Jewish adversaries? The message or instructions that the judges received from God would constitute at best only a small portion of the Old Testament. What Jesus is stressing in this context is that the statement as written in Psalm 82:6 of the extant scrolls is authoritative. After all, his whole argument rests on this verse. The reason this verse is authoritative is that the entire context, the Old Testament Scriptures, can withstand any test. The Greek text of Jesus' qualification reads literally, "And the writing is not able to be broken." It does not say, "And the writing could not be broken." Therefore the text and the context seem to inform us that Jesus was arguing for the authority of the Old Testament writings common to himself and his adversaries. It is implied, of course, that Jesus thought as highly of the autographs, but this is not his explicit concern in this passage.

Peter, in his second letter, disputes the idea that Jesus was a "cleverly devised myth" by noting his own experience with Christ on the holy Mount of Transfiguration. Then follows, in 1:19-21, Peter's classic reference to the inspiration of Scripture: "And we have the prophetic word made more sure. You will do well to pay attention to this as to a lamp shining in a dark place, until the day dawns and the morning star rises in your hearts. First of all you must understand this, that no prophecy of scripture is a matter of one's own interpretation, because no prophecy ever came by the impulse of man, but men moved by the Holy Spirit spoke from God." The "prophetic word made more sure" is probably a reference to the messianic passages in the Old Testament that had been confirmed by the life and death of Jesus Christ. Therefore, when Peter advises his readers to pay attention to this prophetic word he is referring to the Old Testament books in their possession. These prophetic utterances, which they have in writing, are not like the man-made ideas put forth by the false teachers of their day, so Peter claims, because "men moved [literally, "borne"] by the Holy Spirit spoke from God." In other words the extant Old Testament copies are trustworthy and authoritative because the original prophecies were God-given. There is no explicit indication in this passage that Peter made any *essential* distinction between the originals and the copies. The important teaching is that the Scriptures had their origin in God; therefore the copies that Peter's readers had were also to be considered as being from God and thus worthy of their careful study.

Neither in these key passages by Paul, Jesus, and Peter nor in the rest of the New Testament passages that refer to the inspiration of the Old Testament are there any explicit statements that single out the autographs as being different in kind from copies. The reason is clearly seen from the New Testament as a whole. In proclaiming and defending the "good news," Jesus and the apostles took as their authority the available manuscripts of the Old Testament books. Their Jewish opponents shared this belief, and so the spiritual battle was waged and won on the common ground of the extant copies of Scripture, not on an abstract reference to the autographs.

Theological Value of the Autographs

Notwithstanding the lack of explicit biblical teaching about the autographs, the subject came to have an increasingly prominent place in any discussion on inspiration. The earliest nonbiblical formulations of inspiration were general statements that conceived of Scripture as the trustworthy, authoritative Word of God. Implied in trustworthiness, of course, were the aspects of truthfulness and accuracy of the record because the ancients concurred in Balaam's answer to Balak, "God is not man, that he should lie" (Num. 23:19). For the most part, however, this concept of accuracy was applied to the available copies of Scripture. Difficulties in the text were overcome by the allegorical method of interpretation that disregarded the literal meaning of the text and looked for the hidden meaning.

When it became clear to lovers of Scripture that copies of the Hebrew Old Testament and the Greek New Testament contained some errors, it was quite natural to transfer the quality of accuracy or inerrancy to the original writings. Obviously one reason for this new emphasis was to protect the honor and perfection of God. The basis for this assumption was the syllogism: God is perfect, God revealed himself in the autographs, therefore the autographs had to be inerrant. A closely related reason for this doctrine was to guarantee the value and the authority of extant Bibles. According to this argument, without the presupposition of a perfect original text one could just as well turn to Buddhist or Hindu literature.[2] In brief, even though our Bibles are an approximation of the original manuscripts, their value and authority are ensured, so it is claimed, by the assumption of inerrant autographs.

2. See Cornelius Van Til, "Introduction" to Warfield, *The Inspiration and Authority of the Bible*, p. 46, note 22.

The desire to honor God and to contend for the uniqueness of his revelation is indeed praiseworthy, but the question is whether the assumptions back of the syllogism are in accord with the facts. In other words, do the events of redemptive history reveal the kind of God presupposed by the deduction inherent in the doctrine of inerrant autographs?

Each autograph of a biblical book (coming at irregular intervals over many centuries) served as a standard of reference for only a short time—an exceedingly short time, considering the span of the Judeo-Christian religion. Aside from the few manuscripts copied from the original documents, the autographs had little standardizing control because they soon perished, either through continual use or because of deterioration.

Thus, for centuries before the church came into existence, and for a century after, the Old Testament books were transmitted with no standard text being employed to gauge the accuracy of copies. Yet, in spite of this fact, God's Kingdom grew and spread worldwide. Actually, for more than 99 percent of the people involved in the Judeo-Christian tradition, knowledge of God has come through copies of Scripture, none of which was inerrant. In short, errant copies of biblical books have not hindered the Holy Spirit in his convicting and illuminating activities.

On the other hand, when the role of Scripture is directed toward specific issues of faith and practice, there is a valid basis in appealing to the autographs. For example, persons who justify religious snake-handling on the authority of Mark 16:18 need to know that the last twelve verses of our copies of Mark are not the original conclusion to that Gospel account. It is right and reasonable, therefore, to ascertain as nearly as possible the text of the original manuscripts. Only insofar as the accidents of transmission are removed can one be sure what was originally written. It was primarily in relation to faith and practice that traditional formulations of inspiration ascribed infallibility to Scripture, but inasmuch as all of Scripture does not pertain to faith and practice the task of textual criticism is not necessarily grounded in the assumption of inerrancy. Moreover, since God has seen fit to work through errant copies of Scripture, is one justified in claiming that God *had* to give the autographs inerrantly?

It is very instructive to observe how much stress those who believe in the doctrine of inerrant autographs put on the trustworthiness of our present Hebrew and Greek texts. One representative scholar says of Scripture: "We may truly say that by God's peculiar providence it has been preserved free from serious error. We may say that to all intents and purposes we have the words that prophets and apostles wrote—and this was nothing less than the verbally inspired Word of the living God."[3] If extant texts "free from serious error" are authoritative enough to be considered, "to all intents and purposes," the words of the prophets and the apostles, then is it not valid to acknowledge that the autographs also had some inconsequential errors and were to all intents and purposes the pure, authoritative Word of God? Is it actually true that some defects in the autographs would have reduced Scripture to the level of Hindu or Buddhist sacred literature?

Why Did the Autographs Perish?

The question still remains as to why God permitted the autographs to perish or be lost. These documents, some have suggested, would have become more revered with the passing of time and possibly even worshipped. Others see benefit in the loss of the autographs because it removes any necessity of determining which of our extant manuscripts are copies and which are original. This also removes the further possibility of some person's claiming autograph status for a manuscript with erroneous teachings.

We can be sure that if we had the autographs some persons would revere or even worship them, and still others would doubt their authenticity, but in neither case does the suggestion get at the heart of the problem. The important thing about the autographs is, after all, not the

3. R. Laird Harris, *Inspiration and Canonicity of the Bible*, p. 103.

manuscript itself but the assumed inerrancy of the document. If God, through his Spirit, could have given the original writings inerrantly, then he surely could have enabled the scribes to copy the autograph of each of the Old Testament books without a mistake, maintaining in the copy thereby the precise accuracy of the original manuscript. This process of transmission could have been carried on quite apart from the fate of the autographs once one copy had been made. The real problem, therefore, is not why God let the autographs perish, but why God did not maintain in the copies of Scripture the assumed inerrancy of the original manuscripts.

One proposal in this connection suggests that maybe the benefit reaped during the last century and a half from all the textual, linguistic, and archaeological studies is the reason why God did not transmit the Scriptures inerrantly.[4] But how did errant copies of Scripture benefit those who lived prior to A.D. 1800 or thereabouts?

In the final analysis, is it necessary to attribute reasons to God for the loss of the autographs or the failure to transmit Scripture inerrantly? God did not have to set forth any *special* purpose with respect to the fate of the original manuscripts. He knew what would happen to them in the natural order of wear and decay. What is plain, however, is that God did not purpose to maintain in transmission the accuracy of the autographs. He could allow his revelation to flow through human channels, for he knew that the accuracy of certain human minds devoted to him would be sufficient to maintain the level of truth necessary for achieving his purposes.

Transmission of Source Material

Transmission of biblical material has many more implications for the doctrine of inspiration than the questions of the autographs. It is generally acknowledged that any

4. See Unger, "H. H. Rowley and the New Trend in Biblical Studies," *Inspiration and Interpretation*, ed. by Walvoord, pp. 197-198.

extended bit of scribal activity results in some kind of error. The book of Jeremiah, as we have observed, was compiled over a number of years with units being added after the completion of the second scroll in 604 B.C. Even if one considers this document to have been inerrant, is one warranted in claiming that in all the scribal activity of copying and inserting the new material the compiler was inerrant? If the facts necessitate the redefining of "autograph" in terms of an anthology or collection, then is it not imperative that the doctrine of inerrancy cover all phases of that complex process as well? Let us turn to the biblical data, therefore, to see what is involved.

An excellent example of the difficulty that *process* poses is the historical account presented in Chronicles as compared with that in Samuel-Kings. As a general rule, the figures in Chronicles are larger than the corresponding figures of the parallel accounts in Samuel-Kings. In 2 Samuel 24:9, Joab reports 800,000 "valiant men who drew the sword" available in Israel, and 500,000 in Judah. 1 Chronicles 21:5 has 1,100,000 men in Israel, and 470,000 in Judah. The latter statistic is an example of some instances in which Chronicles has the smaller figure, but this is the exception. 2 Chronicles 13:17 speaks of 500,000 "picked men" of Israel being slain by Judah, and 2 Chronicles 14:9, 13 report that Zerah the Ethiopian came up against Judah with 1,000,000 men, none of whom remained alive.

If, as some believe, the Hebrew expression "thousand thousands" means a vast army rather than precisely a million men, then one wonders why 1 Chronicles 21:5 adds 100,000 to the supposedly round number represented by 1,000,000. Furthermore, the other reference to 470,000 is hardly intended as a round number. Another method of accounting for the excessive figures is to consider them as scribal mistakes in the transmission of the books of Chronicles. Errors of this kind would tend to level out, however, and occur as frequently in Samuel-Kings as in Chronicles. Evidently the large numbers must be accounted for in still another manner.

The available data indicate that 2 Kings was not complete until about 560 B.C. (the thirty-seventh year of the captivity of Jehoiachin, noted in 2 Kings 25:27). If, as the late William F. Albright (1891-1971) and tradition contend, the Chronicler was Ezra, then the books of Chronicles would date from around 425 B.C. While Ezra employed some sources that were overlooked by, or not known to, the compiler of Samuel-Kings, the bulk of the material concerning Judah, the southern kingdom, was common to both histories.

There was at least one significant difference, however. Ezra's sources had acquired the enlarged figures during the period of transmission since the compilation of 2 Kings. It is a well-known fact that numbers in inscriptions of the Assyrian kings, for example, tended to increase with each new edition of the annals. This was due partly to the human tendency to magnify gradually the glories of the past as time widens the gap. Some of the enlarged figures were no doubt accidental errors of the scribes because numbers were indicated, more often than not, by a series of marks or tallies instead of being spelled out. Possibly both of these tendencies helped to account for the exaggerated numbers, but regardless of how they came to be, they probably appeared in the original manuscripts of Chronicles.

After 1 Chronicles 8:32, in his renowned commentary on the Bible, Matthew Henry (1662-1714) acknowledges quite frankly: "As to the difficulties that occur in this and the foregoing genealogies we need not perplex ourselves. I presume Ezra took them as he found them *in the books of the kings of Israel and Judah* (ch. ix.1), according as they were given in by the several tribes, each observing what method they thought fit. Hence some ascend, others descend; some have *numbers* affixed, others *places;* some have historical remarks intermixed, others have not; some are shorter, others longer; some agree with other records, others differ; some, it is likely, were torn, erased, and blotted, others more legible. Those of Dan and Reuben were entirely lost. This holy man wrote as he was moved by the Holy Ghost; but there was no necessity for the making up of the defects, no, nor for the rectifying of the mistakes, of these genealogies by inspiration."[5] Thus Henry, the saintly student of Scripture, felt quite free to admit that the autograph of Chronicles was mistaken in some of its details.

Other evangelical scholars have preferred, however, to seek the solution to the difficulty in the providence of God. According to this view the biblical writers were providentially conditioned men, both by birth and education. Knowledge was conveyed to them by supernatural and natural means. Natural knowledge came through the intuitions, observations, and thought processes of their own experiences, but it also came through sources, both oral and written. These sources were under the general providence of God, so that there was no conflict between the natural knowledge and the supernatural knowledge.[6]

But if this were true, then one of two means had to be employed to ensure the inerrancy of the original biblical scroll: either God's providence guaranteed the inerrant transmission of the source material or the Spirit of God warned the writer of the mistakes in his sources and then supplied the correct data. There is no biblical support for either of these theoretical possibilities, and it would appear that Matthew Henry chose the better course in coming to grips with the data of Scripture. This happier solution was also suggested by James Orr (1844-1913): "Where sources of information fail, or where, as may sometimes happen, there are *lacunae* [omissions], or blots, or misreadings of names, or errors of transcription, such as are incidental to the transmission of all MSS. [manuscripts], it is not to be supposed that supernatural information is granted to supply the lack. Where this is frankly acknowledged, inspiration is cleared from a great many of the difficulties which misapprehension has attached to it."[7]

5. Henry, *Commentary on the Whole Bible*, II, 858. Italics his.
6. See Warfield and Hodge, *Inspiration*, pp. 14, 16. Reprinted from *Presbyterian Review* (April, 1881).
7. Orr, *Revelation and Inspiration*, p. 165. Italics his.

Transmission of Biblical Manuscripts

The recognition of scribal errors in manuscripts of the Hebrew Old Testament and the Greek New Testament raises the question as to whether God's honor and veracity are really protected by contending for inerrant autographs when one has to turn around immediately and admit that God could not, or did not care to, keep the text inerrant in transmission. After all, if God bore the prophets and apostles along inerrantly in the autographs, then why should it be unthinkable that God could bear up the scribes in such a way that their copies would have the same accuracy as the original manuscripts? In either case God is working through human instrumentality and there is no *inherent* reason why he should have any more difficulty performing the latter feat than the former.

Some evangelicals sense the implications of this apparent inconsistency and so they contend for a God-protected text.[8] But this way out of the difficulty is also inconsistent because one must finally admit that none of our present manuscripts is a perfect reproduction of the autograph. The theory of a God-protected text, therefore, must answer the question, How much imperfection of the text will inerrancy permit?

A good example of the attempt to reconcile copies with autographs is found in the writings of the seventeenth-century theologians. The Lutheran dogmatician D. Hollaz (1648-1713) contended that the apographs (a technical term from Greek, meaning "copies" of Scripture) were the very words and content of the autographs. J. A. Quenstedt, the older contemporary of Hollaz, reasoned in a similar vein. He acknowledged that the autographs of the Old Testament had perished, but he contended that the copies that Paul described as *theopneustos* had the attributes of the original manuscripts because careful transcribing had preserved the precise sense and wording of the autographs. In theory, therefore, Quenstedt was assuming

8. See Edward F. Hills, *The King James Version Defended!*, pp. 25, 27, 114-116, 122, 141.

exact transmission of the Old Testament books from their origin down to Paul's time, but it is doubtful that he would go much beyond this period. As Robert Preus comments: "There is certainly no reason to doubt that he, like Hollaz, was aware of the fact of variant readings among the manuscripts then accessible. He would hardly have considered the apographa of his time in the same category as those which Paul and Timothy used. However, this statement indicates that he is not alive to the significance of the fact of variant readings."[9]

The remarkable fact is Quenstedt's recognition that *theopneustos* in II Timothy 3:16 referred to the apographs of Paul's time. Most likely this objectivity with respect to the biblical statement resulted from his failure to recognize the significance of textual variants. The oversight permitted him to take Paul literally while still holding to the assumption of inerrant autographs. All he had to do was claim that the words of Paul's apographs were precisely the same as the autographs.

But for some years now, evangelicals have been "alive" to the significance of textual variants, and so they have not been able to accept Quenstedt's easy answer. Knowing that any extended bit of scribal activity results in errors, they have admitted, for the most part, that all *copies* of the Old Testament were errant to some degree.

This implication received partial confirmation in 1947 and the subsequent years by the discovery of the Dead Sea scrolls. The biblical books among the scrolls, dating from the second and first centuries B.C., exhibit a number of scribal errors. Without doubt this condition prevailed in the manuscripts of the first century A.D. as well. Nevertheless, when the Sadducees tried to trick Jesus with a question, he answered them (Mark 12:24), "Is not this why you are wrong, that you know neither the scriptures nor the power of God?" Here, as in John 10:35, Jesus was grounding his appeal in the copies of the Old Testament extant then.

If Jesus and Paul and Peter considered the errant manu-

9. Preus, *The Inspiration of Scripture*, p. 49.

scripts of their time as trustworthy and authoritative, should we not have the same attitude toward our manuscripts today? On the basis of 2 Peter 1:21 some evangelicals contend that there is a very important distinction between the autographs and copies. If "men moved [literally, "borne"] by the Holy Spirit spoke from God," then only what was given at the moment of the Spirit's aid can really be inspired. Because Scripture does not state specifically that scribes and copyists were borne along by the Holy Spirit, one is not warranted, so it is claimed, in maintaining that copies are also inspired.[10]

Obviously, the scribes who made copies of biblical books were not inspired in the unique sense in which the prophets and the apostles were, but does this fact prevent copies from being authentic records of the original experiences of inspiration and revelation? The way in which Jesus, Peter, John, and Paul handle passages derived from their Old Testament copies implies that they considered these copies as preserving both the results of inspiration and the authority that characterized the autographs.

Nowhere does the Bible teach that copies of Scripture are not the result of inspiration. What, then, is the basis for this concept? Evidently it stems from an assumption that equates inspiration with inerrancy. This deductive approach to the matter assumes, as we have seen, that God had to reveal himself inerrantly. When the sacred writers were borne along inerrantly by the Holy Spirit their words were truly inspired. Once this assumption is granted, it is clear that scribal errors automatically eliminate copies from the category of inspired literature. But the question still remains, What is the biblical support for this teaching? Can one really claim biblical authority for this view when it is in the theological and philosophical discussion that normally follows the treatment of the biblical passages that the idea of the autographs is brought in?

The teachings and the data of Scripture indicate that the New Testament writers considered the errant manuscripts of the first century A.D. as inspired (that is, the product of

10. See Edward J. Young, *Thy Word Is Truth*, pp. 55-56.

God's revelation to the inspired Old Testament authors), trustworthy, and authoritative. The extent to which they understood the implications of scribal errors and variant readings is not important. The extant Scriptures had been opened to them by the life and teaching of Jesus, and also the Holy Spirit, working through these errant manuscripts, had wrought a marvelous change in their lives. It is little wonder, then, that from a practical, popular point of view they considered the Scriptures as the very message of God to them. They were not concerned about the autographs as such, nor were they exercised over the difficulties in transmitting the original text. What really mattered was the "here and now"—the reality and power of the Old Testament copies they had. Are we not justified, therefore, in considering the errant copies of our day, both Old and New Testaments, as the product of God's inspiration of his messengers, and thus trustworthy and authoritative?

Translation and Inspiration

A step removed from the problem of manuscript transmission is the issue of translation into another language. Scholars, regardless of their theological views, accept the fact that all translations err in some measure because no one language has terms that correspond exactly to similar terms in another language.[11] Differences of opinion arise when inferences are made from this sound premise. If inerrancy of the autographs is assumed, the logical inference is that no translation, not even the Septuagint, can be inspired. But again the question is whether this assumption is supported by evidence from the New Testament and contemporary sources.

Origin of the Septuagint (LXX)

While the story of the Septuagint's origin (recorded in the letter of Aristeas to Philocrates) has been proved to be

11. See, e.g., Robert Dick Wilson, *Studies in the Book of Daniel,* I, 85.

a late, fanciful explanation, some features are of importance. This story says that the idea of translating the Hebrew Pentateuch into Greek came from Demetrius, the librarian at Alexandria, Egypt. He proposed it to the king, Ptolemy II (Philadelphus), who reigned 285-247 B.C. The suggestion met with approval and Ptolemy sent a letter to Eleazar, high priest at Jerusalem, requesting seventy-two elders (six from each of the twelve tribes) known for their exemplary life, knowledge of the law, and ability to translate.

The request was granted, and the Jewish scholars went to Alexandria, where they were given a royal reception by the king himself. Seven banquets were held for them, all of which observed strictly the dietary laws of the Jews. To avoid the distractions and oppressive conditions of the city, the translators were taken to the island of Pharos in the harbor of Alexandria. Here in magnificent surroundings, with everything provided for their convenience, the translators set to work. The account in the letter relates: "And so they proceeded to carry it out, making all details harmonize by mutual comparisons. The appropriate result of the harmonization was reduced to writing under the direction of Demetrius."[12] After explaining some of the daily routine, the letter states, "And so it came about that the work of transcription was completed in seventy-two days, as if this coincidence had been the result of some design."[13] Whatever the historical basis for this story, it shows that the Alexandrian Jews considered the Septuagint as the product of God's providence, given by inspiration.

Most certainly Philo knew something of this tradition (although he shows ignorance of the letter of Aristeas to Philocrates) because his account of the Septuagint's origin has certain features of the story in expanded form. He believed, for example, that the translators, "under inspiration, wrote, not each several scribe something different,

12. *Aristeas to Philocrates* (*Letter of Aristeas*), ed. and tr. by Moses Hadas, p. 219.
13. *Ibid.*, p. 221.

but the same word for word, as though dictated to each by an invisible prompter."[14] There was no need to harmonize the seventy-two translations because all of them agreed word for word. This was an even greater coincidence than that of completing the translation in exactly seventy-two days.

In trying to support the authenticity of this marvelous feat, Philo proceeds to explain: "Yet who does not know that every language, and Greek especially, abounds in terms, and that the same thought can be put in many shapes by changing single words and whole phrases and suiting the expression to the occasion? This was not the case, we are told, with this law of ours, but the Greek words used corresponded literally with the Chaldean [Hebrew], exactly suited to the things they indicated. For, just as in geometry and logic, so it seems to me, the sense indicated does not admit of variety in the expression which remains unchanged in its original form, so these writers, as it clearly appears, arrived at a wording which corresponded with the matter, and alone, or better than any other, would bring out clearly what was meant. The clearest proof of this is that, if Chaldeans have learned Greek, or Greeks Chaldean, and read both versions, the Chaldean and the translation, they regard them with awe and reverence as sisters, or rather one and the same, both in matter and words, and speak of the authors not as translators but as prophets and priests of the mysteries, whose sincerity and singleness of thought has enabled them to go hand in hand with the purest of spirits, the spirit of Moses."[15] For Philo, then, the Septuagint was as divinely inspired and authoritative as the Hebrew Scriptures because the translators were endued with such a measure of God's Spirit that they were in the category of the prophets and the priests, even the greatest prophet, Moses. Philo spanned the first centuries B.C. and A.D., and there is every reason to believe that his views represent those held by many Jews of that time.

---

14. Philo, *Life of Moses,* Book II, par. 37, as tr. by F. H. Colson, *Philo with an English Translation,* VI, 467.
15. *Ibid.,* pars. 38-40, pp. 467-469.

The New Testament and the Septuagint

More than half of the quotations from the Old Testament are from the Septuagint rather than being the New Testament writer's own translation of the Hebrew text into Greek. The book of Hebrews quotes extensively, and invariably the source is the Septuagint. Many of the quotations in Paul's letters are also derived from the Septuagint.

In fact, the arguments of the New Testament writers often hinge on the reading in the Septuagint. In Hebrews 10:5-9, for example, the author is talking about the "offering of the body of Jesus Christ once for all." Into Jesus' mouth are placed the words of Psalm 40:6-8, the heart of the quotation from the Septuagint being "a body hast thou prepared for me." But the corresponding line in the Hebrew text reads, literally, "Ears thou hast dug for me," meaning, "Thou hast given me an open ear." Yet this meaning (while somewhat related to the meaning in the Septuagint) was not the precise idea that the author of Hebrews had in mind. His key word in the unit in chapter 10 is "body," and because this word occurs in the Septuagint passage he makes use of the quotation.

Moreover, the inference "translation = no inspiration" poses a real problem in the Gospels. Probably most of what Jesus said in public and to his disciples was in Aramaic. But the *inspired original Gospels were written in Greek;* that is, the *autographs* of the Gospels *were translations* for the most part. Consistency would mean denying the Gospels the rank of inspired Scripture, but no one has dared follow the inference to its ultimate conclusion.

Under the pressure of accounting for different words in the Gospels, some evangelicals are quite eager to explain them as differences in translation of the original Aramaic statement back of the Greek autographs. As a corollary of this argument, they affirm that translation does not impair the original teaching. It is even recognized by some that the Christian church would not suffer unduly should all the Hebrew manuscripts perish and only the Septuagint remain.[16] Yet having made these very accurate and valid

16. See, e.g., R. Laird Harris, *Inspiration and Canonicity of the Bible*, p. 100.

statements, these same persons are constrained to deny
inspiration to any translation. The apparent reason for this
conclusion is the inference that since all translations err,
no translation can be inspired. Here, as in the case of
manuscript transmission, inspiration is tied to inerrancy.

As observed previously, there is a sense in which the
autographs can be distinguished from copies of the original
records. The uniquely inspired servant of God is involved
with the autograph, whereas the scribe who produces
copies has only that degree of inspiration common to all
devoted men of God. When viewed solely as written records, however, there is no reason, aside from the doctrine
of inerrancy, to distinguish a copy from the autograph. As
long as the copy has the essential results of God's revelation to the prophet or apostle, one is warranted in considering the copy as the product of inspiration. This seems to
have been the view of Jesus and the New Testament
writers.

The next question is whether they held the same respect
for the Septuagint. We have already observed that Paul's
use of *theopneustos* in 2 Timothy 3:16 applies to the
manuscript copies of his day. In verse 15 Paul refers to
"the sacred writings" with which Timothy has been acquainted from his childhood. But what were these writings? The Hebrew, or the Septuagint, or both?

Timothy lived in Derbe or Lystra in Asia Minor. His
father was a Greek and his mother a Jewess (Acts 16:1).
He received his spiritual heritage and training from his
grandmother Lois and his mother Eunice (2 Tim. 1:5).
When Paul wanted Timothy to accompany him "he took
him and circumcised him because of the Jews that were in
those places, for they all knew that his father was a Greek"
(Acts 16:3). This information, along with the popularity
of the Septuagint among the Jews of the Dispersion (such
as in Asia Minor) and the widespread belief in its inspiration, makes a very strong case for the Septuagint as "the
sacred writings" in Timothy's religious experience.

It is beyond doubt that the New Testament writers
considered the Septuagint as inspired in a secondary or

derivative sense. Like the copies of the Hebrew text, it shared the inspiration of the autographs. The problem is whether they followed Philo's belief in the primary inspiration of the Septuagint due to special aid given the translators by God's Spirit. Pierre Benoit, the well-known Dominican on the faculty of Ecole Biblique in Jerusalem, has contended for many years that there was a special inspiration associated with the Septuagint.[17] He interprets the fathers as teaching this doctrine; therefore their witness becomes the basis of his argument.

Since Augustine's mother tongue was Latin, he read as his Bible the Old Latin translation, the extant copies of which swarmed with scribal mistakes. Thus, in a letter to Jerome, he comments: "If I do find anything in those [canonical] books which seems contrary to truth, I decide that either the text is corrupt, or the translator did not follow what was really said, or that I failed to understand it. . . . I do not believe that you want your books to be read as if they were those of prophets or apostles, about whose writings, free of all error, it is unlawful to doubt."[18]

This affirmation has been commonly interpreted to be a clear reference to the inerrancy of the original writings of Scripture, but with respect to the Old Testament it contends rather for the inerrancy of the Septuagint. This is made quite clear in another context where Augustine declares: "In emending any Latin translations, we must consult the Greek texts; of these, the reputation of the seventy translators [that is, the Septuagint] is most distinguished in regard to the Old Testament. . . . Who, then, would venture to put anything on a level with this authority; still less, esteem anything better? . . . Therefore, even if we discover something in the Hebrew original other than

17. "La Septant est-elle inspirée?" in *Vom Wort des Lebens, Festschrift Max Meinertz*, pp. 41-49, and "L'inspiration des Septant d'après les Pères," in *L'homme devant Dieu, Mélanges Henri de Lubac*, I, 169-187.

18. Augustine, Letter 82, p. 392, in *Augustine, Letters* (1-82), Vol. 12, The Fathers of the Church.

they have interpreted it, it is my opinion that we should yield to the divine direction."[19] Thus, the wording of the manuscripts of the Septuagint extant in Augustine's day was to be preferred over the wording of the available Hebrew manuscripts. In this context it is clear that Augustine's designation "Hebrew original" means the extant Hebrew manuscripts, and, accordingly, the term "original" refers to the original language in which the Old Testament books were written, not to the original writings (autographs). Furthermore, Augustine made no specific reference to the original copy of the Septuagint. He assumed, along with Philo, the New Testament writers, and Irenaeus, that the authority of the Septuagint rested in the wording of the available manuscripts.

It would appear, therefore, that Augustine did believe in the special inspiration and authority of the Septuagint, but it is not possible to show that the New Testament writers held this view or that they even recognized the difference between primary and secondary inspiration. A number of Roman Catholic scholars dissent from Benoit's theory, one being the Canadian Jesuit R. A. F. MacKenzie. In the second century A.D., Theodotion's Greek translation of the book of Daniel was substituted for the regular Greek text of Daniel in the Septuagint, presumably because it was a more accurate rendering of the Hebrew-Aramaic text available then. "If then," MacKenzie comments, "Church authorities rejected part of the LXX just because it differed from its original, they could hardly have regarded those differences as of divine origin and divine authority."[20] Undoubtedly some of the Christians were more alert to textual differences and their implications, but it is unlikely that those who made the textual shift were successful in educating any large segment of the church. Augustine, two centuries after Theodotion, does not recognize the textual problem nearly as well. In truth, there

19. Augustine, *Christian Inspiration*, Book 2, ch. 15, p. 80, in Vol. 2, The Fathers of the Church.
20. "Some Problems in the Field of Inspiration," *The Catholic Biblical Quarterly*, XX (1958), 6.

were probably many views concerning the Septuagint, but in the Roman world where Greek was the common language of communication the majority of Christians believed in the inspiration of the LXX because it was their Bible and it spoke to them.

A very sane evaluation of the situation was made by the translators of the King James Version. In the preface, "The Translators to the Reader," they comment concerning the Septuagint: "It is certain, that that translation was not so sound and so perfect, but that it needed in many places correction; and who had been so sufficient for this work as the apostles or apostolic men? Yet it seemed good to the Holy Ghost and to them, to take that which they found, (the same being for the greatest part true and sufficient) rather than by making a new, in that new world and green age of the church, to expose themselves to many exceptions and cavillations, as though they made a translation to serve their own turn, and therefore bearing witness to themselves, their witness not to be regarded." The King James translators, unlike Philo, recognized mistakes in the Septuagint, yet they believed in its sufficiency. They were also wise enough to see that if God had wanted the apostles to make their own Greek translation of the Hebrew, he would have set them to the task. Rather, a new translation would have posed a problem, because the Jews would have continually accused the Christians of reading their own ideas into the translation. As it was, the Septuagint had been translated by Jews long before the coming of Christ and the Christian church, and so it could serve as the common ground of appeal.

In spite of some mistakes, all reasonably accurate translations of Scripture share secondarily in the inspiration of the original books. How far can one take this principle? Only God can say. In some cases translations have been pitifully weak because the earnestness of the missionary translator was not matched with a corresponding facility in the native language of the translation. But in spite of errors scattered throughout these translations, enough of the truth was retained to bring the readers under the convicting power of the Holy Spirit. As a result, lives were transformed and whole churches came into being. When one observes God working his purpose through such imperfect means, has one the right to exclude such a translation from the category of inspired writings?

Chapter Eight

Inerrancy and
the Phenomena of Scripture

The discussion thus far has dealt with biblical teachings and data that are instructive with respect to the autographs, manuscript transmission, and translations. This evidence, when viewed inductively, seems to indicate that the Bible makes no essential distinction between the three categories of Scripture. All three are considered as trustworthy and authoritative because they derive ultimately from God. However, the biblical writers did not express themselves on many technical aspects related to the doctrine of inspiration; therefore there is the genuine problem of trying to determine just how far implications and areas of silence can be elaborated and still be true to the intent of the writers. Those who approach the issue deductively with the assumption that God, if he were truly God, had to reveal himself inerrantly are inclined to see this teaching as a clear implication of the biblical passages.

Both approaches are sincere, but both can hardly be correct in the areas where they come to opposite conclusions. In the interests of truth, there needs to be some careful consideration of the phenomena or data of Scripture that have relevance for the concept of inerrancy. Let it be said at the outset, however, that it is not the writer's intention to parade the difficulties of Scripture. Those to be considered have been known for many years, but additional information warrants a new discussion of the issues.

Jude 14

Jude says in verse 14 of his one-chapter letter, "It was of these also that Enoch in the seventh generation from Adam prophesied, saying," and then follows a quotation that is found in 1 Enoch 1:9. The latter is one of a series of Jewish books not included within the Old Testament canon. These were written, for the most part, in the period between the Old and New Testaments. The general term for these noncanonical books is the Greek word *apocrypha* (meaning "hidden," either because they were thought to be too difficult for the common person to understand, or they were considered spurious). But the book of Enoch is usually classified among the *pseudepigrapha* (literally, "false writings") because the author, employing a fictitious name, gives the impression that the work comes from a biblical character.

The specific problem concerning us here is not, however, the quotation from an apocryphal or pseudepigraphic book. The difficulty lies in Jude's qualifying statement "seventh from Adam." Every known manuscript of Jude has this qualification, so there is good reason to believe that it came from Jude himself. But what did Jude mean by inserting this additional phrase? Some have interpreted the insertion as a literary device identifying the source of Jude's quotation in terms commonly accepted by his readers. According to this view, then, the insertion would not express Jude's actual thoughts as to the ultimate source of the quotation. In brief, "seventh from Adam" is taken as the claim in the book of Enoch; for example, Enoch is reported as saying, "I was born the seventh in the first week, while judgment and righteousness still endured" (1 Enoch 93:3), and Noah, the grandson of Enoch, purports to mention "the garden where the elect and righteous dwell, where my grandfather was taken up, the seventh from Adam, the first man whom the Lord of Spirits created" (1 Enoch 60:8). These references to "seventh" stem from the genealogical table found in Genesis 5.

On the other hand, Jude quotes 1 Enoch 1:9 as a *prophecy* that is being fulfilled in his day. Would he have done so had he thought the book and the passage originated during the period between the Testaments? Does not the cruciality of the quotation indicate, rather, that Jude thought the authority of his source derived from Enoch, the preflood patriarch, who was taken up by God when he was 365 years old? At least for many centuries this was the traditional interpretation of Jude's intent. When the book of Enoch came to light, tradition generally solved the problem by claiming that Jude's source was oral tradition and that Enoch was a later book that copied from Jude.

This attempt at solving the difficulty has proved to be baseless, however. Portions of various copies of 1 Enoch have been found among the Dead Sea (Qumrân) scrolls. These date mainly from the first century B.C., so without question Jude got his quotation from a copy of the book of 1 Enoch. There is good evidence (for example, the defense of a solar calendar) to show that the Enoch literature originated within the Qumrân (Essene) tradition. Mainstream Judaism, on the contrary, followed a lunar calendar; consequently the book of Enoch was considered heretical. Even though the book was not incorporated in the Septuagint, the early Christians (with many affinities to the Qumrân group) accepted it. This is quite evident because the New Testament is influenced more directly by the book of Enoch than by any other noncanonical book. Jude clearly alludes to the book in verse 6 and he quotes it in verses 14-15, but his apparent conviction that the quotation derived from Enoch the patriarch is untenable. As the late Edward Carnell (1919-1967) observed, "Of course, orthodoxy can always say that Jude knew by inspiration that the seventh from Adam spoke the words that now appear in the book of Enoch; but the explanation sounds suspiciously affected."[1]

1. Carnell, *The Case for Orthodox Theology*, pp. 98-99.

If one is to contend that the book of 1 Enoch represents an oral tradition stemming from the patriarch, one should also account in similar fashion for the mass of literature that appears in the intertestament period under the names of various Old Testament characters. It is exceedingly strange that not one reference is made in the Old Testament to any such literature. One reads of the book of Jashar but never the book of Enoch. Is it possible that Abraham, Isaac, Jacob, and the Israelites knew of this oral tradition and yet failed to mention it? Hardly. It is equally difficult to show that God preserved the material by an oral tradition distinct from Abraham and the people of promise.

The facts at hand would seem to indicate that Jude did not realize the origin of his source. However, this view is criticized by some because it is made on partial evidence. Maybe further information would vindicate Jude, so it is reasoned. But an *argument from silence* is recognized by all to be quite weak. It implies that one must have almost total evidence before demonstration is possible. If this is the case, one could argue just as cogently that there may have been airplanes in the time of Christ. By this period, man had conceived of the idea of human flight and he knew how to work metals, etc., so why not airplanes? While this proposition sounds fantastic, it would be difficult to produce sufficient data to disprove the claim in the mind of the proponent. He could always say that someday the evidence would be forthcoming to prove his point. Likewise, in the case of Jude's quotation from Enoch, absolute proof will probably never be accessible, but is this justification enough for the fond hope of having the problem resolved in favor of Jude?

There is, of course, a place for the argument from silence, but it should not be used unless the available evidence permits a *genuine probability*, not a theoretical possibility, that the proposition is true. In far too many cases the argument from silence is resorted to only when the facts are on the side of one's opponents. On the contrary, it is amazing how little evidence it usually takes to convince a person of a point when it agrees with his presuppositions. To some extent every human being is guilty of wishful thinking, but there must come a time when the facts become determinative, and in the case of inerrancy Jude 14 is as good a place to start as any.

Either the quotation originated with Enoch the patriarch or it did not. Aside from Jude's claim, all the evidence indicates that it did not. Jude did not intend to deceive or falsify the issue. His error was an innocent one that he made in common with his fellow Jews and Christians. But sincerity of motive did not eliminate the mistake. Moreover, the Holy Spirit did not override the human concept of Jude. How, then, does this accord with the dogma that the Holy Spirit "bore" the writers along, guiding them inerrantly in all that they wrote? The seriousness of the problem is also indicated by the fear of many even to recognize the difficulty; for example, commentaries by evangelicals seldom discuss the problem.

Jude 9

The little book of Jude is a warning against false brethren who have infiltrated the Christian ranks and undermined "the faith which was once for all delivered to the saints" (v. 3). Jude reminds his readers that God will punish such sinners, and as proof he cites three examples: the unbelieving Israelites who died in the wilderness (v. 5), the fallen angels chained in nether gloom (v. 6), and the immoral residents of Sodom and Gomorrah who perished by fire (v. 7). The first and last examples are described in the Pentateuch, and without question the author considered them as historical events in God's dealing with mankind. Apparently Jude considered God's condemnation of the fallen angels (described in an expansion of Gen. 6:1-4 found in the book of Enoch) as an actual happening in the past.

In contrast to the revilings of the false brethren, "loudmouthed boasters" (v. 16) who "boldly carouse" (v. 12) at love feasts, Jude cites in verse 9 the example of the archangel Michael: "But when the archangel Michael, contending with the devil, disputed about the body of Moses, he did not presume to pronounce a reviling judgment upon him, but said, 'The Lord rebuke you.' ''

The event to which Jude alludes is not recorded in the canonical Old Testament. According to early tradition, his source was a portion of The Assumption of Moses that has been lost during the transmission of the apocryphal book. After the death of Moses, according to this account, the archangel Michael had to contend with Satan for the body. Satan claimed the body because Moses had been a murderer (Ex. 2:11). This blasphemous charge was intolerable to Michael, but rather than accuse Satan of blasphemy he simply said, "The Lord rebuke you."

While some have interpreted Jude's allusion to the apocryphal book as an argument *ad hominem* in which he cites the passage because the book was respected by his opponents, one gets the impression, just as in verse 6, that Jude believed the incident was an actual fact and thus a valid basis for refuting his adversaries.

But Jude 9 (which was also a part of the autograph of Jude) is, according to the traditional view, just as much inspired as John 3:16. If it is inspired, then why be hesitant about discussing the implications? Either the archangel Michael contended with the devil for the body of Moses or he did not. Joshua and the prophets never refer to any such struggle, so there is no biblical reason, aside from Jude's allusion, for believing in the actuality of the story. On the other hand, does not the authoritative function of Jude's illustration show the importance that he attached to it? If, as the evidence seems to indicate, Jude accepted the current tradition with respect to the body of Moses, what becomes of the doctrine of inerrancy?

The Reign of Pekah

According to 2 Kings 15:27, "in the fifty-second year of Azariah king of Judah Pekah the son of Remaliah began to reign over Israel in Samaria, and reigned twenty years." For some years now, the figure 20 has been known to be wrong. James Orr, speaking of the cross references or synchronisms in the books of Kings, said, "Pekah's twenty years in 2 Kings 15:27 . . . is shown by the Assyrian syn-chronisms to be a mistake."[2] He did not explain further, and nothing was generally accessible to the layman until Edwin R. Thiele's *The Mysterious Numbers of the Hebrew Kings* appeared in 1951.

The chronology of the kings of Israel and Judah is one of the most complex problems in all the Bible, but Thiele has given sufficient evidence to clinch the matter concerning Pekah's twenty years. In the ancient world there were two systems for reckoning the years of a king's reign, the difference between the two being a matter of one year. Since Israel followed one system and Judah the other during part of their histories, there is often a difference of one year in the records. To simplify the discussion, both of Pekah's reign and of Hezekiah's reign (which is to follow), a single date will be used in each case, although technically the actual date may be a year off one way or the other. Furthermore, unless indicated otherwise, all references in the two sections will be from 2 Kings.

The verse in question (15:27) says Pekah began to reign in the fifty-second year of Azariah (another name for Uzziah). Azariah's death, coming in the fifty-second year of his reign, occurred about 739 B.C., and therefore Pekah's reign began then. This was also the year in which Isaiah the prophet "saw the Lord . . . high and lifted up" (Isa. 6:1). If Pekah is given his twenty years, then he finished in 719. The biblical record says Hoshea, the last king of Israel, followed Pekah and reigned for nine years. This would mean that Samaria, the capital of Israel, fell in 710. However, archaeological evidence has confirmed be-yond doubt that Samaria submitted to the Assyrians in 722. It is impossible, then, to give Pekah his twenty years after 739 B.C.

Accordingly, some early commentators figured back twenty years from 731, the end of Pekah's reign and the beginning of Hoshea's. But this reconstruction is equally impossible. Pekah was preceded by Pekahiah (two years) and Menahem (ten years). If Pekah's reign began in 751,

2. Orr, *Revelation and Inspiration*, p. 180.

then Menahem reigned from 763 to 753. Yet 15:19 informs us, "Pul the king of Assyria came against the land; and Menahem gave Pul a thousand talents of silver, that he might help him to confirm his hold of the royal power." "Pul" was the Babylonian nickname for the great Assyrian king Tiglath-pileser III, whose dates (745-727) have also been settled beyond question. The annals of Tiglath-pileser refer to this same event, mentioning Menahem by name. Since the payment of tribute was made in 743 or later, Menahem could not have reigned 763-753. If Menahem cannot be moved, Pekahiah's reign must remain 741-739, with Pekah's rule beginning in 739. Inasmuch as his reign closed in 731, the twenty years ascribed to him shrink to eight.

In the first edition of his book (1951), Thiele suggested that Pekah took credit to himself for the twelve years that Menahem and Pekahiah had ruled.[3] This seemed logical, especially since Pekah was a *shalish* ("captain, official") under Menahem's son, Pekahiah, the man he slew in order to gain power (15:25). This same verse notes, however, that Pekah had a band of fifty Gileadites when he slew Pekahiah. Working with this bit of evidence, Thiele contends in his revised edition (1965) that Pekah became king of Gilead, in northern Transjordan, in the same year that Menahem killed Shallum and began his reign in Israel.[4] In short, rather than assuming that Pekah took credit for the reigns of Menahem and Pekahiah (a total of twelve years), Thiele is endeavoring to give full credence to the biblical claim that Pekah reigned for twenty years (twelve in Gilead and eight in Israel). This latter view may well be correct, but in either case the important fact is that the court records of Israel credited Pekah with a twenty-year reign. Moreover, it should be noted that Thiele's revised theory does not lessen the problem for the inerrancists. 2 Kings 15:27 states quite unambiguously that Pekah reigned in Samaria twenty years after he became king of Israel, and this is precisely what did not happen.

3. Thiele, *The Mysterious Numbers of the Hebrew Kings* (1951), p. 114.
4. *Ibid.*, rev. ed. (1965), p. 124.

Most scholars recognize that the twenty years assigned to Pekah are in error, but some are still inclined to account for it as a scribal error in transmission of the text of 15:27. This argument fails to reckon, however, with two synchronisms in 15:32 and 16:1. The text of 15:32 notes that Jotham began to reign in "the second year of Pekah." Jotham began to reign as a coregent with his father Uzziah (who was a leper, 2 Chron. 26:21) about 750. If this date was considered the second year of Pekah, then his first year would have been 751. In other words, the scribe who compiled this section had assigned 751-731 as the time of Pekah's reign. The most plausible explanation for the scribe's action is that his records also attributed a twenty-year reign to Pekah. He was working up his synchronisms between the kings of Israel and of Judah about 125 to 150 years after the fall of Samaria, and so he had no way to check the accuracy of the data that had come from the northern kingdom. In making his comparative chart, he gave Pekah twenty years, not realizing that it was impossible (as we have noted) to put Menahem's reign 763-753 and Pekahiah's 753-751. This slip may appear a bit foolish, but the scribe in Judah knew nothing of B.C. or A.D. and the specific numbers we are using as dates. He did not have an absolute time scale (with Tiglath-pileser's dates, for example) to warn him that he could not actually give Pekah twenty years.

In 16:1 the scribe notes that Ahaz began to reign in "the seventeenth year of Pekah." This synchronism is obviously based on the assumption that Pekah reigned twenty years. But the interesting fact is that once we grant the original error of twenty years in Samaria instead of eight, the dates that this relative chart gives for Jotham (750) and Ahaz (735) prove to be amazingly accurate. On the other hand, if the original text of 2 Kings had been inerrant (that is, in accord with the actual reigns of Menahem, 751-741, and of Pekah, 739-731), the scribe would have had Jotham beginning in "the second year of Menahem" and Ahaz starting in "the fifth year of Pekah."

Some of those who contend for the doctrine of an inerrant original text take the next logical step by suggest-

ing that the synchronisms are later scribal insertions that
did not appear in the original text of 2 Kings. But again
the suggestion is fruitless. Chapter 15:33 begins, "He was
twenty-five years old when he began to reign, and he
reigned sixteen years in Jerusalem." If 15:32 is dropped,
then "he" refers back to Pekah, who is discussed in 15:31.
This is impossible, however, so there is no other way out
but to admit that the erroneous details of 15:27, 32; 16:1
were in the original compilation of 2 Kings.

The Reign of Hezekiah

Another difficult chronological problem has to do with
the dates of Hezekiah's reign. 2 Kings 18:1 states, "In the
third year of Hoshea son of Elah, king of Israel, Hezekiah
the son of Ahaz, king of Judah, began to reign." Hoshea
began reigning in 731, when he slew Pekah (15:30). According to 18:1, then, Hezekiah began to reign about 728.
But 18:13 notes that Sennacherib invaded Judah in "the
fourteenth year of King Hezekiah." Since Sennacherib's
campaign against Judah and Jerusalem was in 701, Hezekiah began his reign in 715. He ruled for twenty-nine years
(18:2), that is, down to 686. This conclusion is also in line
with the inference from 20:6 that after Hezekiah's illness
(which occurred about the time of Sennacherib's campaign) God spared his life fifteen years. Practically all
scholars are agreed now that Hezekiah reigned 715-686.
Then what is to be done with 18:1, which seems to begin
Hezekiah's reign in 728?

In discussing this problem, Thiele writes, "Long after
the original records of the kings had been set in order and
when the true arrangement of the reigns had been forgotten—certain synchronisms in II Kings, chs. 17 and 18, were
introduced by some late hand strangely out of harmony
with the original pattern of reigns."[5] In Thiele's opinion,
some scribe gave Pekah his twenty years, but this time the
reign was started at 739 and pushed down twenty years.
Thus Hoshea's reign was 719-710. On the basis of this

5. *Ibid.*, 1951 ed., p. 268.

chart, the scribe noted that it was in the third year of Hoshea, about 716, that Hezekiah began to reign. With this interpretation both 18:1 and 18:13 indicate the same time (716-715) for the start of Hezekiah's reign.

Chapter 17:1 indicates that Hoshea began to reign in "the twelfth year of Ahaz." Ahaz' reign of sixteen years (16:2) began in 731; therefore his twelfth year was 719, the year (according to the scribe's chart) that Hoshea began to rule. The scribe went farther and noted in 18:9-10 that the siege of Samaria began in Hezekiah's fourth year and ended in his sixth. Thus, in Thiele's judgment, the synchronisms in 17:1; 18:1, 9-10 are errone-ous because the scribe allotted Pekah twenty years, 739-719.

In the joint article, "Chronology of the Old Testament," K. A. Kitchen and T. C. Mitchell state that Thiele's inter-pretation of the four synchronisms is invalid.[6] They feel that "the twelfth year" noted in 17:1 refers to Ahaz' last year of a twelve-year coregency with Jotham, rather than to the twelfth year of his sole reign. Hoshea began in 731; thus according to this assumption Ahaz became a coregent with his father Jotham in 743. Chapter 16:2 ascribes to Ahaz a sixteen-year reign (undoubtedly the period 731-715), but the previous verse (16:1) tells us that his reign began in 735. Mitchell and Kitchen interpret this to mean that Ahaz became a "senior partner" at that time. It is even more probable that the pro-Assyrian group in Judah forced Jotham (who, like his father Uzziah, was anti-Assyrian) to relinquish the rule to his son Ahaz. The policy of Ahaz was decidedly pro-Assyrian (2 Chron. 28:16), and it was he, not Jotham, who was the active king when Rezin and Pekah came up (about 734) against Jeru-salem (Isa. 7:1). Ahaz was twenty when he began to reign (16:2), but the text does not make it clear which begin-ning (735 or 731) was intended. If the former date was meant, then Ahaz was twelve years old in 743; otherwise he was eight. In 751, when he began his twelve-year coregency with Uzziah, Jotham was twenty-five (15:33).

6. *The New Bible Dictionary*, pp. 212-223.

The question is whether in fact Ahaz began a twelve-year coregency in 743 when he was only twelve (or possibly eight) and when Jotham, his father, was himself technically a coregent (because Uzziah did not die until 739).

To account for 18:1, 9-10, Kitchen and Mitchell have also to postulate a twelve-year coregency for Hezekiah (beginning about 728, when he was thirteen years old). In other words, their solution necessitates twelve-year coregencies for three successive kings: Jotham, Ahaz, and Hezekiah. This solution is theoretically possible, but the probability is exceedingly remote. What Kitchen and Mitchell are really saying, whether they realize it or not, is that somehow Uzziah (who died at 68), Jotham (who died at 45), and Ahaz (who died at 36) happened to appoint their sons as coregents exactly twelve years before each of their deaths. This takes some credulity. The plain fact is that the so-called twelve-year coregencies resulted from a scribe or some scribes in Judah trying to make sense of Pekah's twenty years when he reigned only eight in Israel. Accordingly, the synchronisms in 2 Kings 17 and 18 are just as erroneous as the information in 2 Kings 15:27 and 16:1.

Genesis 5

Genesis 5 contains the genealogy of man from Adam on through the three sons of Noah: Shem, Ham, and Japheth. The interpretation of the chapter varies from individual to individual; but regardless of this, the pattern of the writer is clear. He gives the age of a man at the birth of his son, how much longer he lived after that, and finally his age at death. On the strength of this and other genealogies in the Old Testament the Jewish and Christian communities reckoned the date of creation.

Since the numbers in the Hebrew and Septuagint texts vary, the two systems vary as well. The year 1973, being the year 5733 in Jewish tradition, puts the creation in 3760 B.C. On the other hand, many Christians have accepted the date 4004 B.C., determined by Archbishop James Ussher (1581-1656).

It was not until the nineteenth century that enough evidence was available to disprove the 4004 date as the beginning of the world, and even today some Bibles still carry the old chronology. During the latter part of the nineteenth century, however, some evangelical scholars became aware of the problem and attempted to reckon with it. The genealogies of Genesis, according to these studies, were to be considered trustworthy only for the purpose that the biblical compiler had in mind. This issue hinged, therefore, on one's interpretation of the compiler's intent.

We do not know who worked up the material as it is in our Bible. Whether it was Moses or someone else, he certainly did so on the basis of ancient records or oral tradition. If he intended the genealogy merely as a survey highlighting the main men in the long history of the preflood world, why did he retain, evidently from his sources, the three precise numbers of years (age at birth of son, years lived afterward, and age at death) for each of the men named? True, the ancient Orientals were selective in their genealogies at times, but when doing so, they did not pay such close attention to exact figures as in Genesis 5. A selective list may have been the intent at the beginning of the oral tradition that transmitted the information, but it is hard to reconcile this intent with the specific figures that are an integral part of the present list. When the writer claims that Adam lived 130 years and then begat Seth, and that he lived 800 years afterward, making his total age 930 years, it is apparent that the writer intended the figures literally.

Until geological information disproved the 4004 date, most Jews and Christians (including many alert, even brilliant, persons) thought the genealogy in Genesis 5 was intended to show the consecutive history of man. Inasmuch as some evangelicals in the nineteenth century felt the force of the new geological information, they were inclined to stretch the genealogy enough to provide gaps for the scientific data. But how did this relate to the intent of the author? If the geological and other scientific data known today had not been made available to us, would we have doubted that Genesis 5 was intended to be chronological? Not likely. The biblical evidence is too explicit at this point. It is our scientific knowledge that causes us to ignore the clear meaning of the passage. Obviously, then, the intent of the biblical writer can hardly be accommodated to the scientific facts made available from generation to generation.

Acts 7:4

Stephen's speech before the council, which appears in Acts 7:2-53, begins with the details of Abraham's call. In verse 4, Stephen states: "Then he departed from the land of the Chaldeans, and lived in Haran. And after his father died, God removed him from there into this land in which you are now living." According to Genesis 11:26, Terah was 70 at the birth of Abraham, and he died in Haran at the age of 205 (11:32). Abraham, therefore, was 135 at the death of his father. However, Abraham left for Canaan when he was 75 (12:4), sixty years before the death of his father. On what grounds, then, does Stephen declare that Abraham left for Canaan "after his father died"? Neither the Hebrew nor the Septuagint supports this claim.

This same idea is found in the writings of Philo, the Jewish scholar at Alexandria. Apparently Stephen and Philo were drawing from some kind of oral tradition that was alive in Judaism and the early church. Most likely Stephen's Jewish audience did not pick any flaws in his historical survey because they shared the same interpretation of history from the factual point of view.

It is difficult to determine why Philo, a student of the Pentateuch, believed that Abraham left Haran after his father died, because neither the Hebrew nor the Greek texts (as we have them now) would support such an interpretation. Possibly he had access to a Greek text that had Terah dying at 145 instead of 205. In any event there is strong evidence to show that it formed a part of an oral tradition.

Further support for this conclusion is found in Acts 7:23, where Stephen says Moses was forty years old when he felt he should visit his own people. This too is found in Philo, not in the Old Testament. Moreover, Stephen added in verse 25, "He supposed that his brethren understood that God was giving them deliverance by his hand, but they did not understand." This concept is not based on any Old Testament passage, and so it may well be another bit of the traditional interpretation of that day.

Stephen, after all, was speaking with his very life at stake. He had no scrolls to consult. He spoke out of the fullness of his heart and the store of information in his mind. He thought he was portraying a correct historical picture, and evidently his audience did too, but again honesty of intent does not rectify the difficulty. There is hardly any way out but to admit that Stephen, even while under the inspiration of the Holy Spirit, probably made a mistake in declaring that Abraham left Haran after Terah died.

Acts 7:15-16

Another statement in Stephen's speech demands attention also. In verses 15-16 we read, "And he [Jacob] died, himself and our fathers, and they were carried back to Shechem and laid in the tomb that Abraham had bought for a sum of silver from the sons of Hamor in Shechem." Jacob was buried at Hebron (Mamre) in the field of Machpelah (Gen. 50:13), which Abraham had purchased from Ephron the Hittite (Gen. 23:16-18). Joseph, on the other hand, was buried at Shechem in the plot of ground that Jacob had purchased from the sons of Hamor (Josh. 24:32). According to Josephus (*Antiquities* II, 8, 2), all the sons of Jacob, except Joseph, were buried at Hebron.

This is the Old Testament and traditional evidence. What can we make of Stephen's statement? One of the most popular explanations of the older commentators was that of Daniel Whitby, which Matthew Henry quotes in his commentary: *"Jacob went down into Egypt and died, he and our fathers; and (our fathers) were carried over into Sychem; and he, that is, Jacob, was laid in the sepulchre that Abraham bought for a sum of money, Gen. xxiii 16.*

(Or, they laid there, that is, Abraham, Isaac, and Jacob.) *And they*, namely, the other patriarchs, were *buried in the sepulchre bought of the sons of Emmor, the father of Sychem.* "[7] Thus, Whitby splits the verse up and supplies words to make Stephen mean what Genesis and Joshua say.

Others solve the difficulty by regarding the name "Abraham" as a scribal error for "Jacob," supposedly the original wording of the text. This conjecture, however, is without any textual basis. Still others, recognizing the weight of the textual evidence, suggest the possibility that Jacob bought again at a later time a field previously purchased by Abraham. The better part of wisdom is to accept the evidence we have, and frankly admit, as F. F. Bruce does, "The two purchases of land are telescoped here in much the same way as two separate calls of Abraham are telescoped in v. 2 and two separate Pentateuchal quotations in v. 7."[8]

Some commentators readily acknowledge that Stephen was mistaken, but they claim inerrancy for the autograph of the Acts in that Luke accurately copied Stephen's words, mistakes and all. However, this easy answer ignores the clear biblical statement that Stephen spoke under the influence of the Holy Spirit. The difficulty, as Bruce implies, may well have arisen with Luke when he condensed Stephen's sermon. But with respect to the doctrine of inerrant autographs it makes no essential difference whether the telescoping occurred in Stephen's original speech or in Luke's condensation.

Galatians 3:17

In Galatians 3:16, 17, Paul writes: "Now the promises were made to Abraham and to his offspring. It does not say, 'And to offsprings,' referring to many; but, referring to one, 'And to your offspring,' which is Christ. This is what I mean: the law, which came four hundred and thirty

---

7. Henry, *Commentary on the Whole Bible*, VI, 80.
8. Bruce, *Commentary on the Book of Acts, The New International Commentary on the New Testament*, p. 149, note 39.

years afterward, does not annul a covenant previously ratified by God, so as to make the promise void." All the Greek manuscripts have 430, so in all likelihood Paul's original letter had it as well. There is a problem with this figure, however. Abraham was 75 when he went to Canaan (Gen. 12:4), he was 100 when Isaac was born (21:5), Isaac was 60 when Jacob was born (25:26), and Jacob was 130 when he went to Egypt (47:9). Adding together 25, 60, and 130 gives 215 years in Canaan. The Hebrew text of Exodus 12:40 notes, "The time that the people of Israel dwelt in Egypt was four hundred and thirty years." Therefore, the time from the promise to Abraham to the giving of the law was 645 years (215 + 430). Did Paul get his information from another source, or did he mean something else when he wrote the number 430?

The Septuagint of Exodus 12:40 reads, "The time that the people of Israel dwelt in Egypt and in the land of Canaan was four hundred and thirty years." Thus, the Greek translation allots 215 years to Canaan and 215 to Egypt. It is quite possible, therefore, that Paul was following the LXX figure.

Another concern is the question whether the Hebrew or the LXX is correct. While the genealogies indicate only four generations from Levi through Moses, the preponderance of evidence that archaeology offers at the present time favors the 430-year stay in Egypt as noted in the Hebrew text.

Paul's reference to "the promises" is, according to one interpretation, a reference to the entire patriarchal period down to Jacob's descent into Egypt. Similarly "the law" is taken to mean the period beginning with Moses and the Exodus. Granting this interpretation of the passage, Paul was correct and in accord with the Hebrew text of Exodus 12:40.

But Paul's argument in Galatians 3:16-17 hinges not on periods of time but on events in Israel's history. At first he relates the promises both to Abraham and to his descendants, but later he makes his intention clear by referring to "a covenant . . . ratified by God." What else could this have meant to Paul's readers except the personal covenant that God made with Abraham, ratifying his previous prom-ises? This dramatic event is described in Genesis 15. After the details are noted, verse 18 summarizes, "On that day the LORD made a covenant with Abram." The sign of the covenant, circumcision, came later (Gen. 17:10). Inasmuch as these historic episodes took place within twenty-four years after Abraham arrived in Canaan, the span of time between it and the giving of the law on Mt. Sinai would logically include the 215 years of Canaan and the 430 in Egypt.

What justification is there, then, for interpreting Paul to mean 430 years after the patriarchal period closed (that is, when Jacob went to Egypt)? Had he wanted to say this, would he not have expressed himself more explicitly? As noted previously, Paul used the Septuagint a great deal, so why should one doubt its use here? In fact, because most of his readers probably read the Septuagint, the reference to 430 years would agree with their understanding of history and not distract their minds, therefore, from his main point. Evidently it seemed good to the Holy Spirit to let Paul use the traditional 430 years without informing him that he was technically wrong and should be using 645 years as found in the Hebrew.

Mark 14:30, 72

In Mark 14:30 Jesus says to Peter, "Truly, I say to you, this very night, before the cock crows twice, you will deny me three times." In verse 72 of the same chapter we read: "And immediately the cock crowed a second time. And Peter remembered how Jesus had said to him, 'Before the cock crows twice, you will deny me three times.' "

This same pattern (prediction by Jesus, occurrence of the event, and Peter's remembrance of the prediction) is also found in Matthew (26:34, 74-75) and Luke (22:34, 60-61). However, both of these accounts omit the words "twice," "second time," and "twice." In short, they report that Jesus said, "Before the cock crows, you will deny me three times."

In explaining the difference in detail in Mark's report of

the denial episode, some evangelical scholars suggest that Matthew and Luke generalized the cock's crowing twice to mean "shall not have finished crowing." But why generalize if they knew the cock crowed twice?

Another explanation is the claim that the difficult reading is due to a scribal error. True, the Sinaiticus manuscript of the Greek New Testament omits the words "twice" and "second." In some other manuscripts the word "twice" or "second" is omitted in one of two cases, but never in all three occurrences. Moreover, the majority of the high-quality manuscripts of Mark have "twice" or "second" in all three places.

Furthermore, there is no evidence to suggest that the words "twice" and "second" crept into the text on the basis of some later tradition. How is it that this supposed tradition spread through practically all the Greek manuscripts of Mark and yet had no influence in Matthew and Luke? What basis would there be for any scribe's attempt to insert the words into the text? There is plenty of reason, on the other hand, why a scribe would want to omit the words from Mark and thus harmonize it with the other two Gospels. Mark makes good sense as it is. The source of the scribal activity was most likely Mark himself as he took down bits of information from Peter's lips. The strong probability is that the words "twice" and "second" were in the autograph of Mark.

But what essential difference is there if the other Gospel writers, Matthew and Luke, follow the general tradition of the cock's crowing just once? All three Gospels contain the historical features necessary to convey the truth of the matter: the prediction of denial and Peter's boast, the fulfilment of the prediction, and Peter's remorse on remembering Jesus' words.

1 Corinthians 3:19

Paul, in writing to the church at Corinth, said: "For the wisdom of this world is folly with God. For it is written, 'He catches the wise in their craftiness' " (3:19). The source of the quotation is Job 5:13, which is part of the first speech of Eliphaz the Temanite. Traditionally speaking, Eliphaz has never been considered as inspired. Job, so it is claimed, was the inspired one and he recorded the addresses of Eliphaz and his friends, errors and all.

Certain evangelicals more or less equate the expressions "It is written" and "God says." It cannot mean this in 1 Corinthians 3:19 if Eliphaz is uninspired. Apparently Paul did not care who said it, nor whether he was inspired. The statement was true as far as he was concerned and so he used it in his argument. This illustration does not involve an error as such, but it does show how biblical evidence is often at variance with some of the more precise formulations of inspiration. As Carnell observes, "Whether orthodoxy realized it or not, it was really saying that inspiration, at times, ensures no more than an infallible account of error."[9]

Theological Variations

In addition to the difficulty of squaring all biblical data on the objective level, there is also the problem of subjective interpretations. An excellent example is the theological judgment made by the historian in 2 Samuel 24:1, "Again the anger of Yahweh blazed against Israel when he incited David against them, saying, 'Go, number Israel and Judah.' " David undoubtedly took the census in connection with such material concerns as military draft and assessments to maintain the royal court and administration of the kingdom. At the time of the compilation of 2 Samuel, however, the prevailing view was that Yahweh was responsible for everything that happened. The idea is well expressed in Isaiah 45:7, "I make prosperity and create trouble, I, Yahweh, do all these things."

In 1 Chronicles 21:1, on the other hand, the historian declares, "Satan set himself against Israel by inciting David to number Israel." In general, the Chronicler incorporated older source material (much of which came from a copy of Samuel-Kings) as he found it, but where he differed from

9. Carnell, *op. cit.*, pp. 102-103.

the interpretation of his sources he revised the text, apparently on the conviction that his understanding was more accurate. It is obvious that he simply did not believe that God incited David to take a census in order to express his anger against Israel.

Tradition has harmonized the two interpretations by understanding 2 Samuel 24:1 as the permissive will of God in order to test David, but such an attempt skirts the fact that had the Chronicler met the historian of 2 Samuel there would have been some real theological debate. Although it is difficult to prove an error, it is evident that partial truth is involved in the interpretations. There are numerous biblical examples of theological interpretations of one generation being revised slightly or even rejected by another. The solution to this complex layering of theological judgments is hardly the theory of the inerrancy of these partial truths.

Inerrancy and Consistency

While the specific problems considered thus far in this chapter by no means exhaust the difficulties that biblical phenomena present to Christians, they are sufficiently varied and precise to show the seriousness of the issue. The question is, What are we to make of these findings? The evidence can be viewed from three possible points of view: (1) Scripture teaches the doctrine of inerrancy, but the phenomena of Scripture disprove this claim, (2) Scripture teaches the doctrine of inerrancy, therefore any contradictions or errors are in appearance only; and (3) Scripture does not teach the doctrine of inerrancy, therefore the phenomena of Scripture are to be accepted as an important factor in determining a biblical view of inspiration.

The first point of view frankly acknowledges that Scripture is not consistent in all the evidence relevant to the doctrine of inspiration. While some within the church accept this conclusion, the majority of Christians take either the second or third of the possible interpretations. The basic premise of these latter views is that God, being the author of all truth, was consistent in his revelation.

The determinative factor for the second point of view is the assurance that Scripture teaches the doctrine of inerrancy. The probability of some errors in the autographs is intolerable, therefore, because a perfect God would never have allowed such a thing to happen. As a result, the usual mood is one of caution with respect to the interpretation of the phenomena. Problems are recognized, but there is little inclination to resolve them on the basis of the evidence at hand. Let us not be hasty, so the argument goes, because we do not have all the information. Maybe future discoveries will resolve these apparent contradictions. But is such a fond hope justified? A number of scholars who hold to inerrancy recognize that some of the biblical phenomena cannot be harmonized without employing strained or forced methods. This intellectual honesty is to be commended, but this series of suspended judgments indicates that the totality of biblical evidence does not prove the doctrine of inerrancy to be a fact. It is still a theory that must be accepted by faith.

This conclusion is also supported by the kind of apologetic that is usually employed to parry the thrusts of the phenomena. The chief refutation is a negative one that concentrates on some glaring examples of error that the liberals have made. A favorite target is the German critic Anton F. Hartmann, who said that Moses could not have written the Pentateuch because the Hebrews did not start writing until the period of the judges. Now we know that the Hebrews were literate and capable of writing from Abraham on down. Another example is early liberalism's verdict that Isaiah 20:1 was erroneous in mentioning Sargon, a king otherwise unknown. Since that time a mass of information about Sargon, including his annals, has been discovered.

Of course, the idea back of such an argument is that in numerous instances liberalism has been proved wrong and in due time it will be proved wrong everywhere. But will this suggestion stand up under close scrutiny? The most extreme liberals today recognize the folly of these early statements. In many instances it has been the liberal camp itself that has corrected its earlier excesses. Many of the so-called "assured results" of higher criticism have proved to be "assumed results," but the evidence does not warrant the conclusion that this will happen to *all* of the liberal findings. In some instances, the so-called "assured results" of *tradition* are in reality "assumed results."

Truth is like a two-way street or a double-edged sword. Although facts confirm the biblical record in many instances, they also disprove it in other cases. In the last analysis we must let the truth cut both ways. The true biblical view of inspiration must account for all the evidence of Scripture. The peril of the view of inerrancy is its rigidity and all-or-nothing character. If only one of the illustrations discussed in this chapter is correct, the doctrine is invalidated.

Chapter Nine

Inspiration and Inerrancy

Tradition accepted the biblical emphasis that God initiated the revelatory process, but one of the unanswered problems was that of authorship. Was God the author of Scripture as well as its originator? If so, what part did man play? Some, like Athenagoras, thought completely in terms of the Greek theory of inspiration where the deity dictates his message to his passive human instrument. Others, recognizing differences in style and content between the biblical books, allowed a place for the rational activity of the writers.

The Syllogism of Inerrancy

While in general there was greater stress on the divinity of Scripture, there was some recognition of the Bible as a divine-human book. Inspiration was understood as God's help during the revelation of Scripture, and so comprehensively it extended to all of God's trustworthy, authoritative Word. Implied in trustworthiness, of course, were the aspects of truthfulness and accuracy of the record because most Christians concurred in Balaam's answer to Balak, "God is not man, that he should lie" (Num. 23:19). More often than not, this line of thinking involved the basic syllogism: God is perfect and cannot lie; God revealed himself to humankind; therefore the Written Word must be perfect, that is, free from all error.

Inspiration of Biblical Writers

Just as there are varying kinds of revelation in Scripture, there are different kinds of inspiration. There is no question that the prophets claimed to have the help of God in declaring the revelatory word. Jeremiah, like Moses, had a special sense of divine aid because at his call Yahweh touched his mouth and said, "Behold, I have put my words in your mouth" (1:9). Even on occasions when Jeremiah viewed such ordinary objects or events as a blossoming almond tree, a steaming cooking pot being emptied, a potter at work, and two baskets of figs, his insights were understood as the word of Yahweh.

Other traditions have the overtones of God's inspiration, but the effect is not so overpowering. Occasionally the wise acknowledge that their insights derive from their reverence of Yahweh. Elihu even alludes to his own inspiration when he makes the claim that it is the spirit of the Almighty, not one's age, that leads to understanding: "But it is the spirit in a man, the breath of the Almighty, that makes him understand" (Job 32:8). In general, however, wisdom literature evidences no consciousness that Yahweh is involved in its attempts to offer prudential guidelines for living or to grapple with life's problems. This is equally true of some of the psalmists and the historians of Israel.

Whereas, on the one hand, the concept of inspiration permeates the Bible, the biblical writers, on the other hand, do not give any psychological clues to explain how this inspiration took place. In fact, they seldom report any of their inner feelings during the period of inspiration. The most explicit description is that of Eliphaz, apparently the eldest of Job's three friends. In order to back up his words of counsel with prophet-like authority he relates how he got the message:

> Now a word was brought to me stealthily,
> > my ear received the whisper of it.
> Amid thoughts from visions of the night,
> > When deep sleep falls on men,
> dread came upon me, and trembling,
> > which made all my bones shake.
> A wind [spirit] glided past my face;
> > the hair of my flesh stood up.
> It stood still,
> > but I could not discern its appearance.
> A form was before my eyes;
> > there was silence, then I heard a voice.
> > > (Job 4:12-16)

This revelation by a vision during a deep sleep undoubtedly represents one of the ways the ancients experienced the coming of God's word, but it is hardly the normal method of the wisdom tradition. In any case, in view of the psychological complexity of the revelatory experience and the few descriptions of it, it is certain that the Bible does not explain how God inspires his instruments of revelation. In fact, the "how" is still inexplicable; therefore this study will make no attempt to explain it.

Inspiration of Biblical Books

The inspiration of the biblical writers is beyond question, but because of other biblical evidence and certain difficulties inherent in an emphasis on the inspired person, some have preferred to speak of the "inspired book." Robert Preus summarizes the opinion of the seventeenth-century Lutheran theologians as follows: "Properly speaking, inspiration pertains to the holy Scriptures themselves. It may be said, however, that the writers too were inspired by God: they wrote by the illumination and inspiration of the Holy Ghost."[1]

One reason for stressing the inspiration of the book was the sporadic nature of the inspiration of a number of biblical writers. David, for example, was inspired by God while producing his psalms. But when, after his sin in

1. *The Inspiration of Scripture*, p. 33.

taking Bathsheba, he sent a letter to Joab the general saying, "Set Uriah in front of the hardest fighting, and then draw back from him, that he may be struck down and die" (2 Sam. 11:15), neither David nor his letter was inspired by God. Tradition has considered the writer of the book of Samuel as the inspired one. He gave an accurate account of the event and the letter that God intended to be included in Scripture.

While there is some justification for this distinction between the inspiration of the source of the biblical material and the inspiration of the compiler of that material, the idea has been carried too far in some instances. According to some, Stephen (in his sermon in Acts 7) was just a preacher who made mistakes in his survey of Israel's history, whereas Luke, preserving these errors, was the inspired one. Yet Luke does not claim inspiration for himself. His authorization for writing is not a command from God. He simply says, "It seemed good to me." Moreover, Luke does not consider his Gospel and history of the early church as inspired. "An orderly account" is the only claim he makes.

The clearest evidence for defining inspiration in terms of the book comes from 2 Timothy 3:16. Paul says that Scripture is *theopneustos* ("God-breathed," that is, "inspired by God"). Because Paul was thinking in terms of the extant manuscripts, his primary emphasis was on the book, but this does not mean that Paul would deny the inspiration of the Old Testament writers. He would certainly agree with 2 Peter 1:21: "Men moved by the Holy Spirit spoke from God."

In reaction to the Protestant emphasis on the inspiration of the book, some Roman Catholic scholars contended for a broader definition that would include God's aid to the channel of revelation as well as the Spirit's aid in appropriating the truth of the Bible. Johann Sebastian von Drey (1777-1853), founder of the "Tübingen School" tradition, defined inspiration as a God-wrought change that elevates the spiritual faculties in the mind of the channel of revelation. He could see little need for inspiration to write down on a tenth occasion what the inspired prophet or apostle had preached nine times before. James Orr, an evangelical Protestant, expressed similar sentiments when he declared, "Inspiration belongs primarily to the *person*, and to the *book* only as it is the product of the inspired person."[2]

Inspiration of Biblical Editors

While Drey and Orr were correct in principle, the situation was far more complicated than they realized. They were cognizant of obvious explanations and other insertions by editors (redactors), but they did not realize how many hands were involved in producing some of the biblical books. For example, the original explanation for the removal of the Red (Heb., Reed) Sea from the path of the Hebrews was "a strong east wind" sent by Yahweh (Ex. 14:21). The song of deliverance described this event as the blast of Yahweh's nostrils piling the water in heaps (Ex. 15:8). Later on, someone in the tradition understood the poetry to mean that the Hebrews marched through with walls of water on both sides, and this interpretation was incorporated into the Exodus account (Ex. 14:22). Such a strong wind would have destroyed the Hebrews had they attempted to march against it. Most certainly the editor was sincere in his insertion of this later tradition, and some would claim that he was inspired, but what value is all of this when the reader is led to believe something that never happened? Moreover, what remains of the theory of inerrancy in such a case?

The problem of editorial additions is equally clear in the realm of theological interpretations. As noted earlier, there is a complex layering of traditions that spans centuries. R. A. F. MacKenzie is correct when he observes, "Instead of 'the inspired author' of a given book or pericope or phrase, we should accustom ourselves to speak of 'the inspired authors.' By that I do not mean that any writing or composition was done by a committee, i.e., a group whose members cooperated equally and simultaneously in the work, but rather that historically authorship (and con-

2. *Revelation and Inspiration*, p. 162.

sequently inspiration) was very seldom completely executed and accomplished by one man or on one occasion. Many men contributed to it, at varying levels and in analogical degrees of cooperation. This applies to the New Testament as well as to the Old Testament."[3]

This fact, of course, raises the question as to which editor of the book was the most inspired one. The easy answer is to regard the final editor as the truly inspired person. But as Bruce Vawter, the Roman Catholic scholar, accurately observes, "The final-redactor theory can hardly be the answer to our problem. We have come to realize that the full meaning of the Scripture must be sought in its total literary history, and even in whatever pre-literary history may underlie it. The final redactor must be heard, certainly, but he is only one voice of many speaking in the Bible."[4]

God as Author

While Scripture claims unequivocally that God was the source of revelation and inspiration, it is interesting that nowhere does the Bible teach that God was its author. Vawter comments, "That God is author of Scripture is a patristic formulation, probably a Latin formulation at that, and to some extent at least, influenced by non-Jewish and non-Christian conceptions of inspiration as well as by the Bible."[5] The problem is the ambiguity of the Latin term *auctor*. Like the equally ambiguous English term "author," it can mean "originator, founder, architect, literary author, etc." The majority of the fathers undoubtedly understood the formulation to mean that God was actually the literary author of the Bible.

This interpretation gained new support in medieval times when Aristotle's concept of instrumental efficient causality was used to explain prophetic revelation. "An instrumental efficient cause," Vawter explains, "is one

3. "Some Problems in the Field of Inspiration," *The Catholic Biblical Quarterly*, XX (1958), 7.

4. *Biblical Inspiration*, pp. 105-106.

5. *Ibid.*, p. 96.

that truly acts, and with a power of its own, but does so in fact only when employed by another, principal efficient cause, which in activating its potential also extends it to the production of an effect of which alone it would have been incapable."[6] A favorite example of this logic was a piece of chalk in the hand of a writer. Even though the analogy was most appropriate in the case of inanimate objects, it was applied to the biblical writers. Vawter describes the reasoning as follows: "God, the principal cause, had moved the instrumental cause, the Prophet, to speak, to act, or to write. The effect produced is the word of God: it is God who uttered it through the Prophet, who of himself would have been incapable of it. Yet it is a word into which the Prophet also has truly entered, for it is the work of his mind and will and other faculties, that the principal cause utilized and 'elevated' in the process. The words are Jeremiah's wrung from his heart and experience; and the word is God's."[7]

The doctrine of God as author became such a strong tradition that it has persisted in Roman Catholic pronouncements down through Vatican II. Karl Rahner, the renowned Roman Catholic theologian from Germany, has wrestled with the problem of how God and the biblical writer could be true authors at the same time. "It is precisely not a question of the instrumentality of a secretary in regard to the author," Rahner notes, "but of a human authorship which remains completely and absolutely unimpaired, which is permeated, embraced, but not diminished, by the divine authorship."[8] In other words, God's authorship is of a different kind than that of the human author. "If God's authorship of the Scripture really means anything at all," Vawter declares, "if the term, in other words, intends to enunciate something other than the banality that He is the transcendent cause of every human effect—then God and man can hardly both be called authors in the same sense of the word."[9] "The

6. *Ibid.*, p. 48.
7. *Ibid.*, pp. 48-49.
8. *Inspiration in the Bible*, p. 14.
9. *Biblical Inspiration*, p. 100.

Church has endorsed the analogy," Vawter continues, "to the extent that it ever has endorsed it, for whatever virtues it has and not for what it cannot do or for what it does ineptly."[10] Finally, even though Vatican II affirmed the doctrine of God as author of Scripture, Vawter thinks "it is very doubtful that—in or out of the Council—a theological consensus could be found in our times that would attach to the term the literary signification it has had for many in the past."[11]

Kinds (Degrees) of Inspiration

The Jews took a view of the Hebrew canon that amounted to degrees of inspiration. The Torah was supreme—no prophet was inspired as Moses was. Philo accepted this view and evidenced it in practice by confining almost all of his activity to the Pentateuch. The second part of the Hebrew Bible, the Prophets, was next in authority, and finally came the Writings.

As noted previously, for the greater part of the church's existence the two terms "revelation" and "inspiration" were considered almost synonymous. Benjamin B. Warfield and Alexander A. Hodge were correct in declaring: "The word 'Inspiration,' as applied to the Holy Scriptures, has gradually acquired a specific technical meaning independent of its etymology. At first this word . . . was used in a sense comprehensive of supernatural revelation."[12] In defense of this technical refinement they contended: "It is important that distinguishable ideas should be connoted by distinct terms, and that the terms themselves should be fixed in a definite sense. Thus we have come to distinguish sharply between Revelation, which is the frequent, and Inspiration, which is the constant attribute of all thoughts and statements of Scripture."[13]

The assertion that revelation is the variable element in Scripture while inspiration is the constant factor, applying

10. *Ibid.*, p. 101.
11. *Ibid.*
12. *Inspiration*, p. 5.
13. *Ibid.*, pp. 5-6.

equally well to every word of the canon, is a theologian's deduction, not an explicit teaching of the Bible. The line of deductive reasoning commences with the assumption that God had to reveal himself infallibly. Then the argument moves on to claim that to guarantee the absolute accuracy of the written records the Spirit of God superintended all the activity of the chosen instruments so that every word was inerrant and equally inspired. Most certainly the ideas of "revelation" and "inspiration" are not precisely the same. The former has to do with an experience and its content whereas the latter is the means by which the revelatory event takes place. Accordingly, the teachings and data of Scripture do not warrant the "fixed" meanings assigned by Warfield and Hodge.

In reaction to the concept of "constant inspiration," as advocated during the nineteenth century, the idea of "degrees of inspiration" was renewed and expanded. William Sanday (1843-1920) espoused this view in his Bampton Lectures of 1893. He explains briefly: "In other words, there are some books in which the Divine element is at the *maximum* and others in which it is at the *minimum*. When we come to reflect, it may be seen that the lower modes have a place in relation to the Divine purpose (which includes both high and low) that is not less appropriate than the higher, but from our present standpoint they must be described as lower."[14]

George Tyrrell (1861-1909), the Dublin Protestant who became a Jesuit at eighteen, was a contemporary of Sanday, and in his search for a valid view about Scripture he also came to believe that "the Scriptures are inspired in varying degrees by the spirit of Christ."[15]

With respect to the intuition, illumination, dictation, and dynamic views of inspiration, Olin A. Curtis (1850-1918) states: "There is, I am convinced, no worthy reason for holding one of these theories to the exclusion of the remaining three. The probability is that the Word of God was given by a combination of all four methods; but

14. *Inspiration*, p. 398.
15. *The Church and the Future*, p. 162.

it is not now possible for us to decide in every case precisely what took place. The data are not sufficient." [16]

Curtis ties in this more comprehensive view of inspiration with the long historic process of God's redemptive activity. In this process "men were chosen, each one in his own peculiar situation, to speak, or to write, or to do, whatever was essential to further the redemptional movement."[17] Then he elaborates: "For this furtherance, these chosen men received only such divine help as was needed. At one time it was necessary only to emphasize a common moral fact before the people, and any brave soul could do it. At another time it was necessary to lift a commonplace into spiritual ideality, a work which only genius can do. At another time it was necessary to organize a nation, and it required the highest order of statesmanship. At another time it was necessary to have a Christian testimony, and it could be given out of any overflowing Christian experience in the early church. At another time it was necessary to catch and to express a doctrine of grace entirely beyond the possibility of natural discovery; and for this work a man was extraordinarily helped, raised to a higher power, without being erased as a free person. At another time it was necessary for the man of God to have an absolutely transcendent experience, an experience to which he could make no individual or personal contribution whatever; and he was, for the occasion, actually coerced by the Holy Spirit. He had no more freedom than the sky has in accepting a sunset. Perhaps he is a prophet, and he looks down the centuries, in the swift, clear vision of God himself, until he can see 'a man of sorrows'—'smitten of God,' 'wounded for our transgressions.' Or perhaps he is an apostle, and he is transported into a realm of immeasurable glory, and hears 'unspeakable words, which it is not lawful for a man to utter.' There are, too, some places in the Bible where the best explanation of the very phrase is that it came directly from God. And when I say the best explanation, I mean the explanation which naturally grows

16. *The Christian Faith*, p. 177.
17. *Ibid.*, p. 178.

out of the Christian conception of God's relation to man in redemption. How extremely absurd it is for any Christian thinker to hold that God could not or would not, in the furtherance of redemption, give a prophet or an apostle a message as definite as human speech. Even the most incipient Christian theist should be ashamed of such fundamental inconsistency."[18]

All these activities of God's servants derived from inspiration of some sort, and so we can speak of the Bible as being inspired from cover to cover, human mistakes and all. On the other hand, all of Scripture does not involve special or primary revelation, and so there is no need to posit *unique* inspiration for every word of the Bible. There are degrees of something in Scripture, and it is more than just degrees of revelation. As Orr observes, "It does not follow that all inspired persons possess the Spirit in a *like* eminent degree. Inspiration in Scripture is of different kinds, and for different ends. It is certainly too narrow an idea of inspiration to tie it down to the production of the written record. There is inspiration in speech as well as in writing; and there are lower grades of inspiration in the form of special *charismata* (wisdom, artistic skill, physical powers), shading off till it becomes difficult to distinguish them from heightened natural endowment."[19] He explains further as follows: "But the fact is obvious that, whereas at some periods and in some souls the Spirit of revelation is working, if one may so say, at a maximum, at other times, and in other persons, He is operating on a lower plane, and, still to speak reverently, with feebler energy. Every one, by a species of 'higher criticism' of his own, recognizes this in practice, whatever he may do in theory. No one . . . would compare the Books of Chronicles, in point of spirituality, with the prophecies of Isaiah or the Gospel of John, or the books of Esther and Ecclesiastes, as to the canonicity of which the later Jews themselves had doubts, with the Epistles of Paul. The prophets after the exile stand, on the whole, on a lower plane than the earlier

18. *Ibid.*, pp. 178-179.
19. Orr, *op. cit.*, p. 177. Italics his.

prophets—Hosea, Amos, Isaiah, etc. In the natural body, as Paul reminds us, all members have not the same office, and so is it here. Some parts of Scripture have a humbler function to fulfill than others."[20]

Vawter concurs with Curtis in the broad range of inspiration: "In the concrete, scriptural inspiration must have been as diverse as the human efforts that conspired to produce the Scripture."[21] But in recognizing these various expressions of inspiration he shies away from using the term "degrees" to designate the difference: "To think of one Biblical work as less inspired than another, and less the word of God, is to engage in a false problematic: it is to assume what we have just insisted can hardly be, namely that inspiration is something univocal that admits only of degrees. Rather, we must learn to think of one book as inspired differently from another, as therefore being, or mediating, the word of God in its own proper fashion." [22] Vawter is attempting to get away from qualitative, hierarchical judgments that are rather demeaning to parts of Scripture. He notes, for example, "The genealogy of Keturah's children (Gen. 25:1-4) may, when investigated by the right person, advance Biblical religion quite as much as a prayerful meditation on Ps. 23."[23] The semantic problem still exists, but perhaps he is correct that it is preferable to speak of different "kinds" rather than different "degrees" of inspiration.

Inspiration Without Inerrancy

As noted earlier, the theory of inerrancy became dogma in the Roman Catholic Church during the latter part of the nineteenth century. As a result of the *Syllabus of Errors* in 1864, most of the university and seminary teaching positions were under fairly strict church surveillance, but there were some posts that allowed scholars a little freedom. Leo's encyclical *Providentissimus Deus*, promulgated in

20. *Ibid.*, p. 178.
21. *Biblical Inspiration*, p. 163.
22. *Ibid.*, p. 164.
23. *Ibid.*, p. 165.

1893, aroused these and other free-thinkers to express themselves. The liberal ideas had begun to appear about 1850, but by 1900 a group of scholars with widely variant backgrounds and motives rallied in common cause against the papal teaching concerning inerrancy. The English and French were slightly predominant, but the Germans and Italians contributed as well. The rising tide of scientific knowledge made it increasingly difficult to square the teaching of the church with the data of Scripture. This keen sense of embarrassment was felt first in England. The most important contributing factor was the group of articulate, highly trained converts to Roman Catholicism, starting with John Henry Newman.

One of Newman's disciples, the outspoken Richard Simpson (1820-1876), was the first to get embroiled with the church. He retreated from the field of battle after 1864, but the liberal cause was carried forward by such scholars as John Acton (1834-1902), Robert Francis Clarke, Friedrich von Hügel (1852-1925), and George Tyrrell (1861-1909). In France the leaders were Jules Didiot (1840-1903), Eudoxe-Irénée Migot (1842-1918), and Alfred Loisy (1857-1940). This entire liberal wing of the church was purged or excommunicated during the inquisition against the modernists carried out 1907-1910, and so a systematic statement of the liberal position never was developed. The main features were clear, however, and Burtchaell summarizes them as follows:

> The first step was a recognition of literary forms. In concert with Lagrange and his followers, they insisted on a respect for ancient oriental idioms, which in their non-literal way taught far more theology and far less history than Latin interpreters had been led to believe. Second, they tended to assert that since the purpose of the Book is to impart salvific wisdom, only matters germane to religion enjoyed immunity from error. Newman had proposed a limited inspiration; they inclined toward plenary inspiration with limited effects. Lastly, it was felt that since Scripture was to stand as a record of revelation, it must necessarily contain all those impurities which contaminated the faith during the early

years of growth. Of all the theories . . . , this one alone allowed itself to countenance without a blush that there were errors in the Bible; errors actually believed and affirmed by the sacred writers.[24]

Inerrancy and the Unity of Scripture

As noted in Chapter 5, the statement (schema) on revelation presented to the first session of Vatican II was revised twice and then presented for discussion in the third session. In anticipation of this debate, Norbert Lohfink, the German Jesuit, published a very interesting article. [25] As a historical survey, Lohfink states, "A reading of the Church fathers, medieval theologians and modern tracts on inspiration shows that biblical inerrancy is predicated of three different grammatical subjects: the Bible (simply), the biblical books, and the biblical authors (technically called sacred writers). The three ways of speaking are used side by side; the context indicates the correct choice of meaning."[26]

Lohfink suggests that the inerrancy of the sacred writers was more precisely the understanding of the doctrine, but that it was permissible to speak of the "inerrancy of the books," or even the "inerrancy of the Bible." He observes that this was so because at the turn of the century the Roman Church had the traditional, simplistic view that all of the biblical books were written by a few inspired persons. Now that the complexity of the Bible's origin is known, a stress on the inerrancy of the authors produces "a new content of belief which cannot be shown by the method of positive theology to be part of the older faith."[27]

Accordingly, one must "make an attempt to say the old truth in a new way—precisely so that the old may thus

24. *Catholic Theories of Biblical Inspiration Since 1810*, pp. 165-166.
25. "Über die Irrtumslosigkeit und die Einheit der Schrift," *Stimmen der Zeit*, Band 174, Jahrgang 89 (Juni, 1964), pp. 161-181.
26. *Ibid.*, p. 162.
27. *Ibid.*, p. 165.

remain."[28] The new description acknowledges that "everyone who made a real contribution to the phrasing and sense of a biblical book should be considered as directed infallibly by God in view of the future book, that is, as 'inspired.' "[29] The end result, however, is an inerrant book, and so Lohfink is willing "to let the formula 'inerrancy of the sacred writers' fade into the background." [30]

But shifting the emphasis to the book is not the answer either: "Even in the matter of defining the relation between 'biblical book' and 'the Bible as a whole' our conceptions have shifted because of the results of historical-critical study. The individual biblical 'books' in their distinctive quality as 'books' are questionable. This too, of course, has its consequences for the application of biblical inerrancy."[31] Lohfink moves on, therefore, to the Bible as a whole as the proper object of inerrancy. "Jesus and the early Church recognize that in Jesus the end of time has come. The process of revelation itself has come to a conclusion with Him. According to their conviction, after the expression of Christ there can be nothing new and decisive on its way to determine the meaning of the Old Testament further."[32] It is Christ who "welds the Old and New Testaments together into a single book," and it is only with this unity that "biblical inerrancy can meaningfully be predicated."[33]

Lohfink recognizes difficulties in the details of Scripture, and he grants partial errors in teaching during the revelatory process that led up to Jesus Christ. Yet, working on the principle that "the meaning of a statement can never be defined apart from the whole relational system in which the statement appears," he affirms, "The whole includes and preserves the individual part. . . . Hence one can and must say that every statement of the Bible is inerrant."[34] One must note, however, that Lohfink wrote

28. *Ibid.*
29. *Ibid.*, p. 166.
30. *Ibid.*, p. 168.
31. *Ibid.*
32. *Ibid.*, p. 172.
33. *Ibid.*
34. *Ibid.*, p. 173.

this article with the knowledge that the first draft of the schema on revelation, offered to the first session of Vatican II, November, 1962, declared that " ... the entire Sacred Scripture is absolutely immune from error." Clearly, he was trying to stay within bounds of his church's dogma, but he was being required to say too much because by no stretch of the imagination can Pekah's twenty-year reign be called an inerrant statement just because it is in the context of Yahweh's redemptive history leading up to Christ. Vawter appreciates Lohfink's recognition of "a true divine condescension to a genuine human condition," but his theory "seems to demand an unnecessary denigration of the Old Testament and its writers and to rely too heavily on the anthropomorphism of God as literary author of the Bible."[35]

Fortunately, the more objective scholars of the Roman Church were able to revise the schema on revelation. A definite breakthrough came with the fourth draft: " ... the books of Scripture teach firmly, faithfully, and without error that truth which leads to salvation." Some revision, to meet conservative objections, resulted in the fifth draft, the statement finally approved and promulgated by the Council on November 18, 1965: " ... the books of Scripture must be acknowledged as teaching firmly, faithfully, and without error that truth which God wanted put into the sacred writings for the sake of our salvation."[36] Biblical problems were reduced immeasurably when the dogma of inerrancy was limited to the area of saving truth.

Inductive Inerrancy

The necessity for the inductive approach to the problem of inerrancy is well expressed by Everett F. Harrison: "It would seem that the only healthy attitude for conservatives is to welcome criticism and be willing to join in it. No view of Scripture can indefinitely be sustained if it runs

35. *Biblical Inspiration,* p. 149.
36. *The Documents of Vatican II,* ed. by Walter M. Abbott, p. 119.

counter to the facts. That the Bible claims inspiration is patent. The problem is to define the nature of that inspiration in the light of the phenomena contained therein." [37] But there is still the problem of interpreting the phenomena, and conservatives differ considerably at this point.

In a short article "Inductive Inerrancy," [38] John Warwick Montgomery of Trinity Evangelical Divinity School claims to have the answer to the problem of "induction vs. deduction in relation to the inerrancy of Scripture." The essence of his solution is as follows:

> To know how to treat biblical passages containing apparent errors or contradictions, we must determine what kind of book the Bible is. A doctrine of limited biblical authority derived from passages manifesting difficulties is as false an induction and as flagrant a denial of the analogy of Scripture as is a morally imperfect Christology derived from questionable acts on Jesus' part. In both cases, proper induction requires that we go to the express biblical teaching on the subject (Jesus' deity; Scripture's authority) and allow this to create the pattern for treating particular problems.

Montgomery explains further, "Christ's attitude toward the Old Testament was one of *total trust:* nowhere, in no particular, and on no subject did he place Scripture under criticism. Never did he distinguish truth 'in faith and practice' from veracity in historical and secular matters, and he told the Evil Foe in no uncertain terms that man lives 'by *every word* that proceedeth out of the mouth of God' (Matt. 4:4, quoting Deut. 8:3)." Finally, he declares, "Inerrancy? Yes. Induction? Yes."

Inerrancy and Matthew 5:17-18

Most certainly Jesus put his whole trust on the Hebrew Bible, and it is equally true that he did not place Scripture under criticism, but in neither case does this prove that Jesus taught the doctrine of inerrancy. In preparation for

37. "The Phenomena of Scripture," *Revelation and the Bible*, p. 239.

38. *Christianity Today* (March 3, 1967), p. 48.

his discussion on the law, Jesus assures his audience: "Think not that I have come to abolish the law and the prophets; I have come not to abolish them but to fulfil them. For truly, I say to you, till heaven and earth pass away, not an iota, not a dot, will pass from the law until all is accomplished." For the last part of verse 18, the King James Version translates, "One jot or one tittle shall in no wise pass from the law, till all be fulfilled." Jesus intends to refute some Jewish interpretations of the law ("It has been said to you . . . , but I say to you"); therefore, he is very careful to preface his remarks with a statement expressing his confidence in the law. "Do not think for a moment," Jesus assures them "that I have come to tear down the law or the prophets piece by piece. [The same verb is used in Matt. 24:2 concerning the temple.] I have not come to tear down, but to fill to the full."

This law, Jesus affirmed, was as sure as "heaven and earth." To the Jewish mind this was the ultimate in stability, for as Psalm 89:29 stated, "I will establish his line for ever and his throne as the days of the heavens," and as Psalm 119:90 declared, "Thy faithfulness endures to all generations; thou hast established the earth, and it stands fast."

Jesus' use of the term "iota" (translated "jot" in the King James Version) is a reference to the Greek letter *iota*, which in turn goes back to the Hebrew letter *yod*, the smallest letter of the alphabet (in the Aramaic or square script that was commonly employed to write Hebrew from the third century B.C. on). The "tittle" or "dot" is a reference to the small features that distinguish certain letters of the Hebrew alphabet from other letters that are very similar in appearance. Jesus is making it clear, accordingly, that the smallest item of the law is important.

Not one of these items will pass from the law "until all is accomplished." From the King James translation "fulfilled" in verse 18, the reader would think the verb was the same as in the previous verse, but such is not the case. The Greek reads literally, "until all has become." The idea back of this "coming to be" is the *purpose* for which the law was given. So long as the heavens and the earth exist, so long will the law continue to work out or accomplish its purpose. Some portions of the law would "come to be" (that is, achieve their purpose—for example, the ceremonial law) and so pass away. Jesus was *not* saying that all the law would continue until the heavens and earth would be dissolved.

How, then, are we to interpret Jesus' use of "iota" and "dot"? Traditionally, the passage has been taken to refer to the *words* of the law (a description for the whole Old Testament), and thus a witness for the doctrine of inerrant, verbal inspiration. But this view fails to take into account the fact that the Hebrew manuscripts of the Old Testament in Jesus' day swarmed with variant spellings and forms because of the omission or addition of *yods*. It is recognized that Jesus argued at times from the accuracy of specific words, but in this overall statement concerning the law, his emphasis can hardly be on the words or letters. The prevailing tendency of Jewish interpretation, to stress the letter instead of the spirit of the law, is the very thing Jesus is refuting in Matthew 5:17-48.

An illustration of Jewish concern for the very letters of the Hebrew text is a rabbinical comment on Ruth 3:14. The text reads, "So she lay at his feet until the morning, but arose before one could recognize another; and he said, 'Let it not be known that the woman came to the threshing floor.' " The Hebrew word translated "before" has the letter *waw*, a distinctive spelling not found elsewhere in the Old Testament. The Jewish commentators felt that the occurrence of the letter *waw* (which, as the sixth letter of the Hebrew alphabet, has the numerical value 6) was intended by God to inform the readers that Ruth lay on the threshing floor at Boaz' feet for *six hours*. But this explanation given to a scribal mistake is hardly proof of the author's intent in 3:14.

Zeal for the letter, the object of Jesus' criticism, was also a plague to the apostle Paul. Legalists from Jerusalem and thereabouts visited the young churches that Paul had started and they caused great unrest among the young Christians. In his letter to the Romans he speaks of this vital issue: "He is a Jew who is one inwardly, and real circumcision is a matter of the heart, spiritual and not literal [the Greek reads "in spirit not in letter"]" (Rom. 2:29). In Romans 7:6, Paul comments further, "We serve not under the old written code [Gk. "in oldness of letter"], but in the new life of the Spirit [Gk. "in newness of spirit"]." This concept is also treated in 2 Corinthians 3:6, where Paul declares, God "qualified us to be ministers of a new covenant, not in a written code, but in the Spirit; for the written code kills, but the Spirit gives life." Thus Paul asserts with Jesus that the essence of the law is its spirit, the principles it embodies, not its letter. Accordingly, to interpret Jesus in Matthew 5:17-18 as pleading for the inerrancy of the smallest detail of the Old Testament is to misinterpret him.

Inerrancy and Reason

Harrison cautiously acknowledges, "Inerrancy is not a formally stated claim made by the Scriptures on their own behalf. It is rather an inference that devout students of the Word have made from the teaching of the Bible about its own inspiration."[39] *But it is precisely this "inference" which is at issue.* Montgomery claims that it is an assured result and that all the phenomena, accordingly, must be interpreted in the light of inerrancy. It is at this very point, however, where there is an unconscious shift from the inductive to the deductive method. The assumption that God had to reveal himself inerrantly becomes determinative for interpretation. Thus it is claimed that Jesus believed and taught the doctrine of inerrancy. This view is to be accepted on the authority of Christ whether or not it accords with all the facts. But this is reasoning in a circle, of course, because the doctrine of inerrancy has attributed its own ideas to Jesus and then turned around to claim as its authority its own interpretation of what Jesus taught.

The only way to break out of this circular reasoning (with its implicit claim of inerrant interpretation) is to

39. "Criteria of Biblical Inerrancy," *Christianity Today*, Vol. II, No. 8 (Jan. 20, 1958), p. 16.

employ our reason objectively with respect to all the
evidence, biblical and otherwise. At the same time, however, we must acknowledge that perfect objectivity is never
achieved. In spite of our sincere efforts we bring to the
task of interpretation certain unconscious presuppositions
that have become a part of us during our formative years.
Yet, having made this concession, we are nonetheless dependent on reason; for we must use it to help isolate and
set aside, as far as possible, even our restricting assumptions. The extent to which we can do this will determine
the objectivity with which we can interpret the evidence at
hand.

An appeal to the use of reason usually draws objections
on the ground that reason is human and necessarily carnal.
One cannot rule out a legitimate use of human reason
aided by the Holy Spirit on the grounds that unaided
reason leads to serious error and eventually considers the
gospel as foolishness. Another objection to reason and its
right to detect error is that man becomes thereby the
arbiter of truth and error. But this argument fails to see
that the human mind does not create the evidence that is
determinative in the separation of truth from error. All
human reason can do is to function properly with the data
that are furnished it. Every human being has the power
and the right to observe the data. The factor of truth or
error is settled before human reason comes on the scene.
While reason can function correctly with the evidence and
ascertain the true and the false, it is also possible for it to
work improperly and to come to inaccurate evaluation of
the data. In neither case, however, is human reason the *real*
arbiter of truth or error.

Ultimately there can be no valid objection to the use of
reason. Every reader of Scripture uses his reason to some
extent. The "inference" leading to the doctrine of inerrancy involves reason, but it is the deductive method.
Reason is indispensable; the crucial factor is *how* we use it,
not that we do. In highlighting the basic issue between true
doctrine (the correct use of reason) and one's definition of
doctrine (the faulty use of reason), Llewelyn J. Evans
(1833-1892) declares: "If the theories of other days will

not bear the pressure of ... facts, they must go to the wall. There is no help for it. If your definition of inspiration, your definition of the infallibility of the Bible—mark what I say! not the doctrine, but your definition of the doctrine—if that definition will not stand the test of the established results of criticism, if it will not harmonize with ascertained facts, then so much the worse for the definition."[40]

Those evangelical Christians who do not find the doctrine of inerrancy in Scripture are free to recognize that the phenomena indicate the presence of some errors in the autographs (for example, the erroneous synchronisms of 2 Kings 17 and 18). Instead of trying to determine implications of the text and to fill in areas of silence, they emphasize the explicit teachings of Scripture. In this way there is no need to choose between teaching and phenomena. They both arrive at the same conclusion.

False in One, False in All

During the last thirty years or so there has been an increasing awareness of the difficulties facing the doctrine of inerrancy and some have felt an inclination to follow the phenomena and explicit teaching of Scripture. At the same time there has usually been a reluctance to make the change on account of the haunting fear implicit in the legal maxim, "False in one, false in all." If a person on the witness stand proves to be inaccurate in his testimony in one instance, the presumption is that he may be inaccurate in other places as well. The presumption is even greater in case of perjury because the intent to deceive involves a whole series of falsehoods. In no case, however, is this legal rule-of-thumb adhered to rigidly in the courts. On what authority, then, must this principle be applied with absolute consistency to the Scriptures?

The tradition of this maxim in theological circles goes back at least to the sixteenth century. Laelius Socinus (1525-1562), a very brilliant and inquisitive person, left his

40. *Inspiration and Inerrancy*, pp. 30-31.

homeland Italy in 1544 and went to Switzerland. There he put many difficult questions to Calvin, who rebuked him for his "luxurious inquisitiveness" and urged him to correct his ways. In 1575 his nephew, Faustus Socinus (1539-1604), left Italy to come to Basel, Switzerland. He not only inherited some of his uncle's unpublished manuscripts, but he also accepted some of his uncle's views, the most heretical being his rejection of Christ as part of the Trinity; in short, God, he held, was a unity.

This unitarian heresy set Socinus at odds with both the Reformed and the Lutheran theologians. Oddly enough, however, Socinus was pretty much of a literalist, and he contended that if a person could doubt concerning one passage, there was no reason why he could not doubt concerning all of them. In the bitter battle that ensued between Socinus and the Lutherans, his opponents accepted his dictum and thus was begun the challenge to prove just one error.

Once the method of reasoning became grounded in the maxim, "False in one, false in all," it was inevitable that the issue of inspiration would become an either-or: either the autographs were inerrant, or else human fallibility infected all of Scripture. Consistency would permit no mediating point of view. Either the inerrancists were right or the rank liberals.

Even John Wesley resorted to this argument in later life. In general, he had for his day a well-balanced view of Scripture in which he recognized the use of reason and experience in interpreting the Bible. Like Calvin, Wesley knew the problems of the text, and in the calm of biblical exegesis he acknowledged the difficulties. On the other hand, in a moment of threat he sprang to the defense of Scripture. Under the date of Wednesday, August 24, 1776, he noted in his *Journal* of having read a tract by a Mr. (Soame) Jenyns in which the author commented, "All Scripture is not given by inspiration of God, but the writers of it were sometimes left to themselves, and consequently made some mistakes." This was more than Wesley could take, and so he retorted, "Nay, if there be any mistakes in the Bible, there may as well be a thousand. If there be one falsehood in that book, it did not come from the God of truth."[41]

The dedication of J. Gresham Machen's highly respected book *What Is Faith?* reads: "TO FRANCIS LANDEY PATTON this book is dedicated as an inadequate but heartfelt expression of gratitude and respect." Patton (1843-1932) was president of Princeton University from 1888 to 1902, and president of Princeton Theological Seminary from 1902 to 1913. Concerning this either-or position, Patton declares: "The trouble is that there is a disposition on the part of some, apparently, to show that unless the Bible is inerrantly accurate in everything, you cannot trust it for anything. There are those who seem to say that the order of a man's thought must be first the inspired Bible and secondly the divine Christ. To that position I cannot consent; and I am unable to make the *in terrorem* argument that unless you believe in the inerrancy of the Bible, you have no right to believe in Christ. It is surely a strange apologetic that says, 'Faith in Christ is all you need for salvation'; and then says, 'You have no right to your faith in Christ unless you believe that the Bible is without error.' Moreover, a more fallacious argument could not be used than that which is sometimes employed in a misuse of the legal maxim, *Falsus in uno, falsus in omnibus.* How much history could stand this test? The real question is whether the Bible is true, not whether it is inspired. Must a book on every subject be inspired in order to be true? Have we lost all faith in inductive logic? Have we abandoned human testimony as a source of information? Is there no longer a place for the common sense of mankind?"[42] While some evangelicals regret this so-called low view of inspiration, they confess, nevertheless, that there is much good in Patton's book. But how can one accept the "much good" when, according to the maxim, "False in one, false in all," the unfortunate (presumably inaccurate) statements lead to the logical conclusion that

41. *The Journal of the Rev. John Wesley, M.A.*, Standard Edition, VI, 117.

42. *Fundamental Christianity*, pp. 146-147.

nothing in Patton's book can be trusted? Evidently the maxim applies only to Scripture.

Rationality and Irrationality

Inasmuch as method implies a process of reasoning it is valid to inquire how far human reason and logic can go in solving the problem of inspiration. We have seen that logic has been a basic tool in developing the theory of inerrancy. But logic founded on a false premise can lead to exceedingly erroneous conclusions; for example, the assumption "error = no inspiration." The Bible, however, does not teach that unless a thing is *totally* true it cannot be inspired. Therefore, when this rational dogma is confronted with the biblical data it finds the going quite difficult. It is usually at this point that those who hold to inerrancy become irrationalists. They speak of the disturbing facts as an area of "mystery" and suggest withholding judgment. Sooner or later we all come to a point of mystery and we do well to acknowledge that we have entered the suprarational realm, but the crucial question is where this transition is made. Whereas the logical system of inerrancy must dismiss logic when it comes to biblical phenomena, those who hold to a strong doctrine of inspiration, without accepting inerrancy, can accept all the facts, even though they are not always able to explain the precise relationship of the data. In other words, if reason is to play any part in determining the doctrine of inspiration, we must allow it to go as far as it can. Patton comments on this point: "You cannot license Reason to seek truth and deny her right to see error. And it is a hazardous thing to say that being inspired the Bible must be free from error; for then the discovery of a single error would destroy its inspiration. Nor have we any right to substitute the word 'inerrancy' for 'inspiration' in our discussion of the Bible unless we are prepared to show from the teaching of the Bible that inspiration means inerrancy—and that, I think, would be a difficult thing to do."[43]

43. *Ibid.*, pp. 163-164.

According to Patton, therefore, the primary task of inspiration was not to secure the inerrancy of the record. His views are considered with alarm, however, for he is supposedly splitting the rock foundation on which Christianity rests. But the crack that appears is not in the foundation; it is only in the encrustations of interpretation that have been added gradually.

"The Bible as Divining Rod"

As a postscript to this discussion a word of caution is in order concerning some statements by the late world-famous archaeologist Nelson Glueck (1900-1971). In an article, "The Bible as Divining Rod," he relates how archaeology has thrown much light on biblical passages and, in turn, how the Bible has aided archaeologists in making new discoveries. "It is worth emphasizing," writes Glueck, "that in all this work no archaeological discovery has ever controverted a single, properly understood Biblical statement."[44] Many who hold to the doctrine of inerrancy have taken comfort in this assertion, for it appears that one of the foremost biblical scholars has spoken out in their behalf. In order to ascertain the precise meaning and implications of this claim, the author of this book questioned Glueck personally. The latter made it quite plain that he had no intention of supporting the doctrine of inerrancy. His primary concern was to point out "the amazing accuracy of historical memory in the Bible."[45]

Deuteronomy 8:9, for example, refers to Canaan as "a land whose stones are iron, and out of whose hills you can dig copper." This would not be true if the "land" meant only traditional Canaan "from Dan to Beersheba" (Judg. 20:1), but the Bible also speaks of Israel's boundaries as extending "from the entrance of Hamath to the Brook of Egypt" (1 Kings 8:65). Understood in this larger perspective, the claim in Deuteronomy 8:9 is indeed accurate, for the copper mines of Solomon have been found in the Wadi of the Arabah, south of the Dead Sea.

44. *Horizon*, Vol. II, No. 2 (Nov., 1959), p. 6.
45. *Ibid.*

The vindication of this and many other biblical passages led Glueck to affirm that the Bible "can be regarded in effect as an almost infallible divining rod, revealing to the expert the whereabouts and characteristics of lost cities and civilizations."[46]   Again, however, this statement cannot be taken as supporting the doctine of inerrancy. It is conditioned by "almost," and also it relates primarily to the geography of Palestine and the Near East. The Pekah problem, on the other hand, involves an interpretation of data which the historian did not completely understand and which he had no means of verifying. While Glueck was convinced of the amazing accuracy and essential trust-worthiness of Scripture, he readily acknowledged that the biblical writers were not inerrant historians. He was a friend of all those who cherish Scripture, but he cannot be claimed as a champion of the doctrine of inerrancy.

46. *Ibid.*

Chapter Ten

Verbal and Content Inspiration

Closely related to the concept of inerrancy is the idea of verbal inspiration. Various interpretations have been given to the term "verbal," but, generally speaking, this view conceives of inspiration as extending to the individual words of Scripture.

Jeremiah 36

As noted previously, the clearest description of the origin of a canonical book is to be found in Jeremiah 36. Jeremiah is told by the LORD to take a scroll and write on it "all the words that I have spoken to you against Israel and Judah and all the nations, from the day I spoke to you, from the days of Josiah until today" (v. 2). This message came to Jeremiah in 605 B.C. (the fourth year of Jehoiakim), and he was ordered to put in writing all God had said to him from the day of his call in 626 B.C. (the thirteenth year of Josiah).

The account informs us that Jeremiah called Baruch, his scribe, who then wrote on the scroll "at the dictation of Jeremiah [literally, "from the mouth of Jeremiah"] all the words of the LORD which he had spoken to him" (v. 4).

Some have interpreted this verse to mean that God "dictated" the words to Jeremiah. However, this assumption has no basis in the biblical account. The Hebrew text does not say that Jeremiah was dictating the words that the LORD *was speaking* to him. Rather, Jeremiah dictates the words that the LORD *had spoken* to him previously. Jeremiah must have repeated some of the oracles of God time and time again, so that after twenty-one years the basic themes were well fixed in his mind. Since the memory of the ancient Oriental was exceedingly well developed, there is no need to postulate "dictation by God" during the recording of the oracles given previously.

Another factor to be considered is the use of the word "all" in verses 2 and 4. Evidently it was intended extensively. Jeremiah could very well have dictated from memory messages covering in extent the whole of God's oracles to him. Undoubtedly some of the words that the LORD spoke to Jeremiah during the twenty-one-year period were omitted from Jeremiah's first book, for in 36:32 we read, "Baruch . . . wrote . . . at the dictation of Jeremiah all the words of the scroll which Jehoiakim king of Judah had burned in the fire; and many similar words were added to them." These "similar words" must have been some aspects of God's oracles that did not occur to Jeremiah at the writing of the first book.

Verbal Inspiration and 1 Corinthians 2:1-16

A key passage for ascertaining a biblical doctrine of inspiration is 1 Corinthians 2:1-16. Since Paul's authority as a true apostle was being questioned by some in the church at Corinth, he took the pains to remind them that when he began working with them his speech and message "were not in plausible words of wisdom, but in demonstration of the Spirit and power" (2:4). The "secret and hidden wisdom of God" (2:7) was revealed, so Paul claims, "through the Spirit" (2:10). He explains further: "Now we have received not the spirit of the world, but the Spirit which is from God, that we might understand the gifts bestowed on us by God. And we impart this in words not taught by human wisdom but taught by the Spirit" (2:12-13). While Paul's claim here refers primarily to his *preaching*, he states later on in this same letter, "if any one thinks that he is a prophet, or spiritual, he should acknowledge that what I am writing to you is a command of the Lord" (14:37). Thus Paul attached as much authority to the written form of his message as to the oral.

While Paul appears to claim that his teaching was verbally inspired, not everything in his letters deals with the "secret and hidden wisdom" that God revealed to him. Can Paul's statement be extended to mean inerrancy of every detail of his writings? In 1:14 of this same letter, Paul writes, "I am thankful that I baptized none of you except Crispus and Gaius." But two verses later Paul remembers others he baptized, and so he inserts into his letter: "I did baptize also the household of Stephanas. Beyond that I do not know whether I baptized any one else." If verse 16 is correct, then verse 14 is not. If the "none of you except" in verse 14 was breathed to Paul by God, word for word, why did it have to be corrected? Paul's uncertainty as to just how many people he baptized in Corinth is hardly to be placed in the same category as his confidence regarding his teaching. It would appear, therefore, that in the New Testament, as in the Old, neither the phenomena nor the claims of the biblical writers justify a strict doctrine of verbal inspiration.

Words or Ideas Inspired?

One of the vexing problems in the area of inspiration is the relationship between words and ideas. This issue exercised the Lutheran theologians of the seventeenth century a great deal. Their definitions varied slightly, but in general they made a clear distinction between words as form or symbols (called *materia*) and the content or ideas (called *forma*) expressed by these symbols.

Yet having made this distinction, they still realized that the content could not be separated from the words. Preus, expressing the common view of the seventeenth-century Lutherans, writes, "The letters and words of Scripture not only signify the inspired content of the Scriptures but actually impart this divine meaning and therefore cannot be separated from it."[1] From a superficial reading of such statements one gets the feeling that the dogmaticians worshipped the very letter. But as Preus observes: "The efficacy of the Word of God does not inhere in the letters and syllables and words as they are written. These are merely symbols, the vehicle (*vehiculum*) of the divine content, the *forma*, of the Word which alone is the Word of God, properly speaking. The dogmaticians will have no part of that ancient superstition which supposed that the words of the Bible as words could cure sickness and exorcise devils. In medieval times it was the practice of some to carry the Bible on their shoulders in the hope that it would ward off evil spirits and calamities. Only the inspired content of the Word which is the mind and counsel of God has the power to work conversion and other spiritual realities in man."[2]

Roman Catholic scholars kept an eye on everything the Protestants did, especially the Lutherans, and so it is not surprising to find them wrestling with the same problem. From the Council of Trent on, the two basic views were verbal inspiration and content inspiration, each having periods of success only to be displaced by the other. The dominant view in the sixteenth century was probably verbal inspiration. It was based on the church's teaching, "Sacred Scripture is the Word of God." Unless God dictated the very words to convey his ideas, the result would not be God's Scripture, but man's word. This view continued on into the seventeenth and eighteenth centuries. One of the foremost supporters was Charles R. Billuart (1685-1757).

The Jesuit Leonhard Leys, commonly known as Lessius (1554-1623), elaborated the idea that the infallibility of Scripture was due to the assistance of the Holy Spirit in preventing the sacred writer from making any errors. Although the Holy Spirit encouraged the writer to record what he saw, heard, and felt, he did not supply the exact

1. *The Inspiration of Scripture*, p. 22.
2. *Ibid.*, p. 174.

words and statements for the human author. In short, Holy Scripture resulted from the negative activity of the Spirit in prevention of error rather than the positive assistance of dictating the words and statements. Lessius expressed his theory with three propositions, the most influential being the first: "For anything to be Holy Scripture, its individual words need not be inspired by the Holy Spirit."[3]

Content Inspiration

Centuries later, other Jesuits expanded this proposition into the theory of content inspiration (known in German as *Realinspiration* and in Latin as the *res et sententiae* theory). It was Giovanni Perrone (1794-1876), the special counselor of Pope Pius IX, who brought the concept into prominence. He rejected the old verbal theory because the Bible itself indicates that the writers were given great freedom in expressing the ideas that God gave them. The most famous advocate of content inspiration was Johannes Baptist Franzelin (1816-1886), who was the papal theologian for the Vatican I Council. He, like the Lutherans earlier, distinguished between the truths of the "formal word" and the expressions of the "material words."[4] His point of departure was the dictum "God is the originator of a sacred book." The sacred writer was inspired only to the extent that he would "write down those truths which God wished to communicate to his Church through Scripture."[5]

Actually, the old verbal theory and the content theory were simply different emphases of the ambiguous teaching of the magisterium about Scripture. As Burtchaell observes, "Billuart is saying that if Scripture is God's *Word*, he must take sole responsibility for its very wording. Franzelin says that if God is Scripture's *author*, he need

3. Burtchaell, *Catholic Theories of Biblical Inspiration Since 1810*, p. 45.
4. *Ibid.*, p. 98.
5. *Ibid.*

not take responsibility for the wording."[6] "Further," Burtchaell continues, "despite the fact that one system affirms what the other denies, both operate on the same principles of divine-human collaboration. It is agreed by all that, in any joint endeavor, God and man divide up the responsibility between them. To the extent that God's causality intervenes, man's initiative must correspondingly recede."[7] Long after the content theory had begun to wane, the pugnacious German Jesuit Christian Pesch (1835-1925) continued to defend the theory that God was responsible for the ideas but that man supplied the words.

The Theory of Partial Inspiration

John Henry Newman (1801-1890), the famous English convert to Roman Catholicism, spent a great deal of his life wrestling with the problem of inspiration. He realized that a number of biblical statements (classified as *obiter dicta* ["words (statements) in passing"]) were not authoritative in the realm of faith and morals. In essence he was not far from the content theory, which attributed the ideas to God and the words to man. Back of Newman's thought, however, was the idea that inspiration involved inerrancy. Accordingly, if inerrancy applied only to faith and morals, then the temporal, unimportant statements need not be considered inspired. Burtchaell summarizes the situation well: "Over a span of 45 years John Newman had had the biblical question put to him three times, and his method in each encounter was the same: somehow to disengage the Word, the divine element, from its human integument. In 1838-45 he did this by calling it an Idea, hidden beneath the scattered, unsystematic expressions, and gradually clarifying itself with time in the mind of the Church. In 1861-3 the Word was called an *aspect* of Scripture, a respect; it is that face of Writ which looks towards faith and morals. In 1884 the Word had at last become materially separable as those *portions* of the Book

6. *Ibid.*, p. 122.
7. *Ibid.*

that treat of faith or morals. Newman's thoughts gradually worked themselves round to a theory of partial inspiration."[8]

The New Theory of Verbal Inspiration

The major advocates of content inspiration were the Jesuits, and their influence with the popes and Curia in Rome made this the dominant view of inspiration for almost half a century. Leo XIII (Pope, 1878-1903) reversed the trend in 1879 with his encyclical *Aeterni Patris*, in which he decreed that the philosophy and theology of Thomas Aquinas were to be the standard teachings of the church. He purged the Roman schools of Jesuit influence, and the Dominicans assumed the leading role as teachers and counselors of popes.

One of the pioneers in the renewal of Thomistic scholasticism was Heinrich Denzinger (1819-1883). He set the stage for a new development in the discussion of inspiration when he noted that Aquinas had distinguished the passive (apprehension by the senses) and active (judgment about these objects) operations of the human mind, the latter being the aspect where inspiration functions.

In his encyclical *Providentissimus Deus* (1893), Leo XIII, using the terminology of Franzelin, expressed his own definition of inspiration: "For, by supernatural power, He so moved and impelled them to write, He so assisted them when writing, that the things which He ordered, and those only, they first rightly understood, then willed faithfully to write down, and finally expressed in apt words and with infallible truth." Here was the best of both worlds—the positive inspiration of the ideas and the negative inspiration in the choice of words.

The next important step in the development of the new theory of verbal inspiration was an article written in 1895 by the young Dominican, Thomas Pègues (1866-1936). In trying to explain Leo's teaching more fully, Pègues developed Aquinas' concept of instrumental causality more

8. *Ibid.*, p. 79.

fully than Denzinger had done: "God, the principal cause, puts all man's powers to work, to write exactly as God wishes. The resulting book, which no man or group of men could have produced unaided, expresses God's mind. Within this scheme it is impossible to ascribe any element of Holy Writ to man alone. The two causes conspire in the whole, each in his own manner. The human instrument God uses is a crude one, so there are crudities in his work; but God has his reasons for wishing it this way."[9] When confronted with apparent errors and contradictions, Pègues took refuge in Augustine's famous statement, "I decide that either the text is corrupt, or the translator did not follow what was really said, or that I failed to understand it."

The formulator of the classic Roman view of verbal inspiration was Marie-Joseph Lagrange (1855-1938). From his school in Jerusalem he issued a number of articles and rebuttals, and, like Newman, he revised his views over the years. In order to get beyond the troublesome discrepancies he urged at the outset that the key was to determine what the authors really intended to teach. Inspiration for Lagrange involved God's influence of both the will and the intellect. Whereas the sacred writer was conscious of God's help in supplying the material and information of revelation, inspiration was an unconscious gift of inerrant judgment in the use of revelation.

In the middle period of his thought, Lagrange realized that a number of clear teachings of the Old Testament were hardly in accord with the gospel. Regardless of whether the sacred writer intended to teach or not, God inspired him to record the ideas as historical information for future generations. But this theory did not apply very well to the New Testament, and so Lagrange returned to his old theory of inerrancy—that whatever the writer teaches God does likewise.

Verbal Inspiration in Protestantism

The pressing problems of defending Scripture against the criticisms of the humanists and scientists occupied the

9. *Ibid.*, p. 131.

thoughts and time of the Protestants just as much as they did the Roman Catholics, and in both instances the result was a bitter controversy between the conservatives and the liberals. There were mediating scholars, however, who faced the difficulties with empathy and irenic spirit. Concerning the issue of words and ideas, the late John Baillie (1886-1960) quoted Frederick Denison Maurice (1805-1872) as expressing his own point of view: "When you speak to me of verbal *inspiration*, though I do not like the phrase, though it seems to me to involve a violent—a scarcely grammatical—ellipsis, yet I subscribe most unequivocally to the meaning which I suppose is latent in it. I have no notion of inspired thoughts which do not find for themselves a suitable clothing of words. I can scarcely, even in my mind, separate the language of a writer from his meaning. And I certainly find this difficulty greater in studying a book of the Bible than in studying any other book."[10]

B. F. Westcott (1825-1901) expresses a similar view in the following, often-quoted passage: "The slightest consideration will show that words are as essential to intellectual processes as they are to mutual intercourse. For man, the purely spiritual and absolute is but an aspiration or a dream. Thoughts are wedded to words as necessarily as soul to body."[11] The truth of this statement is beyond question, but some very false implications have been drawn from it. Since ideas are wedded to words, it follows, according to some evangelicals, that inerrancy of ideas necessitates inerrancy of *all* words.

This conclusion, however, is only partially true. In Galatians 3, for example, Paul argues for the supremacy of grace over law because the promise was given before the law. If he had inverted the words, arguing instead for the priority of the law, obviously the wrong words would have led to the wrong concept. But granting the necessity of correct *key* words does not imply inerrancy for all the words. Paul's argument holds true whether he says the law came 430 or 645 years after the promise to Abraham.

---

10. *The Idea of Revelation in Recent Thought*, p. 116.
11. *An Introduction to the Study of the Gospels*, p. 14.

Although Paul's reference to 430 years could technically be termed an incorrect "idea," it is a nonessential idea in relation to the primary issue that Paul is attempting to communicate. Accordingly, we must always keep in mind the distinction between the essentials and the nonessentials in Scripture.

Mark's account of Peter's denial is another good illustration of this principle. Whether the cock crowed once, twice, or a dozen times makes no essential difference as far as God's purpose and our response are concerned. This minor detail varied with the human memories of the writers, but all the writers agree on the basic facts.

As a universal truth, applicable to biblical and nonbiblical literature alike, we may lay down the following principle: a true concept necessitates correct key words, but there may well be some inaccurate details that are incidental to the argument or presentation of the chief idea. Recognition of this fact is even found in the writings of most scholars who defend the doctrine of inerrancy or verbal inspiration, especially when they deal with such biblical phenomena as variations in parallel accounts and differences between New Testament quotations and the Old Testament sources.

Calvin recognized the difficulty of squaring some of the New Testament quotations with their Old Testament sources. He frankly admitted that some quotations from the Septuagint involved inaccuracies, but his out was the claim that the incorrect portion of the quotation was never used to prove the writer's point. As Kenneth Kantzer comments: "Interestingly enough, Calvin argues that quotation of the Old Testament by the New Testament is no guarantee of the correct text of the Old Testament. The New Testament writer, however, never uses the incorrect element in the quotation to prove his point. Luke, for example, in quoting an inaccurate text from the Septuagint, is merely using the commonly accepted version with which folks were familiar. The point which Luke wishes to make, nevertheless, is derived from that part of the Septuagint text which is absolutely correct."[12] But does this line

12. "Calvin and the Holy Scriptures," *Inspiration and Interpretation*, p. 147.

of reasoning prove the inerrancy of the erroneous words that were not involved in the argument?

Verbal Inspiration and Ideas

Because the term "verbal" has the unfortunate feature of seeming to claim inspiration for each separate word of the text, some conservative scholars have proposed what amounts to a doctrine emphasizing inerrancy of ideas. In parallel accounts, "verbal" agreement is not to be expected because the writers of Scripture never thought in terms of the precise accuracy associated with the scientific age. Calvin, for example, recognized this fact. After giving his explanation for differences between Matthew 21:10-22 and the parallel accounts in Mark and Luke, he says, "But anyone who will consider how little care the Evangelists bestowed on pointing out dates will not stumble at this diversity in the narrative."[13] Moreover, "verbal" exactness is not to be expected in quotations, because the interest of the New Testament writers centered in the *sense, not the exact wording*, of the Old Testament source. In effect, then, the term "verbal" is broadened so as to refer ultimately to ideas rather than to every word.

Verbal Inspiration and Truth

In conjunction with this broadened definition of "verbal," some have defined truth as that which corresponds to the nature and purpose of God. The expressed purpose of this new orientation has been to consider the problem of inerrancy in terms of standards current in biblical times rather than to impose on Scripture the demands of twentieth-century accuracy. While this attempt may alleviate some of the difficulty inherent in the doctrine of inerrancy or verbal inspiration, it is not able to account for all the phenomena. Are the erroneous synchronisms in 2 Kings 17 and 18, for example, in accord with the nature and purpose of God? If so, why even raise the issue of inerrancy? If not, how can they be true?

13. *Commentary on a Harmony of the Evangelists, Matthew, Mark, and Luke*, III, 10.

Others have defined truth in terms of the intent of the biblical writers. There is much to be said for this approach to the problem. When the Gospel writers compile events in topical fashion, one is not justified in expecting a precise historical sequence. No fault can be found with Luke when he changes the Jewish expression "kingdom of heaven" to "kingdom of God." On the other hand, what is one to make of Jude's quotation from the book of 1 Enoch? If, as the text indicates, Jude believed his quotation was actually from the preflood patriarch, how can his intent convert the misunderstanding into truth? The intent of the compiler of 2 Kings 17 and 18 was to inform the reader of the specific relationship that Hoshea and Hezekiah bore to each other, but his intent did not make it so.

Ultimately, therefore, truth must be defined in terms of reality or facts. Aside from this absolute formulation of truth, the doctrine of inerrancy is pointless. Regardless of the motivation or intent of the biblical writers, if any portion of the Bible deviates from reality, it is far better to speak in terms of the essential accuracy and trustworthiness of Scripture. For a person in the period of transition there may be some psychological value in clinging to the term "inerrancy" while filling it with new meaning, but eventually this contradiction will have to be given up.

The older apologists for the doctrine of inerrancy realized that the view did not permit any exceptions. Therefore in practice their defense of the claim that every word of the autographs was breathed by God and protected from error usually took the form of a challenge to prove just one error. This is all the more reason why evangelical Christianity must shift its defense to the point where it has the protection of the facts. In terms of absolute truth, Jude was in error because his qualification "seventh from Adam" cannot withstand the test of reality. But this need not cause any alarm because the essential truth of Jude's argument does not hinge on the validity of his proof text. This same principle applies to some of the arguments employed by other biblical writers as well. An excellent example is Matthew 2:14-15, which reads: "And he [Joseph] rose and took the child and his mother by night, and departed to Egypt, and remained there until the death of Herod. This was to fulfil what the Lord had spoken by the prophet, 'Out of Egypt have I called my son.' " The quotation is from Hosea 11:1, where the prophet, speaking for God, states, "When Israel was a child, I loved him, and out of Egypt I called my son." The context is a passage in which God is reiterating his gracious dealings with Israel in the past, one of the greatest being the deliverance from Egypt. The sense of the passage and the intention of the prophet point backward, not forward. There is not the slightest hint that the statement was intended as a prophecy.

Tradition has contended that any adaptation of the original is allowable as long as it proceeds by a true interpretation of the passage. The question is whether Matthew's use of Hosea 11:1 is really a true interpretation. It is also claimed that any neglect of the context of the original is allowable so long as the sense is not falsified. There was apparently a definite cause-and-effect relationship in the mind of Matthew, and so he quoted the passage as being authoritative proof from the Old Testament for an event in the life of Jesus. Although unintentional, is not his use of Hosea 11:1 in a sense a distortion of the context? Is Matthew's appeal to Hosea actually true to the sense of the passage when he picks words out from the context and uses them for another purpose in the New Testament?

Christians today believe that Jesus Christ was the Son of God and that he was anticipated in the Old Testament, but they do so largely on the basis of observations and reports in the biblical record. The essential truth of Matthew's account is not dependent on his proof-text method. This Jewish mode of thinking, so common to the first century A.D., was suited to Matthew's Jewish readers, but it has no validity for the twentieth-century mind that thinks in terms of precise accuracy. In other words, what Matthew was trying to demonstrate (namely, that Jesus of Nazareth was the promised Messiah, the Son of God) is true, but his method of proving his conviction does not conform to all the facts. Matthew's logic in this instance bears the mark of his day, and as such one is not compelled to accept his method of reasoning any more than one is required to wear sandals and a tunic in order to be a Christian. Inasmuch as erroneous nonessentials do not invalidate the essential truth, it is unnecessary to contend for the unique inspiration and accuracy of every word of the autographs. By shifting the line of defense from "absolute truth" to "essential truth," it is possible to reckon with all the phenomena and teaching of Scripture and to have a sound view of authority as well.

Verbal Inspiration and Dictation

While formulations of verbal inspiration have often been characterized by critics as the dictation view, the charge has been rejected repeatedly. The problem is well illustrated by the theologians of the seventeenth century. They declared, on the one hand, that every word in Scripture was inspired and dictated by God. On the other hand, they could claim with equal sincerity and feeling that the writers wrote willingly and without loss of their own styles and idioms. In short, God *accommodated* himself and his message to the intellect, emotions, natural endowments, and normal speech of ordinary men. Concerning this paradox, Preus comments: "If these two parallel thoughts seem paradoxical, if they seem to contradict each other, the orthodox teachers make no effort to harmonize them. Such a lacuna in their theology will of course trouble those who study them, but the minute the dogmaticians are represented as crossing this lacuna they are certain to be misrepresented. This habit of blandly refraining from drawing what seem to be the logical consequences of their tenets was not uncommon among the Lutheran theologians of the sixteenth and seventeenth centuries; in fact, it was a principle with them."[14]

While those who have made formulations of the doctrine of verbal inspiration during the nineteenth and twentieth centuries have been quite aware of the inherent

14. *The Inspiration of Scripture*, pp. 196-197.

paradox, still the claim has been made that every word of Scripture is equally from man as it is from God. How each word can stem from a free, responsible individual and still be God's intended communication is frankly admitted to be a mystery. Indeed, Scripture does not tell us the mode or means by which God revealed his message to his inspired servants, but is not this fact good reason for refraining from any claim of inerrancy in Scripture? Jude's qualification "seventh from Adam" is *man's word* because it represents the opinion current in his day. But how can it be *God's word* at the same time when it is not in accord with the facts? Although the Holy Spirit did not overrule the erroneous words, this does not mean that God was responsible for placing the words in the mind of Jude.

Notwithstanding repeated denials of the charge, the doctrine of inerrancy leads eventually into the mechanical or dictation theory of inspiration. God could not have given a verbally inerrant Scripture through human channels without dictating the correct information directly to the biblical writers where they or their sources were in error.

Verbal Inspiration and Language

Another issue pertaining to the doctrine of verbal inspiration (defined broadly to include both the words and the ideas wedded to them) has to do with the characteristics of language. Can one legitimately speak of human language as being capable of inerrant communication from God? Undoubtedly God was capable of thinking in terms of Hebrew, so direct communication with the prophets did not involve the difficulties inherent in translations. However, unless God dictated his revelation word for word, there is no assurance that the Old Testament writers caught all the nuances or overtones of God's self-disclosure. Words are symbols that cover areas of meaning, and the area varies from individual to individual, depending on the background or experience of the person (for example, the complex terms "capitalist" and "communist"). Consequently no two people speaking the same language necessarily mean the same thing by the same word. In the process of any extended communication something is added to, or deleted from, the precise meaning intended by the communicator.

Scripture is no exception to this linguistic fact. Certainly this is true of the metaphorical language that had to be employed in expressing those spiritual realities extending beyond the realms of the five senses. Furthermore, in the case of biography, or even autobiography, language cannot possibly convey to the reader all the facets of personality and character of the individual under discussion. How much less could words describe the incarnate Christ completely. For this reason we should always bear in mind the difference between Jesus, the Living Word, and Scripture, the Written Word.

A very helpful discussion of language and its role in Scripture is *The Inspired Word* by the Spanish Jesuit Luis Alonso-Schökel. He notes the threefold role of language: the third person function of stating objective facts; the first person function of expressing feelings and thoughts; and the second person function of dynamic communication to others.[15] God employed all of these aspects while choosing to express himself in the specific languages Hebrew, Aramaic, and Greek. As Alonso-Schökel notes, "The speech of Israel and the land of Palestine are both crisscrossed by the foot prints of God."[16]

Yet from the symbolism of metaphorical language the human mind is able to distill concepts that amount to literal truth. Although some would describe these concepts as "absolute truth," they are more properly classified as truths about absolutes. In any case, *effective* communication has always been possible. In spite of the marred "image of God" in mankind, regenerate man has always had the mental and spiritual qualities requisite for receiving communications from Scripture and also for communicating these spiritual truths to his fellow men. With the aid of the Holy Spirit the Scriptures have always been able to

15. *The Inspired Word, Scripture in the Light of Language and Literature*, p. 134.
16. *Ibid.*, p. 127.

communicate sufficient truth to meet the needs of the sincere, inquiring reader. On the other hand, since language is incapable of absolute communication, we are hardly warranted in describing Scripture in terms of inerrancy. As Westcott put it, "For man, the purely spiritual and absolute is but an aspiration or a dream."

Chapter Eleven

Plenary Inspiration and the Canon

During the last century or so, the doctrine of inerrancy has been known generally as the "verbal plenary" view of inspiration. It is necessary now to turn our attention to the "plenary" aspect of this formulation. The term comes from the Latin *plenus* ("full"). According to the plenary view, every word of the autographs was equally inspired.

This general statement does not become definitive, however, unless precise limits are set. To speak of *fullness* of inspiration one must determine which books come under the category. "Canon," the usual term for designating the limits of the Bible, comes from a Greek word meaning "straight rod," "bar." Gradually the word acquired the sense of "rule, standard of accuracy"; therefore the books considered authoritative were termed "canonical."

The primary purpose of this chapter is not to settle the issue between the Roman Catholics and the Protestants concerning the extent of the canon. This matter will be discussed, but only secondarily to the problem of ascertaining whether inspiration applies constantly to all the material within the limited Protestant canon. Since the points at issue apply equally, if not more so, to the Roman

Catholic canon, the discussion will have merit for both communions.

Plenary Inspiration and Duplicates

Although the King James Version does not indicate it, the book of Psalms is actually a collection of five smaller books or compilations: Book 1 (Ps. 1-41), Book 2 (Ps. 42-72), Book 3 (Ps. 73-89), Book 4 (Ps. 90-106), and Book 5 (Ps. 107-150). These books are noted in the American Standard, Revised Standard, Berkeley, New English, and New American Bibles. The RSV, NEB, and NAB also indicate, by footnotes, portions or whole psalms that are repeated elsewhere. For example, Psalm 14 is the same as Psalm 53. Both begin, "The fool says in his heart, 'There is no God.'"

While most scholars who hold to plenary inspiration recognize that much of what the prophets of God spoke has been lost and that even some of their writings may have perished as well, they attribute the existing canon directly to the providence of God. Only those writings which God decreed for us have been preserved. Did God determine that Psalm 14 should be repeated as Psalm 53? No doubt God inspired the psalmist, and in turn the psalm accredited itself to the hearts of the people, so that they felt like preserving it. But its occurrence twice in our collection of psalms is probably an accident of collection. Apparently when Book 2 was added to Book 1 the editor did not go through Book 2 deleting the similar passages. Scholars learn something about the transmission of biblical books from comparing the two psalms (Ps. 14 tends to use "LORD," whereas Ps. 53 has "God"). From the standpoint of theological significance, however, what function does Psalm 53 serve in the Old Testament canon beyond that of Psalm 14?

There are a number of duplicate passages in Scripture. With the exception of Hezekiah's psalm (Isa. 38:9-20), Isaiah 36 to 39 is similar to 2 Kings 18:13 to 20:19. Moreover, Psalm 18 is repeated in 2 Samuel 22; Psalm

40:13-17 = Psalm 70; Psalm 57:7-11 = Psalm 108:1-5; and Psalm 60:5-12 = Psalm 108:6-13. Most of these duplicates occurred in the process of compilation, yet the stress that inerrancy places on every word of the canon makes it necessary to attribute the duplicates to God's providence. Inasmuch as there are many portions of Scripture with greater theological significance (for example, Isa. 53), one wonders why God did not have such passages repeated if it was his intention to teach redemptive truths through repetition.

Plenary Inspiration and Trivialities

According to the seventeenth-century Lutheran theologians, Scripture has no trivialities (*levicula*). In keeping with this view, as Preus comments, "Everything in Scripture pertains somehow to Christian doctrine."[1] Matters of very little consequence are related in some vital way to the total truth of Scripture because God has placed them there for an express purpose.

In Judges 12:5-6 occurs the following narrative: "And the Gileadites took the fords of the Jordan against the Ephraimites. And when any of the fugitives of Ephraim said, 'Let me go over,' the men of Gilead said to him, 'Are you an Ephraimite?' When he said, 'No,' they said to him, 'Then say Shibboleth,' and he said 'Sibboleth,' for he could not pronounce it right; then they seized him and slew him at the fords of the Jordan. And there fell at that time forty-two thousand of the Ephraimites." This interesting little story has great value for the student of Semitic languages. In English the letter *s* is pronounced as a dental normally (for example, "sing"), but there are times when it has a palatal pronunciation (for example, "sure" and "sugar" where *s* = *sh*). Certain Semitic dialects and languages leveled through the *s* sound, so it was as difficult for these people to pronounce an *sh* as it is for a person of Germanic origin to say the English *th*. The scholar is delighted to find this linguistic example in Scripture, but

1. *The Inspiration of Scripture*, p. 83.

from the standpoint of God's revelation the text could just as well have omitted the "Shibboleth" episode with verses 5-6 reading as follows: "And the Gileadites took the fords of the Jordan against the Ephraimites. . . . And there fell at that time forty-two thousand of the Ephraimites."

The complete literature of Israel must have consisted of many other sources that somehow were lost or destroyed. The linguistic and archaeological data incorporated in these documents would undoubtedly have been of great significance to the scholar, but it is questionable whether their disappearance constitutes any serious theological loss. On the other hand, is it not a bit questionable to attribute the "Shibboleth" story to the providential determination of God? Did God decree that this incident should be in the Old Testament canon? The biblical writers were free to use any sources at hand; but in the case of certain individuals, information was so scarce that the writers included material that has little, if any, bearing on God's purpose in recording his revelation to man.

The case of Ibzan in Judges 12:8-10 is quite illustrative: "After him Ibzan of Bethlehem judged Israel. He had thirty sons; and thirty daughters he gave in marriage outside his clan, and thirty daughters he brought in from outside for his sons. And he judged Israel seven years. Then Ibzan died, and was buried at Bethlehem." Surely if Ibzan judged Israel for seven years, he must have risen to his place of leadership on the basis of other attainments than that of marrying off his thirty daughters outside the clan and getting thirty girls imported as wives for his thirty sons. The compiler of the book of Judges incorporated this information from some old source, but the text could just as well have read: "After him Ibzan of Bethlehem judged Israel. . . . And he judged Israel seven years. Then Ibzan died and was buried at Bethlehem." Because the information about Ibzan's children was in the source material at hand, are we duty-bound to find some providential purpose for its inclusion in Scripture?

Another example is found in Judges 12:14, which informs us that Abdon "had forty sons and thirty grandsons, who rode on seventy asses; and he judged Israel eight years." This is all we know about the activities of Abdon. Are not God's ways exceedingly mysterious if, out of all the good things Abdon must have done, God decreed that we should have only this incident of Abdon's seventy sons and grandsons, each with his own means of transportation?

Inasmuch as revelation occurred in a historical context it is fitting that the historical framework play an important role in the record of that revelation. Notwithstanding some gaps and defects, the historical background enables us to understand the message of Scripture in a way that would never be possible otherwise. Inspiration had to do with the understanding of the historical record, not the inerrancy of every word incorporated from the sources.

Old Testament Canon and the Prophets

Philo and Josephus spoke of the Scriptures as being written by prophets, and in Matthew 26:56 Jesus is reported as saying, "But all this has taken place, that the scriptures of the prophets might be fulfilled." This information, along with the fact that a number of Old Testament books were clearly written by prophets, has led some conservative scholars to the theory that *all* the books were by prophets.[2] Solomon was a prophet, so it is reasoned, because God spoke to him in dreams on at least two occasions. Ecclesiastes, Song of Solomon, and Proverbs are to be classified as prophetic literature because they derive from Solomon. Judges, Ruth, Chronicles, Ezra, Nehemiah, Esther, and Job are considered as prophetic literature because there is no evidence that the authors of these books were not prophets. But does this easy answer not overlook some pertinent biblical and nonbiblical data? New evidence supports the traditional claim that Ezra was the Chronicler, but Ezra 7:6 describes him as being "a scribe skilled in the law of Moses." Verse 10 says, "For Ezra had set his heart to study the law of the LORD, and to do it, and to teach his statutes and ordinances in Israel."

2. See Harris, *Inspiration and Canonicity of the Bible*, pp. 167-174.

The following verse describes him as "the priest, the scribe, learned in matters of the commandments of the LORD and his statutes in Israel." Nehemiah 8:9 refers to "Ezra the priest and scribe." There is no biblical evidence that his contemporaries considered him a prophet.

His fame as a scribe is pictured in the apocryphal book known as Second Esdras (Fourth Ezra). Because God's revelation to man has perished, Ezra prays to God for inspiration to restore the Scriptures. Chapter 14:21-22 reads as follows: "For thy Law is burnt; and so no man knows the things which have been done by thee, or the works that shall be done. If then, I have found favor before thee, send into me the Holy Spirit, that I may write all that has happened in the world since the beginning, even the things which were written in thy Law, in order that men may be able to find the path, and that they who would live at the last may live."[3]

The story is completed in verses 37-46: "So I took the five men as he had commanded me, and we went forth *into the field* and remained there. And it came to pass on the morrow that, lo! a voice called me, saying: Ezra, open thy mouth and drink what I give thee to drink! Then I opened my mouth, and lo! there was reached unto me a full cup, which was full as it were with water, but the colour of it was like fire. And I took it and drank; and when I had drunk, my heart poured forth understanding, wisdom grew in my breast, and my spirit retained its memory: and my mouth opened, and was no more shut. And the Most High gave understanding unto the five men, and they wrote what was dictated in order, in characters which they knew not. And so they sat forty days. They wrote in the day-time and at night did eat bread; but as for me, I spake in the day, and at night was not silent. So in forty days were written ninety-four books. And it came to pass when the forty days were fulfilled, that the Most High spake unto me saying: The twenty-four books that thou hast written publish, that the worthy and unworthy may

3. Charles, ed., *The Apocrypha and Pseudepigrapha of the Old Testament in English,* II, 622.

read (therein): but the seventy last thou shalt keep, to deliver them to the wise among thy people."[4]

The reference to twenty-four books is the ancient counting of the thirty-nine books in our present Old Testament (for example, the twelve Minor Prophets were considered one book). The seventy books were the apocryphal writings, which contained such deep wisdom that only the very wise should read them. The story in its present form is clearly fictional, but there must have been some kernel of truth back of it. Perhaps Ezra played some important part in formalizing the Old Testament canon. At any rate, tradition does not recognize Ezra as a prophet any more than Scripture does.

If there is objection to Ezra as being the Chronicler, there can hardly be any doubt that he wrote the book that bears his name. Nehemiah also must have been largely responsible for the book that bears his name. But he is known as the "cupbearer to the king" in Persia, and "the governor" in Judah. Never is he recognized as a prophet.

Furthermore, Proverbs 25:1 reads, "These also are proverbs of Solomon which the men of Hezekiah king of Judah copied." The editor who added this heading makes no reference to the "men of Hezekiah" as being prophets engaged in compilation of Scripture. Proverbs 22:17 reads, "Incline your ear, and hear the words of the wise," and 24:23 states, "These also are sayings of the wise." These references are to other wise men than Solomon. Jeremiah 18:18 speaks of "counsel from the wise," and Ezekiel 7:26 mentions "counsel from the elders." In other words, there was a clear concept of God revealing himself through some men other than the prophets. Proverbs 30 is attributed to Agur, son of Jakeh of Massa. Massa is an Arabian tribe mentioned in Genesis 25:14, but that is all we know of the place name. Agur was probably no Israelite and less likely a prophet. Chapter 31 of Proverbs is attributed to Lemuel, king of Massa—words that his mother taught him. Was she a prophetess?

The book of Ruth was passed on orally for a long period

4. *Ibid.*, pp. 623-624.

before it was put into written form. It is exceedingly doubtful that the prophets had a significant part in its oral transmission or its recording. It is just as doubtful that Esther or Job was written by the prophetic tradition. In the light of all this evidence, much of it from the biblical text itself, is one warranted in ascribing all the Old Testament canon to the prophetic tradition?

Plenary Inspiration and the Book of Esther

Over and above the difficulties that are caused by duplicates, trivialities, and nonprophetic writings, there are some books that are on the edge of the canonical limits. Esther is one of these books. It purports to tell of God's vindication of the Jews in Shushan (the capital city of the Persian Empire, known more commonly as Susa) during the reign of Ahasuerus (Xerxes), 486-465 B.C. Archaeology has not confirmed any of the events of Esther, but the book reflects Persian history and customs, and it is filled with Persian loan words. Oddly enough the name of God never appears in the book. God is certainly implicit in the whole story and numerous reasons have been given to account for the omission of the name. Later additions were made, apparently to correct this oversight, but these were considered apocryphal and do not appear in the Hebrew Bible.

While most of the rabbis quoted in the Babylonian Talmud with respect to the book of Esther believed that it was "composed [literally, "said"] under the inspiration of the Holy Spirit,"[5] some declared that the scroll of Esther "does not make the hands unclean."[6] The implication is that Esther did not share the unquestioned authority and canonical status of the Torah or the Prophets. These books, because of their holy character, "defiled the hands" of the readers.

In all likelihood the primary reason for Esther's being in the Hebrew canon was to show the origin of the Feast of

5. Epstein, ed., *The Babylonian Talmud*, Vol. 10, Megillah 7b, p. 36.

6. *Ibid.*, p. 35.

Purim (first noted in 2 Macc. 15:36 as the day of Morde-cai). The feast has always been, and continues to be, one of the most joyous of all the Jewish festivals. Raba, one of the Talmudic sages, gave the classical description for cele-brating the feast when he said, "It is the duty of a man to mellow himself [with wine] on Purim until he cannot tell the difference between 'cursed be Haman' and 'blessed be Mordecai.' "[7]

In Christian circles Purim was not recognized as a legiti-mate festival of the church calendar, and so the explana-tion of the feast's origin ceased to have real relevance for Christians. In fact, at one time the Syrian Christians omit-ted the book of Esther from their Syriac Old Testament. As a general rule today, however, Christians accept the canonicity of Esther, but they do so largely because the book shows God's providential care for his dispersed, per-secuted people. Yet the fact of God's providential care is taught quite clearly in the books of Jeremiah and Ezekiel. Did God actually include the book of Esther in the canon for this purpose, or is this an afterthought of Christians to justify the present Old Testament canon? The primary reason for Esther's inclusion has become a dead issue for Christians, and evidently the book did not occupy a very important place in the thinking of the New Testament writers, because it is never quoted in the New Testament. Is it really necessary, therefore, to contend for the unique inspiration of every word of Esther?

Plenary Inspiration and the Song of Songs

The Song of Songs (known also as Canticles or the Song of Solomon) is attributed to Solomon. In general, critical scholarship has discounted this claim, but in recent years new evidence has indicated that the book could well have come from the age of Solomon. Love songs were popular in the ancient world and a book of love songs dating from about 1100 B.C. has been discovered. It consists of seven cantos or units that express alternately the sentiments of

7. *Ibid.*, p. 38.

lovers who call each other "brother" and "sister." Love-sickness plays an important part in the song. In the Song of Songs we find the expression, "I am sick with love" (2:5; 5:8), and in 5:1 the girl is addressed "my sister, my bride." In 5:2 she is called "my sister, my love," while in 8:1 she wishes that her lover "were like a brother to me."

It is the content, however, not the authorship, that is the basic problem relating to inspiration. Human love is expressed in such a frank, open manner that the book has been used sparingly for preaching and public reading. As a general rule Jews have allegorized the book in terms of God's love for Israel, and most Christians have followed suit by interpreting it as Christ's love for the church. This, to most people, was the only interpretation that would justify the book's being in the canon. In fact, Theodore of Mopsuestia was condemned by the Second Council of Constantinople (A.D. 533) because he thought the book was a mere song of human love that Solomon wrote for his marriage to Pharaoh's daughter.

Neither Jesus nor the New Testament writers find occasion to quote the Song of Songs. If the book was intended by God as a type or foreshadow of Christ and his love for the church, it is very odd that neither Jesus nor the apostles make mention of this fact. One factor that may have contributed to the book's inclusion in the canon is that the love song was a part of the great literature of other groups in the Orient, and in like manner Solomon's love song became a part of Israel's collection of great literature. But whether literal truth or allegory, the most obvious reason for the book's place in the canon is the name of Solomon. The Song had its place in the age of Solomon and it is a much needed corrective for the ascetic tendency of the New Testament, but are we, then, to contend for the unique inspiration of its every word?

Plenary Inspiration and Ecclesiastes

The title Ecclesiastes derives from the Greek translation of the Hebrew word *qoheleth*, meaning "preacher." The Preacher identifies himself as "the son of David, king in

Jerusalem" (1:1). Up to the Reformation, both Jews and Christians traditionally attributed the book to Solomon. Luther seems to have been the first Christian scholar to deny the Solomonic authorship. Since his time it has become increasingly apparent that the book is one of the latest compositions in the Old Testament canon. While early portions of the Old Testament tended to acquire some different linguistic features and editorial insertions later on during the process of transmission, they retained many aspects indicative of their antiquity. In the case of Ecclesiastes, however, both the language and the content witness against Solomonic authorship.

In recent years there has been considerable debate among conservative scholars over the date and authorship of Ecclesiastes. Some frankly admit that the author lived after the exile and placed his words in the mouth of Solomon as a literary device.[8] Others conclude that 1:1 clearly attributes the book to Solomon and so they maintain the Solomonic authorship. To do otherwise would be an admission that Ecclesiastes is in the category of the apocryphal book The Wisdom of Solomon.[9] The former view counters with the assertion that the Preacher in verse 1 is not Solomon, and the original readers of the book would never have interpreted the literary device in this way.[10]

It is very charitable to speak of the unambiguous literary character of the book and to affirm that it would have deceived none of its original readers, but what is the *historical* justification for such a view? In 1:12 the text reads, "I the Preacher have been [was] king over Israel in Jerusalem." Apparently, the author was not on the throne at this time, but Solomon, according to the historical books, reigned until his death. To get around this contradiction, the Jewish sages concluded that Solomon's sin resulted in the loss of his regal powers.

In section 20b of the unit "Sanhedrin" in the Baby-

8. See Edward J. Young, *An Introduction to the Old Testament*, p. 340.

9. See Unger, *Introductory Guide to the Old Testament*, p. 390.

10. See *The New Bible Commentary*, p. 135.

lonian Talmud there is an extended passage dealing with the problem of Solomon's gradually restricted authority. The rabbis note (quoting Eccl. 1:12) that at first Solomon was king over all Israel, then (quoting 1:1) they observe that his authority extended only over Jerusalem. They believed that Solomon, becoming like a commoner, was finally stripped of all power, except his own staff. Was Solomon ever restored to power? Some of the rabbinical authorities thought so, but others said he remained a commoner forever.

Further discussion of Ecclesiastes occurs in section 68b of the unit "Gittin." One of the main points in this section is to account for the Solomonic authorship of Ecclesiastes. It is difficult to say how far back these ideas go into Jewish history, but one thing is clear: tradition knows of no time when the Solomonic authorship was doubted.

The book was questioned, but not on grounds of authorship. The Talmud notes: "The Sages wished to hide the book of Ecclesiastes, because its words are self-contradictory; yet why did they not hide it? Because its beginning is religious teaching and its end is religious teaching."[11] From start to finish, the Talmudic discussion of Ecclesiastes assumes Solomonic authorship. Christian tradition followed suit, apparently, although the New Testament writers found no occasion to quote from the book.

On what grounds, then, can one declare that none of the original readers was deceived? At best it is an assumption, and even if one grants its validity, it was not long before tradition attributed Ecclesiastes to Solomon. It is this fact which accounts for the book's being in the canon.

While some of the conservative scholars are willing to deny the Solomonic authorship, they usually date the book prior to 400 B.C. This also is to protect the book because traditionally the canon has been considered as having been completed by 400 B.C., the time, according to later Jewish tradition, that the spirit of prophecy departed from Israel. However, the linguistic features of the book along with evidence from fragments of Ecclesiastes found

11. Epstein, *op. cit.*, Vol. 3, Shabbath 30b, p. 135.

at Qumrân point to the third century B.C. as the date of composition. Thus we are faced with the possibility that a canonical book was composed after 400 by someone putting his message in the mouth of Solomon, yet without actually using his name.

About 180 B.C. a certain Jesus, the son of Sira(ch), a Jerusalem Jew, composed a book in Hebrew. He frankly gave his name, and as a result his teachings, although quite popular, were never granted canonical status by the Jews. However, the book, known as The Wisdom of Sirach, was read a great deal by the Christian church, and for this reason it acquired the title Ecclesiasticus ("Church Book"). In terms of theological relevance and impact on Judaism and Christianity, the book of Ecclesiasticus has had far more influence than has the canonical book Ecclesiastes. Accordingly, the author who uses a literary device, leaving the impression of Solomonic authorship (without actually employing the name), has his book included in the canon, while the author who has much to say, but honestly names himself, finds his work excluded from the canon.

Plenary Inspiration and Inerrancy

The concern to define inspiration as the constant feature of the canon is a theological deduction from the assumption of inerrancy. Thus in order to evaluate the validity of plenary inspiration it is necessary to reconsider the validity of inerrancy from still another perspective. The survey of traditional theories of inspiration (Ch. 6) indicated that there has been a traditional or classic doctrine of inspiration. With few exceptions the church has contended for both the human and the divine character of Scripture. For the greater part of this nineteen-hundred-year history, however, the existing manuscripts (both the Hebrew and Septuagint texts in the Old Testament and the Greek texts in the New Testament) were generally considered inspired.

But with the expansion of scientific knowledge Christians recognized increasingly the problems inherent in any attempt to reconcile the divine and human factors in the extant manuscripts of Scripture. In order to strengthen the essence of the traditional doctrine, more and more emphasis was placed on the original writings (autographs) as the basis of appeal for the inspiration, trustworthiness, and inerrancy of Scripture. We can agree heartily with the general affirmations of the traditional view of inspiration. The difficulties cluster around the *refinements* of the classic view that have come to the front since the beginning of the nineteenth century.

As A. G. Hebert comments, "Hence the inerrancy of the Bible, as it is understood today, is a new doctrine, and the modern fundamentalist is asserting something that no previous age has understood in anything like the modern sense."[12] Notwithstanding the clear historical evidence supporting this assertion, some evangelical scholars reject it with the utmost emphasis. The verbal plenary view of inspiration "is the inspiration which the Scriptures claim for themselves, which the Apostolic Church claimed for them, and what the Reformed Church understood by the Word of God written."[13]

However, such a sweeping claim does not give sufficient weight to the following statement by Warfield and Hodge: "The word 'Inspiration,' as applied to the Holy Scriptures, has gradually acquired a specific technical meaning independent of its etymology. At first this word, in the sense of 'God-breathed,' was used to express the entire agency of God in producing that divine element which distinguishes Scripture from all other writings. It was used in a sense comprehensive of supernatural revelation, while the immense range of providential and gracious divine activities concerning the genesis of the word of God in human language was practically overlooked."[14] This statement is quite an accurate picture of the situation. The early definitions of inspiration were generalized and "in a sense comprehensive of supernatural revelation." It was only as sys-

12. *The Authority of the Old Testament*, p. 98.
13. R. A. Finlayson, "Contemporary Ideas of Inspiration," *Revelation and the Bible*, p. 233.
14. *Inspiration*, p. 5.

tematic theology began to reckon with the data from science that the more technical definitions of inspiration came into being. Some of the general statements of Scripture and church history concerning inspiration appear to be the same as the modern formulations of verbal plenary inspiration, but in most instances the *similarity is in appearance only* because the precise meaning of the words has changed in various ways. Only when Scripture and history of doctrine are read with the presupposition of inerrancy is it possible to extend the twentieth-century formulation of verbal-plenary, inerrant inspiration back through church history and even into Scripture itself.

The untenable nature of inerrancy and its corollary "constant inspiration" is just as evident from the New Testament data as from the Old Testament. The traditional criterion for a canonical New Testament book has been apostolic authorship; that is, every book was written by an apostle or one closely associated with him (for example, Mark with Peter, and Luke with Paul). Some have claimed, on the other hand, that the original basis for canonicity was not apostolic authorship but apostolic authority that imposed (as law) on the churches any book that it deemed worthy, whether the book was written by an apostle or not.[15]

Inasmuch as every New Testament book supposedly has the imprimatur of the apostles, the complete accuracy of every word of the canon is assured. Any conclusion, therefore, that runs counter to a biblical affirmation is inconsistent with the true doctrine of inspiration regardless of the apparent evidence supporting it.

But how does the book of Jude, for example, fit in with this theory? The book purports to have been composed by Jude, the brother of James (leader of the church at Jerusalem and half-brother of Jesus). The book was one of the last to be accepted into the canon because its authorship and validity were disputed. Yet this doubt would hardly have been an issue if Peter, John, or Paul had authorized the book and imposed it on the early church.

15. See Warfield, *The Inspiration and Authority of the Bible*, pp. 415-416.

Moreover, according to the doctrine of plenary inspiration every word of Jude is inspired. But Jude, as we have seen, quotes the book of 1 Enoch in the belief that he is quoting Enoch the preflood patriarch. By definition the quoted words are inspired because they are supposedly from an authoritative, God-given source and they actually occur within New Testament canonical limits.

Some scholars in the past have gone so far as to say that the verse quoted from 1 Enoch was inspired, while the rest of Enoch was not. Jude, so they claim, is not sanctioning the book of Enoch any more than Paul sanctions the words of Aratus, Menander, and Epimenides, the Greek poets whom he quotes in Acts 17:28; 1 Corinthians 15:33; and Titus 1:12. There is, however, a real difference between the two situations. Paul refers to the statements of the Greek poets because they accord with what he already knows to be true, but he does not profess to quote them as Scripture. These true statements serve as a point of contact with his hearers or readers. Jude, on the other hand, says, "Enoch in the seventh generation from Adam prophesied saying, . . . " Enoch is no pagan poet—he is a prophet of God whose prophecy is coming true in Jude's own day.

Jude also refers to other parts of 1 Enoch. Verse 6 reads, "And the angels that did not keep their own position but left their proper dwelling have been kept by him in eternal chains in the nether gloom until the judgment of the great day." This is not a quotation but a summary of the point of view expressed in chapters 6 to 16 of 1 Enoch. We may infer, therefore, that aside from 1:9, Jude considered portions of Enoch as also being authoritative. We have also noted Jude's dependence on the apocryphal book The Assumption of Moses. What are we to make of all these affirmations by Jude? Would it not be preferable to acknowledge the facts and claim inspiration for Jude on the basis of the truths found in the book? In spite of the difficulties, this little book of twenty-five verses has an authoritative ring that sets it apart from the New Testament apocryphal books and from the writings of the early church fathers.

Another bit of pertinent evidence involves the inspiration of Luke. As a physician he was a man of science for his day. He accompanied Paul on some of his journeys and he used his trained mind to search out primary sources. In checking his data he undoubtedly talked to all the eyewitnesses of Jesus he could find. Yet concerning his researches for writing Luke-Acts he says simply, "It seemed good to me also . . . to write." In what precise way was the inspiration of Luke different from that of any man of God today? There are hundreds of well-trained, devoted, meticulous Christians filled with God's Spirit today who could do as accurate a piece of reporting as Luke did. When Luke felt the urge to write "an orderly account," was his inspiration of a *different kind* from that of the Holy Spirit's activity in the hearts and minds of God's servants down through the history of the church? Not likely.

What distinguishes Luke from Christians today is not inspiration as such, but rather the unique period of revelation that he was privileged to witness. The same can be said for Mark, who learned from the lips of Peter the events of Christ's ministry on earth.

On the other hand, Luke refers to many other writers who undertook to compile a Gospel narrative. They wrote prior to Luke, and the implication is that they too had some relationship to this unique period of history. Then why were their accounts rejected while Luke's became a part of the canon? Apparently Luke himself gives us the answer. He had "followed all things closely [accurately] for some time past," and as a result he wrote "an orderly account." The clear implication is that the other accounts were not as orderly or accurate. But Luke's accuracy, while superior to the others he mentions, hardly comes under the category of unique inspiration. Therefore, it is (1) his association with Paul, the uniquely inspired servant of God, and (2) his own experience in that crucial period of history, that constitute Luke's uniqueness as a biblical writer.

Concerning the relation of inspiration to the record of revelation, Orr comments: "It is urged . . . that unless we can demonstrate what is called the 'inerrancy' of the biblical record, down even to its minutest details, the whole edifice of belief in revealed religion falls to the ground. This, on the face of it, is a most suicidal position for any defender of revelation to take up. It is certainly a much easier matter to prove the reality of a divine revelation in the history of Israel, or in Christ, than it is to prove the inerrant inspiration of every part of the record, through which the revelation has come to us. Grant the Gospels to be only ordinary historical documents—trustworthy records of the life of Christ, apart from any special inspiration in their authors—we should still, one may contend, be shut up as much as ever to the belief that the Person whose words and works they narrate was One who made superhuman claims, and whose character, words, and deeds attested the truth of these claims."[16]

The Inspiration of the Canon

The evidence is overwhelming that there are varying kinds and levels of theological relevance, and it seems equally clear that Curtis was correct in recognizing varying degrees (kinds) of divine help or inspiration in the production of Scripture. In terms of the biblical data, therefore, the modern definition of the doctrine of inerrancy is untenable. Although the fringes of the unique collection called Scripture are tattered in places, the essence of the canon is not marred. This principle was recognized by the translators of the King James Version in their preface: "For it is confessed, that things are to take their denomination of the greater part. . . . A man may be counted a virtuous man, though he have made many slips in his life, (else there were none virtuous, for, in many things we offend all) also a comely man and lovely, though he have some warts upon his hand, yea, not only freckles upon his face, but also scars." Because this is also true in the realm of Scripture, we are not justified in claiming that every word in the biblical canon is the product of unique inspiration any more than we are warranted in denying that some portions of noncanonical writings came into being through the working of God's Spirit in the hearts of men.

16. *Revelation and Inspiration,* pp. 197-198.

The Extent of the Old Testament Canon

It is apparent that the books of the Old Testament range from works of unquestionable authority and revelational content to those of limited theological value and authority. Some portions of the apocryphal books appear to have greater worth than some sections of the canonical books, but somewhere a line had to be drawn. Considering books as a whole (not as units or verses), the Jewish community made the decision. It is implicit that Jesus accepted the Hebrew canon (which rejected the apocryphal books), but there is no evidence in the New Testament to indicate what his opinion was regarding some of the canonical books, because he neither quoted them nor alluded to them. For practical reasons, canonical limits were set, but does this mean that every word within these limits is uniquely inspired of God, while every word outside the canon is not inspired?

John Bunyan, with many other great Christians both past and present, would answer, "No!" In his *Grace Abounding* he relates how, in a period of great despondency, the following words came to mind: "Look at the generations of old and see: did ever any trust in the Lord and was confounded?" He searched the Bible for these comforting words, but they were not to be found. He asked his Christian friends concerning the words, but they too could not identify the source. About a year later he found the statement in Ecclesiasticus 2:10. "This at first," writes Bunyan, "did somewhat daunt me, because it was not in those texts that we call holy and canonical; yet as this sentence was the sum and substance of many of the promises, it was my duty to take the comfort of it. And I bless God for that word, for it was of good to me. That word doth still ofttimes shine before my face." Bunyan was wise enough to see that God was the source of all redemptive, moral truth, whether that truth was found in canonical or apocryphal books.

Both among Roman Catholics and Protestants there has been an increasing recognition of the difficulty in drawing a precise canonical line and forming a "hard" canon. John

Newman put the issue of the canon quite well when he wrote: "Providence never acts with harsh transitions, one thing melts into another. Day melts into night, summer into winter. So it is with His inspired Word. What is *divine* gradually resolves into what is human. Yet, as nevertheless summer and winter have for practical purposes a line of division, as St. Paul dissuaded the shipmen from sailing because the fast was already past and sailing dangerous, so we too for practical purposes are obliged to draw a line and say what is safe and sure to take as a canon for our faith, and what we cannot be sure will not mislead us. Without therefore, far from it, denying that God's supernatural hand is in the Apocrypha, yet knowing that it was not included in that Canon which Christ sanctions, and that his church has not spoken so clearly on the subject as to overcome the positive face of the argument deductible from this silence, therefore we do not see our way clear to receive it as canonical."[17] While acknowledging that the Hebrew Bible did not include the apocrypha, Newman still insists that God's "supernatural hand" was present in the production of these "outside books." This halfway or secondary status is clearly expressed in the Roman Catholic designation "deuterocanonical books." Burtchaell comments, "It is not unfair to say that some of our canonical books might have been omitted, or some of the apocrypha included, without altering the character of the collection noticeably."[18]

The Southern Presbyterian John Bright is convinced that the canon of the Hebrew Bible is the safest, and yet he is open to the ambiguity of determining the Old Testament canon. "The problem of the canon is a serious one," he acknowledges, "and perhaps an insuperable barrier to any unambiguous notion of biblical authority. But coming at the subject of authority as we have done, it seems to me

17. Jaak Seynaeve, *Cardinal Newman's Doctrine on Holy Scripture*, pp. 50*-51* in Appendices, "Newman Manuscripts on Holy Scripture," No. III, "On the Connection in Doctrine and Statement of the Books of the Apocrypha with the New Testament" (Anglican period-date unknown). Italics his.

18. *Catholic Theories of Biblical Inspiration Since 1810*, p. 301.

that the sting of the problem is removed. We have argued that the normative element in the Bible, though by no means to be abstracted from the verbal meaning of its texts, does not reside mechanically in certain books or certain texts *per se*, but in the structure of theology, the gospel, that undergirds the whole of the Bible and in one way or another informs, and expresses itself in, each of its texts. It is through its theology that the Bible speaks its authoritative word. Since we have in the writings universally accepted as canonical a wide enough field of evidence for determining what the normative theology both of the Old Testament and the New was, it little affects the problem whether further books are drawn in or not. The normative biblical theology having been established, the question of the deuterocanonical becomes less pressing. Thus, for example, if we were by some unthinkable accident to lose a minor prophet, or one of the pastoral epistles, we should be immeasurably poorer; but the total picture of the theology of the Old or the New Testament would not be seriously altered. On the other hand, were we to find in some yet undiscovered Qumran an authentic new minor prophet, or a new apostolic epistle, we should be enriched; but, again, the total picture of the Bible's theology would not be essentially changed. Indeed, the normative theology of the Bible, as derived from the books universally accepted as canonical, is precisely the standard by which any conceivable new candidate for canonicity would have to be judged. It is also the test of the value to the church of the 'disputed' writings. It is my own conviction that the Masoretic canon of the Old Testament and the accepted canon of the New cannot be improved upon. But add a book or two—and nothing essential is added; leave them off—and nothing essential is lost."[19]

Brevard S. Childs puts the matter succinctly, "The fundamental theological issue at stake is not the extent of the canon, which has remained in some flux within Christianity, but the claim for a normative body of tradition con-

19. *The Authority of the Old Testament*, pp. 158-159. Copyright © 1967 by Abingdon Press. Quotations from this book are used by permission of Abingdon Press.

tained in a set of books."[20] Childs gets to the heart of the issue of authority when he claims that "the canon marks the era in which the modern issues of life and death are defined in terms of what God had done and is doing, and what he demands as a response from his people."[21]

When the ultimate issues are seen from this perspective, ulcerating concern for the minutiae passes away. The message of the canon is too all-inclusive to be discounted by some incidental shortcomings of certain biblical details. The most pressing problem of Christians is not a correct view of inspiration but a correct method of interpreting the canon. The complexity of this process is indicated by the scholarly debate over the last twenty-five years concerning the relation of the New Testament to the Old and whether there is a "fuller sense" (*sensus plenior*) beyond the literal sense of the Old Testament. It is not within the purpose of this book to discuss this very interesting debate, but it can be noted that all of the participants share the common goal of trying to understand the message of the Christian canon as fully as possible. This is true because all of them believe that the canon is God's inspired word to humankind.

The precise refinements of a doctrine of inspiration lose their significance in the interpretive process. The best proof of this lies in the fact that the adherents of inerrancy vary considerably in their interpretation of key biblical issues. It would seem that if God was really so concerned about giving his word inerrantly in the autographs, he would be equally concerned to help biblical interpreters determine that inerrant meaning. This raises the issues of infallible interpretation and the authority of Scripture; therefore it is necessary to consider in some detail the theological and psychological ramifications of the doctrine of inerrancy.

20. *Biblical Theology in Crisis*, p. 99.
21. *Ibid.*, pp. 101-102.

Chapter Twelve

Inerrancy, Infallibility, and Authority

The terms "inerrant" and "infallible" have been used in a variety of ways and contexts. Within the Roman Catholic tradition "inerrant" is usually employed in discussions about the Bible, whereas "infallible" is reserved for consideration of the authority of the church, especially the teaching function of the pope or magisterium. In Protestant circles the authority of the church is not overtly associated with infallibility, and therefore attention is focused on the Bible. While "inerrant" seems to be the usual designation, a number of Protestant writers prefer "infallible." Whether applied to the Bible or the church, therefore, the essential meaning of each term is "freedom from error." But this claim immediately raises the issue of defining error.

Inerrancy and Sovereignty

In line with the syllogism of inerrancy noted earlier, the earliest understanding of error was any deviation from the absolute truth of God. The concern to protect God's honor is rooted, quite obviously, in the doctrine of divine sovereignty. It is no accident, then, that some of the most conservative Protestant scholars are bold to declare, "It is only the followers of Calvin who have a theology that fully fits in with this idea of Scripture."[1]

The sovereignty of God is a crucial doctrine, indeed, for if God is not sovereign, we as Christians are engaged in a hopeless struggle. Essentially, sovereignty means the authority and power to achieve a desired goal. Yet one can believe that God is going to achieve his purpose with mankind and still recognize that God is not restricted to one unalterable method in attaining this goal. Is the most sovereign God the one who must always act in a prescribed way because his nature permits no other, or is he the one who can work in a variety of ways in order that a greater purpose be achieved?

All Christians accept the truth of Numbers 23:19: "God is not man, that he should lie," but all of Scripture does not come under the category of primary revelation. Because God did not override some biblical writers in their use of erroneous sources does not mean that God is a liar. He can hardly be charged with the defects of the human instruments and their sources.

But the view of sovereignty held by some conservatives does not permit this distinction, and so they feel constrained to plead for God's honor in every detail. "Why insist on verbal inspiration," it is asked, "when no one can produce the documents that are to be regarded as thus inspired? . . . If the theory is true, then we would dishonor God if we held any other. Surely, we would not want to do that!"[2] But when the biblical data disprove this theory, how is God honored by it?

The fervor with which some Christians cling to this strict view of sovereignty is illustrated by the following statement: "God, we are being told, had to use the means

1. Van Til, "Introduction" to Warfield, *The Inspiration and Authority of the Bible*, p. 66.
2. Henry C. Thiessen, *An Introduction to the New Testament*, p. 80.

at his disposal. Those means were human beings. Therefore, when God revealed his Word, that Word, in passing through the media of human writers, acquired the characteristics of those writers, including their error, their ignorance, their crudities. Well may we exclaim at the poverty and weakness of such a God! If indeed man can thus thwart him, it is pertinent to ask, Is he really worth knowing after all?"[3] God did not have to use human beings—he chose to do so. In this choice God was showing anything but "poverty and weakness," and in no instance has man really thwarted God. In another context we read: "God has revealed to us his Word. What are we to think of him if this Word is glutted with little annoying inaccuracies? Why could not the omnipotent and omniscient God have taken the trouble to give us a Word that was free from error? Was it not a somewhat discourteous thing for him to have breathed forth from his mouth a message filled with mistakes? Of course, it was discourteous; it was downright rude and insulting. The present writer finds it difficult to have much respect for such a God."[4] Dare one say that God was "rude and insulting" when he determined to use human instrumentality in the giving, transmitting, and the translating of his revelation? This process was intended to honor both God and man. For the good of his ultimate goal God has accepted willingly the "little annoying inaccuracies" even though they plague some of those who love him and would defend his honor.

Concerning this doctrine of sovereignty, Llewelyn J. Evans comments: "God has not so poised the Rock of Ages that the Higher or Lower Criticism, with pickax or crowbar, digging out a chronological inaccuracy here, or prying off a historical contradiction there, is going to upset it. The critic may be all right, the crowbar may be all right, but the Rock of Ages is all right too, and it will stand fast forever. Do not, I beseech you, charge upon God the priggish precision which makes as much of a molehill as of

3. Edward J. Young, *Thy Word Is Truth*, p. 73.
4. *Ibid.*, p. 86.

a mountain. God does not care to be honored in that way."[5]

Inerrancy and Traditional Teachings

The theory of inerrancy is often characterized as the "high view of inspiration," the implication being that "high" means "best" or "true." Is one justified, however, in claiming more than Scripture does? Can there be in actuality a higher view than the biblical view? With respect to the danger of trying to prove too much, Paul K. Jewett acknowledges, "The theologian must never attempt to speak more plainly than God."[6] In more expanded form, James I. Packer affirms: "The humble pupil of Scripture will . . . not be so self-willed as, on the one hand, to build a speculative theological system which will say more about God than God has said about himself, or, on the other, to ignore or tone down what Scripture does say because he finds it hard to fit in with the rest of what he knows. His aim is to learn all that God teaches, and give it all its due place in his own thought. And he will never let himself suppose that now he has finished learning and knows everything; instead, he will keep listening to Scripture for further correction and instruction."[7]

Packer's sentiments are commendable, but he and his fellow inerrancists have so completely fused their emotions and sense of mission with their definition of God's honor that they find it impossible to admit an error when the evidence clearly points in that direction. In 1910 the great evangelical James Orr frankly admitted that the twenty-year reign assigned to Pekah was in error, and the evidence has grown stronger ever since. Rather than accept the clear-cut data, the inerrancists took refuge in the autographs. The error did not exist in the original text of 2

5. "Biblical Scholarship and Inspiration," *Inspiration and Inerrancy*, p. 70.

6. "Special Revelation as Historical and Personal," *Revelation and the Bible*, p. 52.

7. *"Fundamentalism" and the Word of God*, p. 129.

Kings 15:27, so it was claimed. It resulted from scribal activity. But the discussion in Chapter 8 has shown that this escape is impossible because the whole structure of chapters 15-18 involves the assumption of a twenty-year reign. This fact makes it just as impossible to get around the error by claiming that it was not the intent of the historian to claim a twenty-year reign. The alternate attempt of Kitchen and Mitchell to solve the problem by assuming a series of twelve-year coregencies is equally untenable.

In spite of the fact that all escape routes end in blind alleys, still there is no willingness to accept Orr's judgment. As late as 1971, Clark H. Pinnock of Trinity Evangelical Divinity School declared, "The supposedly 'incontrovertible' evidence for biblical errors is, upon careful scrutiny, not that at all. Without wishing to minimize any of them, we regard none as insuperable, and the whole collection of difficulties as unable to shake the strong basis for the verbal inspiration of Scripture. We are open to all facts and threatened by none; but, as Evangelicals, we are still unconvinced that the evidence has yet been fairly set forth which undermines belief in the total trustworthiness of the Bible."[8] In his chapter on the phenomena of Scripture he ignores the Pekah problem entirely, but had he considered it, still the evidence would not have been "insuperable." While admitting that "minor imperfections" in our present Bibles "do not obscure the message of Scripture," Pinnock feels constrained to add, "But unless we wish to blame God for man's mistakes, we have an obligation to try to show that these discrepancies are not original errors."[9] With this basic premise there is no possibility of honestly facing the evidence. The issue has been settled beforehand, and thus it is pious rhetoric to talk about "careful scrutiny" and being "open to all facts."

This reluctance to admit error is equally true of the Roman Catholic Church, but God's honor is more explicit-

8. *Biblical Revelation—The Foundation of Christian Theology*, p. 207.
9. *Ibid.*, p. 196.

ly associated with the human proponent of inerrancy by the dogma of papal infallibility. All externals aside, however, the mentality of the Protestant inerrancist is identical with the papal infallibilist. They are simply back to back at the opposite ends of the theological circle. The basic method of handling problems of infallibility has been, according to Hans Küng, "either it was not an error or—when at last and finally an error could no longer be denied, reinterpreted, rendered innocuous or belittled—it was not an infallible decision."[10]

A prime example is the case of Honorius I, the pope in Rome from 625 to 638. Whereas the Council of Ephesus (431) had decreed that Jesus was one in person, the Council of Chalcedon (451) had declared that Jesus was two in nature. In time, however, there arose a debate as to whether Jesus had just "one will" (*monotheletism*), or "two wills" (*diotheletism*). Emperor Heraclius tried to reconcile the two views by suggesting that Christ carried out his redemptive work by using one divine-human will. Honorius was asked concerning the orthodoxy of this view, and in his letter of reply he used the expression "one will," presumably giving his support. Both the pope and his letter were declared heretical by the Third Council of Constantinople (680) and several subsequent popes. The ruse to get around the problem of the errant pope has been to declare that he did not promulgate the decree *ex cathedra*, and therefore he was not speaking infallibly. The same evasiveness appeared in attempts to explain why Photius (*c.* 820-892), the patriarch of Constantinople, was condemned by the Fourth Council of Constantinople (869) and then recognized by Pope John VIII in a synodical council held in 879-880, but without withdrawing the previous action.

About 1,100 years late, Paul VI officially withdrew the condemnation of Photius, but admission of this ancient error could be tolerated because Rome had never recognized the rescinding synodical council as an ecumenical council. It was a different story, however, when Paul had

10. *Infallible? An Inquiry*, pp. 32-33.

to reckon with the thorny issue raised by *Casti Connubi*, Pius XI's encyclical of 1930 prohibiting contraception. He called in experts on the problem and sincerely expressed his desire to seek the most objective answer to the problem. However, in his encyclical *Humanae Vitae* (1968) he reversed the consensus of his technical advisors. Küng has put his finger on the "neuralgic point: the question of *error* in the traditional teaching of the Church and of the most recent popes."[11] "It is quite clear," Küng comments, "the permissibility of contraception could have been conceded only under the one condition completely unacceptable to Pope and Curia, of disavowing the traditional teaching of the Church and particularly of the last three popes, of admitting an error in this teaching of the Church."[12] It is equally evident, moreover, that the papal infallibilists, like the Protestant inerrancists, are so involved with their dogmas that there is no *real* chance for the evidence to speak objectively on its own merit—the issue has already been decided emotionally.

Humanae Vitae illustrates in a very clear-cut manner the subtlety of defining when a teaching is infallible. Paul did not desire to define his encyclical *ex cathedra*, but he presented it as "the teaching of Christ" with the hope that the faithful would abide by it. When some Roman Catholics concluded that the decree was not infallible, and thus not binding, because it was not defined *ex cathedra*, Cardinal Felici countered with a newspaper article in which he reminded his readers that "a truth can be sure and certain and therefore binding, even without the charism of an *ex cathedra* definition."[13]

Inerrancy and Papal Infallibility

Starting from the sound assumption that "no ecclesiastical tradition may be accepted without examination, but must be judged critically in the light of the original Chris-

11. *Ibid.*, p. 50.
12. *Ibid.*, pp. 50-51.
13. *Ibid.*, p. 61.

tian message,"[14] Küng summarizes the evidence for papal infallibility:

> that the text of Matthew 16:18f., so important for the modern Roman pontiffs, which now adorns St. Peter's Basilica in large black letters on a gold background, does not occur on a single occasion in its full wording in the whole Christian literature of the first couple of centuries; that the text is quoted for the first time in the second century, by Tertullian, and then not with reference to Rome, but to Peter; that only in the middle of the third century did a bishop of Rome—Stephen II, an early type of Roman authoritarianism, making use particularly of excommunication, who calumniated the great Cyprian as pseudo-apostle and pseudo-Christian— claim the better tradition by appealing to the preeminence of Peter; but that only from the fourth century onward was Matthew 16:18f. used (particularly by the Roman pontiffs, Damasus and Leo) to support a claim to primacy, and even then without any formal claim to infallibility. And finally, in all Eastern exegesis of Matthew 16:18 until into the eighth century and beyond, it was considered at best as a reference to Peter's personal primacy, without any serious thought of a Roman primacy. And, with reference to Matthew 16:18 or Luke 22:32, neither in East nor West is there ever a claim raised for the infallibility of the Roman pontiff.[15]

Leo I (400-461) became pope of the Roman Church in 440. He was the first pontiff to assume the title Pontifex Maximus, previously the designation for the pagan high priest, and he tried to have the ecumenical Council of Chalcedon (451) subordinated to him. While the Council did accept his teaching concerning the two natures of Christ, it showed its disdain for Leo's ambitions by granting equal supremacy to the patriarch of Constantinople as head of the Eastern Church. To make the counterclaim even more forceful the Council conferred (Canon 28) the same civic authority on Constantinople (New-Rome) as it did on Old-Rome. The Roman Church, of course, has

14. *Ibid.*, p. 112.
15. *Ibid.*, p. 111.

never been very keen to recognize such non-Roman tradition. As Küng observes in a note, "Heinrich Denzinger, otherwise painfully exact in nosing out quotations for primacy and infallibility from documents which are often of very secondary importance, passes over in silence as in so many cases also this canon of an ecumenical council which does not fit into his system."[16]

On the other hand, documents in Rome ascribe great authority to the teaching office and disciplinary power of the early popes. Pope Lucius, a contemporary of Cyprian (*c.* 200-258), the bishop of Carthage, is reported to have called the Roman Church "Mother of all the Churches of Christ" and then claimed that she had never erred. Thomas Aquinas accepted these sources, and so, because of his towering stature as a scholar, he became the basis for the Roman doctrine of papal infallibility. Unfortunately, for Aquinas and the Roman Church, the sources have proven to be spurious. Küng explains, "The monstrous forgeries of the Pseudo-Isidore Decretals of the ninth century (115 wholly forged documents of the bishops of Rome from the first centuries, from Clement of Rome onward; 125 documents with interpolations) were now employed to buttress the claim of the teaching authority of the pope. These forgeries destroyed all sense of the historical development of institutions and created the impression that the Church in the earliest times had already been ruled in detail by papal decrees: an image of the Church and law of the Church that appears to be concentrated wholly on the Roman authority."[17]

In short, there was no sound biblical or traditional basis for the promulgation of *Pastor aeternus* in 1870, but there were a number of forces that combined to bring it about: the threat to theology posed by liberalism; the threat to Roman supremacy, especially from France and Germany; a widespread frustration over the confusion of the post-Napoleonic period and a yearning for political-religious

16. *Ibid.*, p. 121.
17. *Ibid.*, p. 115.

stability; an increase in the veneration of the pope; and most crucially, the pressure brought to bear by Pius IX himself.

Küng characterizes Pius IX as "a philanthropic, very eloquent, strongly radiant personality, but dangerously emotional, superficially trained in theology, and completely unfamiliar with modern scientific methods, badly advised moreover by zealous but mediocre, unrealistic and dogmatically minded associates."[18]   Pius was convinced that he was God's answer to the satanic threats of the time. "It is only in the light of this basic attitude," explains Küng, "that the pope's desire for a dogmatic definition of his own primacy and infallibility can be understood. Only in the light of the veneration offered to him as pope can it be understood how far a definition of infallibility struck a favorable response on the part of large circles of clergy and people, and how far the process of indoctrination and administrative centralization within the Church, rapidly and systematically urged on by Rome after some initial nervous hesitation, no longer met with opposition."[19]

Bishop Francis Simons, the courageous Dutch churchman, is very perceptive when he observes, "Tradition, education, mental conditioning, play a trick on us. It makes it possible for whole societies to accept as quite probable, as not at all difficult to believe, as 'demonstrated' on only the flimsiest grounds, propositions which to the non-conditioned person appear utterly unlikely or fantastic."[20]   The roles of Rome and the pope are well expressed by the French scholar Yves Congar, "The teaching authority explicitly acknowledged in the pope is more of a religious quality which Rome owes to the fact that it is the place of the martyrdom and the grave of Peter and Paul. Peter is the faith, Paul the preacher of the faith."[21]

18. *Ibid.*, p. 92.
19. *Ibid.*, p. 93.
20. *Infallibility and the Evidence*, p. 76.
21. *L'Ecclésiologie du Haut Moyan Age. De Saint Grégoire le Grand à la désunion entre Byzance et Rome*, 1968, p. 159.

Infallibility and the Marian Dogmas

As noted in Chapter 5, Pius IX proclaimed in 1854 the dogma of the Immaculate Conception of the Virgin Mary. The justification for the decree was the widespread desire of Roman Catholics for a definition of the teaching. Pius referred also to the effective explanation of the doctrine by "eminent theologians." In response to another ground swell of opinion, Pius XII continued the doctrinal development by declaring in 1950 the dogma of the Assumption of the Virgin Mary. Of all the papal decrees, these two are most clearly recognized as having been defined *ex cathedra*, and thus infallible.

But there was a minority of theologians who contended that the theory of the Assumption of Mary should not have been defined as a dogma of faith because it was impossible to trace the doctrine back to the apostolic age. Gabriel Moran states quite frankly, "The Pope, it would seem, did not proceed from the historical evidence of the first Christian centuries but worked according to a regressive method from the consensus of belief of the Church to the necessity of the doctrine in revelation."[22] This fact occasioned a discussion of the question about doctrinal development, but the theory of nonbiblical revelation prevailed. Vatican II, following Vatican I very closely, declared, "This infallibility with which the divine Redeemer willed His Church to be endowed in defining a doctrine of faith and morals extends as far as extends the deposit of divine revelation, which must be religiously guarded and faithfully expounded."[23]

In discussing the meaning of "faithfully expounded," Küng states, "The Roman teaching office seems to be permitted to explicate 'authentically' and—as in the case of the two new Marian dogmas—even to define infallibly all kinds of things on which not a word was said either in Scripture or in early tradition."[24] The irony of this development is most incisively expressed by Burtchaell, "In

22. *Scripture and Tradition*, p. 22.
23. *The Documents of Vatican II*, p. 48.
24. *Infallible? An Inquiry*, p. 74.

fact, there has been some schizoid behavior about the Bible. At the very time when Catholic theologians were making their strongest statements in favor of the Bible's authority and inerrancy, they were most neglectful of it when actually building their theological treatises. Scripture was being apotheosized as peerless among the monuments of the Judeo-Christian past; however, it was the one monument of which Catholic divines seemingly felt they could most safely be ignorant."[25]

Inerrancy, Infallibility, and Doctrine

The avowed purpose of the Roman Catholic doctrines of an inerrant Bible and an infallible pope has been to guarantee true doctrine. Conservative Protestants also claim that the doctrine of inerrancy is necessary to prevent the erosion of doctrine. Pinnock, for example, declares, "What is lost in admitting errors in Scripture is *not* necessarily the truth or efficacy of the revelation it contains (though it discredits it), but rather the consistency and stability of the theology which concedes them. The result of denying inerrancy, as skeptics well know, is the loss of a trustworthy Bible. Limited inerrancy is a slope, not a platform."[26] According to this argument, if the doctrine of inerrancy is given up, confidence in the biblical writers as trustworthy witnesses to doctrine is undermined. If they prove to be wrong in their claim of inerrancy, where are they trustworthy? But this line of reasoning is nothing more than "False in one, false in all" applied to the area of doctrine. There are other options than the either-or presented by this argument.

Take, for example, the problem of Jesus' view of inspiration. We have seen how he and the New Testament writers referred, either explicitly or implicitly, to the manuscripts of the Old Testament current in their day. These were errant, as all are compelled to admit, so the dilemma

25. *Catholic Theories of Biblical Inspiration Since 1810*, p. 286.
26. *Biblical Revelation—The Foundation of Christian Theology*, p. 80. Italics his.

arises. We are told that we must believe either (1) that Jesus taught inerrancy, or (2) that he was fanatical or dishonest. But all of this stems from the assumption that Jesus taught inerrancy. If he believed what the doctrine of inerrancy claims for him, then he was indeed fanatical or dishonest because he did support his theory in practice.

But why must one start with the assumption of inerrancy? The inductive evidence of the New Testament indicates that Jesus taught a strong doctrine of inspiration and authority of Scripture, yet without claiming inerrancy. Once this is recognized, there is no need to discredit Jesus by considering him either a fanatic or a liar.

The threat that denial of inerrancy supposedly poses for doctrine is also expressed in the equation: fallible history = fallible doctrine. It is nonsense, so it is claimed, to speak of fallible history in the Bible and then affirm that it has infallible doctrine. Accordingly, since the Christian faith is rooted in history, it is necessary to contend for inerrancy both in history and in doctrine. The writer has no quarrel on the issue of history's being vital to faith. As noted previously, facts and faith are complementary and mutually dependent. But minor historical errors in Scripture invalidate neither our faith nor true doctrine. This leads us, therefore, to consider whether proven historical errors mean that Scripture also contains some fallible elements in doctrine.

One of the important passages in the New Testament is Jesus' discourse on the Mount of Olives (Matt. 24:1-42; Mark 13; Luke 21:5-36). Concerning the buildings of the temple area, Jesus said, "Truly, I say to you, there will not be left here one stone upon another, that will not be thrown down." According to Mark and Luke the disciples inquire as to when "these things" will happen. Their question seems to refer to the destruction of Jerusalem. Luke makes this explicit, for in 21:20 we read, "But when you see Jerusalem surrounded by armies, then know that its desolation has come near." Luke 21:24 also states, "And Jerusalem will be trodden down by the Gentiles, until the times of the Gentiles are fulfilled."

In Matthew 24:3, however, the disciples are reported as

saying, "Tell us, when will this be, and what will be the sign of your coming and of the close of the age?" Matthew 24:14 makes reference to the "end," and in 24:27 "the coming of the Son of man" is likened to "lightning." Accordingly, Matthew's account implies that the disciples related Christ's second coming and the close of the age to the destruction of the temple. Moreover, in a discussion about the tribulations that were to come, Mark 13:10 notes, "And the gospel must first be preached to all nations." Thus Matthew and Mark bring in matters that clearly refer to Christ's second coming.

Yet after the parable of the fig tree Jesus is reported as saying, "Truly, I say to you, this generation will not pass away till all these things take place." With the exception that Luke omits "these," the text of this verse is identical in all three Gospels. There would be no problem here if the passage referred only to the destruction of Jerusalem in A.D. 70, but what is one to do with the preceding and following verses, which refer clearly to Christ's second coming? The normal way out of the difficulty for conservatives has been to reinterpret the Greek word *genea* ("generation") as meaning something else than the people living in Jesus' day. Some have interpreted "this generation" as referring to the generation that was to see the signs at the close of the age. Others have felt that the expression refers to the unconverted world (for example, Paul's reference to the "perverse generation" in Phil. 2:15). Still others, interpreting "generation" to mean "race," have inferred that Jesus was referring to the Jews.

While these interpretations may answer the problem for some twentieth-century Christians, none of them takes into account the difficulty that the disciples faced. In this same discourse Jesus warns them about being led astray by "false Christs and false prophets." Matthew 24:36 has the additional warning, "But of that day and hour no one knows, not even the angels of heaven, nor the Son, but the Father only." This statement would seem to imply a longer period of waiting, yet there is plenty of biblical evidence to show that the early church expected Christ to return in its day. Would Christ speak to his disciples in such ambiguous terms that they would interpret *genea* literally while he had some hidden meaning whereby he was allowing for many centuries before his return? Is it not more likely that the disciples confused some of Jesus' statements about the destruction of Jerusalem with some of his remarks about his second coming? But whether the difficulty lay in the original statement of Jesus or the interpretation of the disciples, it certainly existed in the original copies of the Gospels. Although it is difficult to give conclusive proof of contradiction, some of the verses noted in the three Gospels were in all likelihood inserted out of context, and, accordingly, they constitute erroneous elements of doctrine.

Christ's personal return is clearly taught in the New Testament, yet this fact hardly necessitates the view that the biblical writers saw eye to eye in all the doctrinal details related to eschatology. The conservative assumption has been that every bit of evidence having anything to do with "end times" has its place in some vast eschatological chart that, not unlike a jigsaw puzzle, was revealed by God to the biblical writers piece by piece. The task of the interpreter, according to this view, is to correlate all the scriptural references to "that day," "the day of the Lord," "the day of judgment," *parousia, apocalypse, epiphany,* and *millennium,* with the expectation that the true picture will emerge when all the pieces have been correctly placed. Is it not a significant fact that all the brains and ingenuity of Christianity have been frustrated in this attempt to get a unified, clear picture? Is there not something wrong in the exchange of charge and countercharge where each interpretation claims the personal aid of the Holy Spirit in arriving at the so-called "biblical doctrine of eschatology"?

This apparent diversity of doctrinal data is also evident in other areas of theology, for example, the atonement of Christ. There are many views, but none of them incorporates all the biblical evidence in its systematic formulation. The clear meaning of some passages does not fit in with the clear meaning of others. Christian theologians have worked diligently and long in attempts to arrange all the contents of Scripture, God's seedplot of objective truth, into one consistent pattern, but no system of theology has achieved this goal. The usual explanation is that the biblical diversity is not really contradiction, but paradox (apparent contradiction), and that someday when our mortal minds put on immortality we will have the answers to all the difficulties in Scripture. Can we, however, really attribute all our problems to faulty interpretation? Is it not equally possible that details of doctrine tend to get fuzzy as one nears the fringes of truth?

This does not mean, on the other hand, that the biblical writers are not trustworthy guides in the area of doctrine. The claim that one error in doctrine undercuts the whole basis for any assurance in doctrine is not valid. We can be sure that the biblical writers were just as consistent and accurate in the realms of faith, morals, and doctrine as they were in the area of history.

But this fact leads eventually to the question, "What is to be the standard for determining trustworthy and authoritative doctrine?" According to the New Testament writers, Christ and the gospel are determinative. To those who doubted that deity would ever have come in the form of human flesh John declared, "By this you know the Spirit of God: every spirit which confesses that Jesus Christ has come in the flesh is of God, and every spirit which does not confess Jesus is not of God" (1 John 4:2-3). The denial of the incarnation was "the spirit of antichrist." To the Corinthians who doubted the resurrection of the dead Paul affirmed, "If Christ has not been raised, then our preaching is in vain and your faith is in vain" (1 Cor. 15:14). The biblical writers shared unequivocally some doctrines that cluster around Jesus, the incarnate Christ, and the way of salvation.

This is evident from the preaching of the apostles in the Acts and Paul's declaration in Galatians 1:6-9: "I am astonished that you are so quickly deserting him who called you in the grace of Christ and turning to a different gospel—not that there is another gospel, but there are some who trouble you and want to pervert the gospel of Christ. But even if we, or an angel from heaven, should preach to you a gospel contrary to that which we preached to you, let him be accursed. As we have said before, so now I say again, If any one is preaching to you a gospel contrary to that which you received, let him be accursed." For most Christians today the kerygma ("preaching, proclamation") of the New Testament writers concerning the "gospel of Christ" is still the authoritative standard for doctrinal formulations. The time-honored Apostles' Creed, which contains most of the kerygma, continues to be repeated as a summary of the essential doctrines of the Christian faith.

But when the biblical writers move away from basic doctrinal statements and attempt to delineate some details of these doctrines, there is generally less uniformity of teaching. The valid procedure, so it would appear, is to accept the pluralism of biblical doctrine and then to determine which views most nearly accord with the basic teaching found throughout Scripture.

Errancy and "Drawing the Line"

The recognition that both biblical history and doctrine are a mixture of truth with some error is being admitted increasingly within Roman Catholic circles. Küng, for example, puts the issue squarely, "If a theology, if a Church, does not take seriously this dialectic of truth and error, then it is inevitably on the way from dogma to dogmatism."[27] An excellent case in point is Pinnock's claim that the admission of errancy "has the effect of leaving us with a Bible which is a compound of truth and error; with no one to tell us which is which. What is lost when errors are admitted is divine *truthfulness*. Evangelicals confess inerrancy because it is biblical to do so. The critic who pontificates on 'errors' in Scripture, which we regard simply as 'difficulties,' has usurped for himself the infallibility which he has denied the Bible."[28]

But the infallibility of the Bible is his interpretation of the Bible, his preconception of what the Bible has to teach, and his judgment, in spite of all the evidence, that

27. *Infallible? An Inquiry*, p. 172.
28. *Biblical Revelation—The Foundation of Christian Theology*, pp. 80-81.

the "difficulties" will be resolved in his favor. This line of reasoning is essentially that of the papists. Simons recognizes the danger in his church and he states correctly, "By her claim to infallibility the Church ruled out in advance all evidence contrary to her dogmas as invalid and inadmissible."[29] This is precisely what Pinnock and his fellow inerrancists do. Moreover, they plead for inerrancy on the grounds that without the doctrine they would not know how to separate truth from error. It is not an easy task, but this is what the inerrancists have to do every day of their lives, their theory notwithstanding. The very situation they fear theoretically and lament over is actually what faces them every time they read their Bibles seriously. The doctrine of inerrancy has to do with the autographs, and since those who hold to the doctrine do not have them, they are as dependent on extant Scriptures as are those who reject the doctrine of inerrancy.

All Christians readily acknowledge that the present manuscripts include some errors. One can say that he believes every word of extant Scripture, but this affirmation does not make every word true. One may think the crisis has been eluded by withholding judgment on many questions or by putting these problems in a "mystery bag," but by this very act one has removed portions of Scripture from the category of indubitable, applicable truth. Whether one realizes it or not, or whether one tries to rationalize the issue or not, everyone who believes in the validity and indispensability of Scripture is confronted with the inescapable duty of being open to the presence of some mistaken elements in Scripture. But this does not mean that one comes to the Bible with a negative, pessimistic attitude that expects to find the pages swarming with mistakes. The essential trustworthiness of the Bible is a fact, and anyone who has experienced the regenerating power of Christ comes to Scripture with the assurance that it "has the words of eternal life." Where new evidence proves that some statement of God's Word is inaccurate, one can readily accept the fact knowing that the essential truths

29. *Infallibility and the Evidence*, p. 119.

will not be altered. In the United States, with its Christian heritage, the individual is innocent until proved guilty. This is no less true of Scripture.

The problem of "drawing the line" between truth and error is excellently presented in the following statement by Llewelyn Evans:

> The Bible is a pneumatic (spiritual) Book. The ground-work, the substance, all that makes the Book what it is, is pneumatic. The warp and woof of it is pneuma. Its fringes run off, as was inevitable, into the secular, the material, the psychic. Can we not, as persons of common intelligence even, much more with the internal witness of the Spirit to aid us, discriminate between the fringe and the warp and woof? Do not the "spiritualities" and the "heavenlinesses" of Scripture distinguish themselves from all that is lower, as the steady shining of the everlasting stars from the fitful gleaming of earth's fireflies? Even if the task of discriminating were immeasurably harder than it is, we should not complain. God lays on us in many matters, in matters, too, of great practical moment, the responsibility of separating the things that differ. "Why even of yourselves judge ye not what is right?" (Luke 12:57.) This responsibility is a part of life's discipline. It is not God's way to do all our thinking for us.[30]

In a similar vein Simons notes, "There is no virtue or sense in faithfulness to tradition as such. Tradition passes on good and bad, truth and error, and efficient and wasteful, graceful and ugly, ways of doing things. Tradition cannot spare us the effort of sifting what is true from what is false or of finding more effective tools for today's tasks and needs."[31] It is evident from the New Testament, with its varying emphases and traditions, that the same problem confronted the early Christians even though they had the Old Testament as their Bible. As noted in Chapter 4, there were a number of traditions in Israel's history, and even there it was necessary to sift the true from the partial

30. "Biblical Scholarship and Inspiration," *Inspiration and Inerrancy*, pp. 81-82.
31. *Infallibility and the Evidence*, p. 105.

truths or errors. If the history of God's people is any indication of reality, there has never been a time when truth was isolated in absolute purity.

This fact is equally evident when Scripture is seen from a linguistic point of view. Doctrines are theological propositions, and like all other propositions they suffer from ambiguity and failure to express precisely what is intended. As Küng notes, "Propositions are prone both to double meaning and also to nonsense, both to confusion and to error."[32]

Inerrancy and Security

Notwithstanding the evidence that has been presented, some concerns of those who cherish the doctrine of inerrancy have not yet been answered satisfactorily. One of these has to do with the proverbial "camel." If one error is admitted, then the camel gets his nose in the tent, and soon there is more of him, and finally he occupies the whole tent. This is a genuine fear for many Christians. While history teaches us the validity of concern at this point, it also shows us that this is only one side of the danger.

Too often the person who believes in inerrancy forgets that his personal experience is beset with many temptations and pitfalls. He needs to be reminded that the closer one comes in fellowship with God the more subtle the temptations become. There is no security outside of daily commitment of oneself as a living sacrifice to God. Creeds cannot protect. The one who holds to inerrancy is in as grave danger as the person who rejects the doctrine.

It is also quite futile to talk of "running from evil." We need to recognize that wherever the genuine is, the counterfeit will be found too. In the doctrine of the Trinity, for example, truth and error are separated only by a fine line. If one runs from the error, one is also running from the truth. This is so in all of our spiritual experience. The Christian life is difficult and requires the wisdom and

32. *Infallible? An Inquiry*, p. 169.

strength of the Holy Spirit. Only in this way can the church maintain its integrity. It must seek the truth, and yet while doing so, it will constantly be in danger of evil. How grateful we should be, then, for the biblical assurance that one can be in the world of evil and yet not of it.

In the eternal quest for security in the Christian life, the usual warning is, "Stay on the right-hand side of the road." This is no solution to the problem either, for as Bernard Ramm points out, "We can sin to the right as well as to the left."[33] This possibility has not come into the consciousness of many Christians, and as a result they tend to be left-eyed. While seeing the dangers on their left hand, they are oblivious to equal or greater dangers on the right. In the area of doctrine a person can postulate too much. The history of theology is replete with examples of "superbelief," a creed beyond that set forth by Scripture. As noted earlier, however, one is hardly honoring God by believing things of him or his will that are not true.

Inerrancy and Apostasy

A major contention of those who hold to inerrancy is that once a person leaves the security of inerrancy he will eventually swing to the opposite side and become an extreme liberal. There have been numerous examples of this transition during the last century or so. In fact, some of the most radical liberals have been men who have had evangelical background and convictions, but because of the rigidity with which they were restrained previously they reacted violently when confronted in college or university with the other side of the problems. This was to be expected, of course, since in the early stages of the struggle between traditionalism and liberalism the alternatives consisted mainly of the two extremes. But during the last fifty years the pendulum has settled down and there has emerged a mediating attitude toward Scripture and theology.

When Pinnock claims that "limited inerrancy is a slope,

33. *The Christian View of Science and Scripture*, p. 29.

not a platform," the implication is that those who deny inerrancy will continue to slide down the slope. The usual analogy is a peaked roof, in the which the inerrancists see themselves as sitting astride the peak while all others are sliding off the roof. In fact, however, the roof is cleated with data so that there are numerous toeholds to prevent a fall. This is fortunate for everyone because it is unlikely that anyone is perfectly balanced on the peak. In any case, many Christians, recognizing the untenable nature of the theory of inerrancy, have maintained a warm vital faith with deep concern for Scripture. The person who claims that history proves "loss of inerrancy = extreme liberalism" has not investigated all the evidence.

Inerrancy as Protection

A clear verdict of history, on the other hand, is the futility of man's attempt to protect himself and his doctrine. Every attempt has failed sooner or later. The Jewish rabbis said, "Make a fence around the Torah." In order to protect the law of Moses they elaborated hundreds of rules to alert an individual before he could break the law. Yet a zealot like Saul of Tarsus was not prevented from breaking the law.

Roman Catholicism erected a similar defensive system when it declared that the "deposit of divine revelation" was to be "religiously guarded" by the hierarchy. These words imply, according to Küng, "that the object of infallible authority includes truths which form a safeguard for the deposit of revelation strictly speaking, even though these truths are not formally revealed (implicitly or explicitly)."[34] But here, as in Judaism, the safeguarding truths did not really protect. In fact, they often served as barriers to effectual implementation of God's will. As Simons puts it, "Infallibility has not succeeded in saving the Church, its popes, bishops, and other members, from error and ignorance."[35]

34. *Infallible? An Inquiry*, p. 74.
35. *Infallibility and the Evidence*, p. 89.

There is no absolute protection against doctrinal deviation. God has not deemed such rigid precautions necessary. Even in the Garden of Eden, with his whole creative plan at stake, God put no other barrier between Adam and Eve and "the tree of the knowledge of good and evil" than his personal prohibition. God took the greatest risk possible.

The only protection God has provided is the Holy Spirit's working dynamically in a committed heart, mind, and body. This is sufficient protection for salvation, but it is still not certain protection against false doctrine. Take, for example, the case of Philip Mauro. As a converted lawyer he devoted his talents to the cause of Christ. He was one of the writers in *The Fundamentals*, the series of twelve volumes published from 1909 to 1911. By 1913 he went into print favoring dispensationalism and the pretribulation rapture of the church. Fifteen years later he published *The Gospel of the Kingdom*, in which he repudiated all his dispensational views. As George E. Ladd observes, "Among the reasons was the sudden realization that the Scofield Bible 'has usurped the place of authority that belongs to God's Bible alone.' "[36] Ladd quotes Mauro further as saying: "It is mortifying to remember that I not only held and taught these novelties myself, but that I even enjoyed a complacent sense of superiority because thereof, and regarded with feelings of pity and contempt those who had not received the 'new light' and were unacquainted with this up-to-date method of 'rightly dividing the word of truth.' ... The time came ... when the inconsistencies and self-contradictions of the system itself, and above all, the impossibility of reconciling its main positions with the plain statement of the Word of God, became so glaringly evident that I could not do otherwise than to renounce it."[37] Neither Mauro's view of inspiration nor the presence of the Holy Spirit in his life protected him from the doctrine that necessitated his "mortifying" experience.

36. *The Blessed Hope*, p. 53.
37. *Ibid.*

Inerrancy as a Barrier

From beginning to end, history warns us that theological Maginot lines or fences fail to achieve their purpose. Not only do they fail to protect, but they also *restrict* the outreach of the truth being guarded. This is the ultimate tragedy of all legalism.

The Jews had erected a fence between themselves and the Gentiles. Paul tells us that Jesus made the two groups one by breaking down "the dividing wall of hostility" (Eph. 2:14). The power of the resurrected Christ has also made unnecessary any man-made defenses of the gospel.

Notwithstanding all the history to the contrary, still the doctrine of inerrancy is cherished as a protection. In his plea to those who made such a claim, Evans said: "You protest against the unsettling of faith. You do well. But they also do well who protest against keeping up needless barriers to faith."[38] It is not the purpose of this book to unsettle the faith of any Christian, but the risk must be taken in order to remove the "needless barrier" that has kept many more from exercising faith in Christ. The younger generation is alert, and in certain areas it is far more advanced for its years than was the older generation. From grade school through university young folks are acquainted with many areas of knowledge and learn to use their human reason inductively.

Yet in the last half century the primary emphasis of many groups working with high school and college students has been the inerrancy of the Bible. This was thought to be the one weapon capable of refuting the widespread belief in the doctrine of evolution. The sign of a Christian was one's courage to contest the views of the science teacher. Since "False in one, false in all" had become the slogan, one dare not admit one error in Scripture or the agnostic college student would go so far as to deny the resurrection. But for all his doubting spirit, even the sincere agnostic knew the difference between minor

38. "Biblical Scholarship and Inspiration," *Inspiration and Inerrancy*, p. 86.

details and key events or teachings in Scripture. Yet to test the Christians, and in some cases to bait them, the agnostics made much of the errors they could find, all the while claiming that because Scripture was false at one point it was false everywhere. When tradition accepted this dogma it was hopelessly on the defensive. Far too often "the sons of this world are wiser in their own generation than the sons of light" (Luke 16:8).

The higher and the more rigid Christians build their fences, however, the less the real gospel gets out. Doubters are seldom inclined to have an open mind to accept any of the positive message because they see that these Christians are not being completely honest in the problem areas. Honesty, after all, is a two-way street. Those being evangelized expect Christians to present the truth all the way down the line, but when the defenders of truth fail to acknowledge the facts in areas where they can be checked, then their hearers are usually alienated.

The harm resulting from such an attitude is a great burden to Hans Küng: "And yet (would it help the Church to pass over this in silence?) it can no longer be ignored that, contrary to the best intentions of the Pope and his advisers, the longer the teaching office is exercised by pope and Curia, the more it is exercised in a way which—as previously in Church history, and from Rome—inflicts the worst damage on the unity and credibility of the Catholic Church."[39] Simons shares the same concern: "It seems we deceive ourselves if we think that the other Christians will ever accept our positions on infallibility and papal power. Our case appears just not good enough. But on the basis of the gospels we can unite. If we are wrong in our claims, then we are the insurmountable obstacle to Christian unity, and we cannot simply go on in order not to disturb the peace. A true and lasting peace can be established only on the basis of manifest truth, the truth that will make us free."[40]

Ultimately all fence-building results from fear. When we

---

39. *Infallible? An Inquiry*, p. 15.
40. *Infallibility and the Evidence*, p. 120.

lose our confidence in God and his power, we go on the defensive. Instead of stressing the many portions of clear, positive teaching in Scripture, and backing up this teaching with a convincing personal witness in word and deed, we tend to save face by shoring up our weak foundations. On the other hand, when we are alive with the dynamic of Christ we are on the move. In the spiritual realm, as in the military, the best defense is a powerful offense. Or as John expressed it, "The light shines in the darkness, and the darkness has not overcome it" (John 1:5). Jesus, the Light of the world, said that his followers were to be the "light of the world" (Matt. 5:14), and that light, even though reflected, is intended to dispel the darkness.

Inerrancy and the Incarnation

Another prominent argument for inerrancy stems from the analogy of Scripture to Christ. Just as the Incarnate Word was human and yet sinless, so the Written Word, coming through human channels, is errorless. Warfield, for example, accepts this conclusion, but he does so with some reservations. He declares: "But the analogy with our Lord's Divine-human personality may easily be pressed beyond reason. There is no hypostatic union between the Divine and the human in Scripture; we cannot parallel the 'inscripturation' of the Holy Spirit and the incarnation of the Son of God. The Scriptures are merely the product of Divine and human forces working together to produce a product in the production of which the human forces work under the initiation and prevalent direction of the Divine: the person of our Lord unites in itself Divine and human natures, each of which retains its distinctness while operating only in relation to the other. Between such diverse things there can exist only a remote analogy; and, in point of fact, the analogy in the present instance amounts to no more than that in both cases Divine and human factors are involved, though very differently. In the one they unite to constitute a Divine-human person, in the other they cooperate to perform a Divine-human work."[41]

41. *The Inspiration and Authority of the Bible*, p. 162.

It is precisely this unique, once-only union of the human and the divine in Christ which makes it different from the blending of divine and human elements in Scripture. The crucial fault in the analogy is most clearly expressed by Vawter, "The attempt to set up a parity between written word and Incarnate Word whereby the sinlessness of the latter seemed to require the inerrancy of the former was never really valid. Sin is in man a disorder that error is not. Lying and deceit are the proper correlatives in the equation, just as the correlative of an inerrant written word would have been an Incarnate Word who could neither suffer nor die."[42]

Furthermore, language, as we have seen, cannot completely express or contain all the factors in human personality. How much less can it do so with the wider scope of divine personality! Paul did not, and most certainly would not, say that "the whole fullness of deity dwells" in the Written Word. Somehow, and this is a mystery too, human personality is capable of expressing more of deity than is human language. For this reason also the rigid analogy between Christ and the Bible breaks down. One can hold to a belief in the sinlessness of Christ and still accept Scripture as being fallible in minor details.

The fear implicit in the various objections to admitting some error, both historical and doctrinal, is unwarranted. God is still working through the Holy Spirit to give conviction concerning the truth of his Written Word. It is a trustworthy record of God's teaching (doctrine), and therefore, as Paul informs us, it will always be profitable for teaching. In the basic matters that are repeated time and again, and which are woven throughout the Bible, one can speak with assurance, but once the Christian interpreter leaves the central path of doctrine he must be less dogmatic because the fringes shade off. In brief, then, the sovereignty of God, the honor of Jesus Christ, and the trustworthiness of biblical doctrine are not at stake in accepting a view of inspiration that rejects the qualification of inerrancy.

42. *Biblical Inspiration*, p. 169.

Inerrancy and Salvation

The doctrine of inspiration has loomed so large and taken up so much of the thought of certain groups within Protestantism during the last century that it has tended to become the pivotal doctrine of the gospel. In many quarters, in fact, popular opinion assumes that Christian faith is impossible without belief in the inerrancy of Scripture. Warfield, however, made it quite clear that Christianity and salvation are not primarily dependent on inerrancy. He declared: "Let it not be said that thus we found the whole Christian system upon the doctrine of plenary inspiration. We found the whole Christian system on the doctrine of plenary inspiration as little as we found it upon the doctrine of angelic existences. Were there no such thing as inspiration, Christianity would be true, and all its essential doctrines would be credibly witnessed to us in the generally trustworthy reports of the teaching of our Lord and of his authoritative agents in founding the church, preserved in the writings of the apostles and their first followers, and in the historical witness of the living church. Inspiration is not the most fundamental of Christian doctrines, nor even the first thing we prove about the Scriptures. It is the last and crowning fact as to the Scriptures. These we first prove authentic, historically credible, generally trustworthy, before we prove them inspired."[43]

Warfield expressed himself even more forcibly as follows: "We are in entire harmony in this matter with what we conceive to be the very true statement recently made by Dr. George P. Fisher, that 'if the authors of the Bible were credible reporters of revelations of God, whether in the form of historical transactions of which they were witnesses, or of divine mysteries that were unveiled to their minds, their testimony would be entitled to belief, even if they were shut up to their unaided faculties in communicating what they had thus received.' We are in entire sympathy in this matter, therefore, with the protest which Dr. Marcus Dods raised in his famous address at the

---

43. *The Inspiration and Authority of the Bible*, p. 210.

meeting of the Alliance of the Reformed Churches at London, against representing that 'the infallibility of the Bible is the ground of the whole Christian faith.' We judge with him that it is very important indeed that such a misapprehension, if it is anywhere current, should be corrected."[44] Notwithstanding this warning, it is not uncommon in some Christian circles today for people to consider as non-evangelical any person who has the courage to speak out against inerrancy. Apparently the views of Warfield noted above have not been propagated as thoroughly as has his doctrine of inspiration.

Inerrancy, Infallibility, and Authority

The dire consequences of faulty reasoning in defending inerrancy and infallibility are well illustrated in the running battle between some segments of Christianity and proponents of new knowledge. This is not a new issue, because the seeds of the conflict were sown back in the sixteenth and seventeenth centuries. Philip E. Hughes notes, "The lessons of the Galileo case are plain enough for those who are willing to perceive them. Absolute authoritarianism, whether in church or state, whether in theology or science, is an evil thing, and must be withstood by those who value truth and freedom and the dignity of the individual."[45] Recent research has shown that there were some understanding church leaders in the Galileo case. Galileo himself was wrong in some of his claims and increasingly wrongheaded in his attitude; therefore the Roman Church does not appear in as bad a light as previously. Nevertheless, the power of the hierarchy was exercised by condemning Galileo.

Far more accurate examples of "absolute authoritarianism" are those purges carried out since Vatican I. A closing statement to *Pastor aeternus*, Pius IX's definition of papal infallibility, warned, "If—which may God avert—anyone should presume to contradict this definition of ours, let

44. *Ibid.*, p. 211.
45. *Christianity Today* (Jan. 18, 1960), p. 34.

him be anathema." Ignaz Döllinger, the leading Roman Catholic theologian in Germany, stepped over the line and was excommunicated. Moreover, schism resulted when segments of the church in Germany, Austria, Switzerland, and the Netherlands broke away.

A more thoroughgoing purge was carried out by Pius X over the years 1907-1910. In his encyclical *Pascendi Dominici Gregis* (Sept., 1907) he urged his subordinate authorities to dismiss ruthlessly anyone holding any of the modernist errors noted in *Lamentabili sane Exitu*, the decree of the Roman Inquisition issued in July, 1907. Burtchaell summarizes some of the results:

> Lagrange, called in from Jerusalem, was forbidden to publish on touchy subjects, and for awhile was removed from his post at the Ecole Biblique. In France, Loisy and Houtin had both had their publications put on the *Index*, and had been unfrocked and excommunicated. Even old Pierre Batiffol fell afoul of the authorities and was dismissed from the rectorship of the Institut Catholique de Toulouse. Franz von Hummelauer lost his teaching position. Giovanni Semeria was sent into exile by his Italian superiors, and Salvatore Minocchi was suspended. David Fleming had been eased out of Rome back to Britain, and Giovanni Genocchi had been dismissed from his chair at the Apollinare in that city. George Tyrrell died excommunicate without a Catholic funeral and Friedrich von Hügel found that he was more welcome in non-Catholic circles than amidst his own folk. Henry Poels was expelled from the Catholic University of America and sent home to Holland.[46]

"Finally," Burtchaell notes, "in 1910 a loyalty oath against Modernism was imposed on all clerics whenever they received holy orders, applied for confessional faculties, took papal degrees, began office as religious superiors, or taught in a seminary or pontifically approved faculty."[47] The real tragedy of such a pogrom is that nothing is really solved—the problems are merely postponed. "The catastrophe of the Modernist purge was," according to

46. *Catholic Theories of Biblical Inspiration Since 1810*, p. 231.
47. *Ibid.*, p. 232.

Burtchaell, "that the exploration of this whole constellation of associated and perplexing problems was for half a century paralyzed. However irresponsible the discussion had become, one is tempted to think that it might have been dealt with more deftly."[48] Equally turbulent purges followed by loyalty oaths have occurred in most Protestant churches, and some are in process or shaping up at the time of this writing.

The fearful have always felt that such measures were necessary, but what they have not seen is that victory for the specific point of view is seldom victory for the purposes of God. His purpose is that his creatures come to the truth in the context of freedom even though the latter is often used to obscure and hinder the realization of God's will. Accordingly, it is imperative to understand and to acknowledge that *the issue of truth will never be solved inerrantly.*

Errors come and go with each new generation, and then they reappear later in a new guise. James Russell Lowell (1819-1891) expressed the situation with great insight: "Yet 'tis truth alone is strong; though her portion be the scaffold, . . . yet that scaffold sways the future."[49] The reason that truth always seems to be on the scaffold is that the process of ascertaining the truth must be repeated every generation. While honest, sensitive parents and traditions cannot hand on a package of truth, they can facilitate the process by which the next generation ascertains and experiences truth for itself. In this process, as Küng declares, "the gospel remains in every case the source, norm, and power for the faith and for the perpetuity . . . of the Church in the truth."[50]

Yet Burtchaell's warning is valid: "Any number of religions could have developed, for instance, and have in fact developed from the Bible, yet they need not all be legitimate developments. It is one thing to prove that your faith has grown out of the faith of our fathers; it is quite

48. *Ibid.,* p. 5.
49. "Once to Every Man and Nation," verse 4.
50. *Infallible? An Inquiry,* p. 190.

another to prove that it is a proper development. Our faith may be educed from its past; it cannot be deduced."[51] A number of religious sects and Protestant groups have sprung from charismatic persons who claimed that their teachings were based on the Bible. But because of various reasons, including limited theological education, their interpretations skewed the gospel considerably. Nevertheless, these writings became the standard of orthodoxy for the various groups.

In some instances reluctance to admit errors of the founders of the traditions hardens into a resolve to save face at any cost. In other groups errors are recognized, but it is not feasible psychologically to slough off the old terminology immediately. The normal procedure involves a halfway point in which the crucial terms are redefined. This is especially true in the case of "inerrancy." In conservative Protestant circles this is done by a cluster of conditional statements that in effect negate a strict interpretation of the term.

A particularly meaningful redefinition is that proposed by Burtchaell for the Roman Catholic traditions. "Yesterday's truth may not be today's error," he observes, "but neither is it today's truth, though the two are as parent and child. Truth can be no eternal possession, no safe investment, no once-for-all deposit. He who would keep up with the truth must make the effort to remain astride a wildly mobile, ever-shifting problematic. It means moving, and never standing still. The etymology of 'inerrancy' lends itself helpfully to this sense. To be inerrant means not to wander, nor go astray, nor lose the path. It does not mean to sit down, but to forge forward with assurance of not getting lost. This, I submit, is a right metaphor to characterize God's gift to his people."[52] "The Church does find inerrancy in the Bible," Burtchaell declares, "if we can agree to take that term in its dynamic sense, and not a static one. Inerrancy must be the ability, not to

51. *Catholic Theories of Biblical Inspiration Since 1810*, p. 296.
52. *Ibid.*, pp. 298-299.

avoid all mistakes, but to cope with them, remedy them survive them, and eventually even profit from them."[53]

Burtchaell's insights are valid and very appropriate, but it is doubtful that the tag "inerrancy" can be reinstated with its original meaning. It is virtually impossible to reverse linguistic history, and in the case of "inerrancy" it is beyond question. There are too many rational and emotional connotations to overcome. Moreover, aside from its value as a psychological crutch during an interim period, there is no need to retain the term. Once the mental adjustment has been made, nothing essential is lost. Those basic issues which the advocates of the doctrine of inerrancy have cherished and sought to protect are still valid, and they can be expressed with greater clarity by using other terms and expressions.

In connection with a plea by the German scholar Oswald Loretz to abandon the term "inerrancy," Vawter confides, "Therefore it is a refreshing experience to be asked to abandon the idea of Biblical inerrancy altogether, and to acknowledge—without recourse to subterfuges that would try to have it both ways—that the Bible, like any other comparable body of human literature, records the mistakes of its authors just as surely as it does their inspired truths. Perhaps this is, after all, the higher inerrancy: that the Bible should be permitted to testify truthfully to the genuine human condition of the individual authors and the people through whom the word of God has been mediated."[54]

In discussing the rise of the doctrine of inerrancy, James Smart observes, "It is important to note that the immediate effect of a theory of literal inspiration was not to reinforce the authority of God's word in Scripture as a word in which man must ever afresh seek guidance in the affairs of life but rather to make the Scriptures useful as the divine validation of a system of doctrine and practice. The infallibility attributed to the Scriptures was transferred directly to the doctrines and practices that were

53. *Ibid.*, p. 303.
54. *Biblical Inspiration*, p. 152.

considered to be founded on Scripture, with the consequence that a static religious order came into being."[55]
This is precisely why "doctrine" is the crucial point with inerrancists—it is their doctrine, attributed to God, that is at stake.

"In short," Smart continues, "it was a method of interpretation that robbed the revelation of Scripture of its freedom. God was no longer free to contradict the established religious order. The doctrine of the infallible inspiration of Scripture had the same effect later in Roman Catholicism, making the Scripture the bastion of an infallible church and denying any possibility that the word of Scripture might seriously set in question the order of the church. So also in scholastic Protestantism it was used to validate the established Protestant doctrine and order and to claim for it an infallibility similar to that claimed by the Roman Church. Doctrines and practices soundly based on an infallible Scripture could not be subject to any essential change. There could be no error in them. Thus has man in different ages used Scripture to establish his own or his own human church's authority over men."[56] The subtlety of evil is that often the good that sincere men do to honor God works against his ultimate purpose. Smart states clearly the ultimate case against inerrancy: "The theory of literal infallibility, far from being an expression of genuine respect for Scripture, is open to the accusation of being a means whereby, subtly, under a semblance of extreme respect, an established order of religion makes use of Scripture for its own purposes and subordinates it to itself, thereby removing from God's word in Scripture its power to revolutionize the existing order."[57]

Since treasured ideas are not given up readily, the most important factor is a scrupulous honesty to know the truth, come what may. In acknowledging the error of some of his early views, John Baillie attributed part of the fault to "certain wrong-headed and illusory ideas" that he "im-

---

55. *The Interpretation of Scripture*, pp. 182-183.
56. *Ibid.*, p. 183.
57. *Ibid.*

bibed from the spirit of the age and from the philosophies that were then in vogue."[58] He goes on to say: "What I now realize very clearly, and am ready to confess, is that much of the trouble in the days when I could not hear God's voice was that I was not really listening. I was partly listening perhaps—giving, as it were, one ear to his commandments; but no promise is made in the Bible to those who partly listen, but only to those who hearken *diligently*. And why did I not thus hearken? It was that there were certain things I did not want to hear. We sometimes speak of people being 'conveniently deaf' to human communications, but there is such a thing also as being conveniently deaf toward God; and it is a malady that afflicts us all. There are certain things we just do not want to be told. They would be too inconvenient, too upsetting, too exacting. The readjustment they would involve would be too painful. They would commit us to tasks more difficult and troublesome than we desire to undertake, or they would interfere with certain indulgences we have been allowing ourselves."[59]

Admittedly, Baillie made these remarks in connection with his discussion of the difficulty that the sophisticated mind of our age poses in accepting objectively the revelation God has given. But when it comes to the matter of accepting new truth, truth that demands a painful readjustment of thought, the attitude of heart and mind is no different for the liberal than it is for the conservative. It is quite evident that the advocates of inerrancy and infallibility have been conveniently deaf to the truth of the matter because of the upsetting consequences inherent in the facts.

The revolution involved in turning from the indulgence of one's own interpretation about inspiration to the facts of the biblical teaching on inspiration may well be a traumatic experience, but through it all one can have the assurance that, irrespective of his fears, the truth will always lead to Christ. Patton expressed his assurance as

---

58. *The Idea of Revelation in Recent Thought*, p. 141.
59. *Ibid.*, p. 140. Italics his.

follows: "I like when I go to sea to know that the ship is provided with bulkheads and watertight compartments, so that in case a collision come, whether it be on bow or bilge, she will float. I do not care to put all my hope of heaven in a theory of inerrant inspiration, so that if a hole were bored in it the great ship would founder. I like to feel that the historicity and the inspiration of the Bible cooperate and help to strengthen faith, so that if either is sufficient how much better both will be."[60]

Difficult though it may be to understand, God chose to make his authority relevant to his creatures by means that necessitate some element of fallibility. Whether we like to think of authority in such terms is beside the point. The facts permit no other understanding of Scripture's inspiration and authority. Concerning this mystery, Evans comments: "How know we what Divine, infallible, and perfect Purpose may be served even by these limitations and fallibilities? Does not Scripture itself intimate that at least there *is* such a purpose, and that it does work through just such channels of human frailty? Is not God's strength always made perfect in man's weakness? . . . If God thus chooses to work out his problems through surds and fractions and zeros, who are we to say him nay? Brethren, this is God's way; this is the law. What right have we to say where that law shall stop? to decide how much of the earthen vessel shall count as a factor? how much or how little of the human folly, weakness, nothingness, is compatible with the Divine Purpose? God is not limited as to his means and methods in communicating his will to men. Had a literal, stereotyped, incorruptible infallibility in every jot and tittle of the record been an indispensable requisite, God had a thousand resources at his command for securing such a record. That he chose men, yes, men, with all their ignorance and weakness and fallibility; that he intrusted his revelation to their stammering tongues and to their stumbling pens; that he deposited the interpretation of his eternal ways in earthen vessels, which could not escape the corruptions and mutilations of time; simply

60. *Fundamental Christianity*, pp. 165-166.

shows that a literal, particularistic infallibility is of less moment in the sight of God than some other things; of less worth, perhaps, than the thrill of a human touch, the glow of a red-hot word, the pulse of a throbbing heart, the lightning of a living eye, the flash of a soul on fire; of less worth—who knows?—than the faltering of the pilgrim's foot; dearer to heaven than the lordly step of Gabriel."[61]

On the other hand, refusal to be open to new truth is sure to have some dire consequences along the line. The people of God during Jeremiah's ministry were convinced, with few exceptions, that God's permanent residence was over the ark in the temple. God tried to tell them through his prophet that he was no prisoner of a box, but they would not listen. As a result they went into exile, and there finally, in their dismay and uncertainty, God was able to speak to them. The sovereign God of Israel, the Father of our Lord Jesus Christ, exercises the same lord-ship today. He will no more be a prisoner of the Book or of church authority and teaching than he was of the box. The corollary is, of course, that if we persist in trying to imprison him, then we face the learning experience of another exile. James A. Sanders states incisively the crucial role of Scripture in exilic experiences then and now: "The emerging identity shifted to the extent that the questions forced by the historical experience were answered by the ancient traditions which proved viable in survival. The two focuses of the dialogue were the questions that the exiles could not avoid and the answers that they heard from their traditions. Their understanding of those answers molded the shape of the traditions into the basic gestalt of the Torah and the Prophets we inherit. In this sense the canon is perhaps the most relevant precisely to the sort of experi-ence the heirs of early Judaism now face, the church and the synagogue today."[62]

But since the human interpreters of the canon have varying understandings of God's will, there can be no absolute human authority. Bright is pertinent at this point:

61. "Biblical Scholarship and Inspiration," *Inspiration and Iner-rancy*, pp. 40-41.
62. *Torah and Canon*, pp. 118-119.

"Is there an authority that can tell a man what he has to believe and what he must do? No, there is not! That is an old-fashioned notion best gotten rid of. It is in a class with the unicorn, the centaur, the hippogriff, and other such mythical creatures. 'There ain't no such animal,' and people ought not to be so gullible as to suppose that there is."[63]

Authority has two basic ways of working. On the *subjective* side is the power of the Holy Spirit working through Scripture to convince and convict so that the response to the challenge of the gospel is an act of faith and commitment. On the *objective* side, Scripture becomes the basis of appeal in all matters pertaining to the content of faith and the practice of Christian living. Bright states the problem well: "Let the right of each free individual to believe what he will without let or hindrance, or threat of coercion, by all means be granted. But must the church then agree that one belief is as Christian as another, provided only that it be held sincerely? Certainly not. But, in that event, how is the matter to be settled? With our fists? By the counting of noses (the voice of the majority is the voice of God)? By appeal to tradition alone (the thing is without precedent, therefore wrong)? By forensic skill (a euphemism, perhaps, for the ability to shout the loudest)? Or is there some authority, recognized by all parties as competent to determine what is, and what is not, in accord with the Christian faith, to which the church may appeal in attempting to referee the matter?"[64]

As noted above, however, even the recourse to Scripture is not the final answer because interpretations of the Bible vary, and each church hierarchy has a different idea of what doctrines and practices are basic. Sincere appeals to Scripture are not enough. "Is it, after all," Bright queries, "really conceivable that any should rise in church court or assembly and say: We freely admit that the solution we propose is not a Christian one and, furthermore, we do not care what the Christian solution is?"[65] Therefore, the

63. *The Authority of the Old Testament*, pp. 19-20.
64. *Ibid.*, p. 22.
65. *Ibid.*, pp. 22-23.

problem eventually comes down to the quality of the interpretation. Not all understandings of the Bible are equally valid, and so the basic criterion for determining God's truth is the proper use of reason working with all the available data. Without this approach there is no way to break into the vicious circle of theological deductions. Yet, after the best efforts of heart and mind some issues will be inconclusive. For this reason human authority cannot exercise absolute control. A church may excommunicate one of its members, but that act does not determine the eternal destiny of the person. According to Jesus, final judgment is God's; therefore no human authority can usurp his absolute authority (Matt. 7:1).

Inerrancy, Infallibility, and Indefectibility

As indicated earlier, the terms "inerrancy" and "infallibility" are absolutes that actually apply only to God. "Instead," Vawter declares, "we should think of inspiration as always a positive divine and human interaction in which the principle of condescension has been taken at face value. To conceive of an absolute inerrancy as the effect of inspiration was not really to believe that God had condescended to the human sphere but rather that He had transmuted it into something else. A human literature containing no error would indeed be a contradiction in terms, since nothing is more human than to err. Put in more vital terms, if the Scripture is a record of revelation, the acts of a history of salvation in which God has disclosed Himself by entering into the ways of man, it must be a record of trial and error as well as of achievement, for it is in this way that man learns and comes to the truth."[66]

The underlying reason for the failure to recognize God's condescension to the humanity of his channels of revelation is "a crude interpretation of divine-human collaboration" that, as Burtchaell notes, divides up the task "like Jack Sprat and his wife."[67] The Sprats could lick the plate

66. *Biblical Inspiration*, p. 169.
67. *Catholic Theories of Biblical Inspiration Since 1810*, p. 289.

clean "only because their appetites complemented each other so well," but in the realm of causality joint human cooperation is impossible because as one of the pair gains control the other loses it.[68] Yet in the realm of divine-human relationships the analogy of human relationships breaks down. According to Burtchaell, "The wrangle over predestination and free will still runs on, for example, because disputants cannot see that God can do what no man can: control the activity of persons without infringing upon their freedom."[69]

In any case, to be human goes beyond the error of the biblical writers. "To err is also ecclesiastical," Küng observes, "to err—as we have recently added—is papal: simply because Church and pope are also human and remain human. Since this has often been forgotten in the Church, we need to be reminded of it forcibly."[70] It was Pope John XXIII, Küng remarks, who "revealed a new ideal of an unpretentious, ecumenically and humanly disposed Petrine *ministry* to the brethren and attached so little importance to the infallibility attributed to him that he could say on one occasion with a smile: 'I'm not infallible; I'm infallible only when I speak *ex cathedra*. But I'll never speak *ex cathedra*.' "[71]

Accordingly, Küng declares, "We would like therefore to give preference to the concept of '*indefectibility*' or '*perpetuity*' *in truth* over that of 'infallibility.' The concept of 'indefectibility' (unshatterability, constancy) and the positive concept of 'perpetuity' (indestructibility, continuance) are just as much traditional concepts in ecclesiology as 'infallibility.' "[72]

The history of the people of God in the Old Testament is a long succession of crises in which the enemies of the community, both inside and outside, did everything imaginable to bring it to destruction, but still a remnant survived! This quality of survival was affirmed for the church as well: "the gates of Hades [the powers of death] shall

68. *Ibid.*, pp. 289-290.
69. *Ibid.*, p. 290.
70. *Infallible? An Inquiry*, p. 186.
71. *Ibid.*, p. 87. Italics his.
72. *Ibid.*, p. 182. Italics his.

not overcome it" (Matt. 16:18). Even during the dark, dreary periods of the ninth and fifteenth centuries the light of God's truth did not go out. But where was this indefectibility manifested? "Not in the hierarchy," states Küng, "and not in theology, but among those innumerable and mostly unknown Christians—and there were always some bishops and theologians also among them—who, even in the Church's worst periods, heard the Christian message and tried to live according to it in faith, love, and hope. Mostly they were not the great and powerful, the prudent and wise, but—wholly in accordance with the New Testament—the 'simple people,' those 'of no account,' who are the truly great in the kingdom of heaven. They were the true witnesses of the truth of Christ and manifested by their Christian life and Christian conduct the indefectibility of the Church in the truth."[73]

Although Luther and Calvin did not use the term "indefectibility," they certainly believed in the perpetuity of the true church because of the work of the Holy Spirit. This has been true of Protestantism in general. Within the last twenty-five years, however, there have been a number of prophets of despair predicting the demise of the church. Where it is wrong or ineffective it will be judged by its sovereign Lord, but the church, whether understood as visible or invisible, will continue long after the prophets of doom have ceased. This is true because the primary mission of the church is redemptive. The severe problems of race, poverty, ignorance, and injustice must be confronted, but with the concerted effort of all people of good will it will take time to heal the malignant areas of modern society. This is where the good news of Jesus Christ can enable changed human beings to carry with courage and assurance the burden of unfulfilled hopes. Even when the blight of social ills has been greatly reduced, there will still be the need for renewed persons. The true church is characterized by a love that will be appropriate when the need for faith and hope has ceased (1 Cor. 13:13).

73. *Ibid.*, p. 189.

Chapter Thirteen

A Comprehensive View
of Scripture and Tradition

With the specific purpose of reconciliation and redemption, God determined to make known his person to, and
his will for, rebellious, estranged humanity. In this long
process of self-disclosure he employed "many and various
ways" to achieve his goal. Of primary importance were his
saving acts in behalf of his covenant people. But these
events in the realm of human history were more than just
charades in which the spectators were left to supply their
own meaning. From the call of Abraham to the birth of
the church at Pentecost, the saving deeds of God were
made intelligible by words of interpretation. God's communication through deeds and words found ready response
in the hearts and minds of some, and at that moment
revelation became an actualized reality. The chief recipients of revelation were the prophets and the apostles.

In order, however, for this primary revelation to be
relevant to each new situation in every generation, the
Spirit worked in a secondary way to aid devoted Israelites
and Christians in educing and extrapolating guidelines for
living in covenant relationship with God. Moreover, per-

sons with the gift for learning from experience compiled their insights and passed this wisdom on to the next generation. God's variegated disclosure included additionally the skill of craftsmen and the gifts of charismatics.

Associated with the giving and receiving of God's revelation of himself was the divine aid (inspiration) of God's Spirit. Varying kinds (degrees) of divine aid were called for by the manifold means employed by God in his self-disclosure. At those special events of primary revelation the servants of God were uniquely inspired by the Spirit of God. At other times only the inspiration of a devoted Israelite or follower of Christ was necessary to achieve God's purpose. Accordingly, there is a sense in which John L. McKenzie, building on the work of Karl Rahner, is correct in speaking of the "social character" of inspiration: "The spokesman of God speaks for his society; when he speaks, he speaks not only in virtue of his own personal experience and knowledge of God, but in virtue of the faith and traditions in which his experience occurs and without which his experience would not have meaning."[1]

However, the social view of inspiration is only part of the truth. Dennis J. McCarthy is correct in commenting, "I submit that this is still a matter of degree; individuals, anonymous to us perhaps, but still individuals, did the work, even though under the pressure of tradition. All literature—not just the ancient Oriental—involves an interplay of an individual and a tradition carried in society."[2] The Hebrew society in Egypt can no more explain Moses than the church at Corinth can explain Paul. There is a God-given "plus" in the inspiration associated with primary revelation. On the other hand, inspiration must operate in the context of society or else there can be no effective communication. McCarthy observes rightly, "If a writer—and this includes the sacred writer—were to demand complete freedom from the conventions of his so-

1. "The Social Character of Inspiration," p. 121, *The Catholic Biblical Quarterly*, Vol. 24 (1962).
2. "Personality, Society, and Inspiration," p. 554, *Theological Studies*, Vol. 24 (1963).

ciety, he would have to give up language and destroy all possibility of communication. Thus, however personal may be the work of a writer, however new the trail he blazes, he must submit in some degree to traditional elements recognized in his society."[3]

The fact that insights of one generation are rooted in and educed from the revelation of the fathers means that inspiration continues throughout the flow of the generations. For this reason Luis Alonso-Schökel is correct in affirming, "We are obliged to allow for some form or other of 'successive inspiration' in order to explain the facts and apply the principles correctly. Wherever there is a real literary and religious contribution, there the Spirit acted."[4]

At first the witness to revelation from God was usually in the form of oral report. In due time some of these reports were reduced to writing, especially the key redemptive, historical events and the compelling "word of Yahweh" that came to the prophets. The pattern of oral tradition followed by written records was equally true of the New Testament. In this whole process of transmitting, recording, and compiling the deeds and words of God, the Spirit of God was active in the hearts and minds of God's servants. But this activity did not extend to inerrant transmission, either oral or written, and neither did it guarantee an absolute inerrancy of the original documents. What the Spirit's activity did guarantee was selectivity of events and accuracy of reporting and interpretation sufficient to achieve God's purpose for each generation as well as the basis for extrapolating into the future.

By the hearing, reading, and study of Scripture, revelation, inspiration, and authority become realities in every earnest heart through the agency of the same Spirit who watched over Scripture's recording and transmission. This result occurs whether Scripture is in the original languages or in translation. Of course, for clarification of specific details, the best extant text of the Hebrew and Aramaic in

3. *Ibid.*, p. 556.
4. *The Inspired Word*, p. 205.

the Old Testament and the Greek in the New Testament
will always have a priority over any translations. But in the
great issues of faith (love for God) and action (love for
man) Scripture in translation is sufficient to achieve God's
purpose. This is true of all translations even though they
have unintentional, and in some cases deliberate, variation
from the clear text of the extant manuscripts. As far as the
translation itself is concerned, and indirectly the reader,
the reason for the variation does not matter. Enough of
the redemptive truth is woven throughout Scripture that
the Holy Spirit can take any translation and use it for the
salvation of the sincere reader.

The whole history of God's redemptive activity is one in
which the Holy Spirit has worked through imperfect
means, both men and Scripture, without the means being a
handicap. Fallible ministers with many imperfect notions
have been God's messengers throughout the history of the
church. In spite of this fact the "hungry and thirsty" have
heard them gladly as being inspired by God and setting
forth a trustworthy message. If the Holy Spirit is willing to
authenticate the message of very fallible servants, how
much more will he authenticate the extant manuscripts
and translations!

In all essential matters of faith and practice, therefore,
Scripture is authentic, accurate, and trustworthy. It is the
indispensable record of revelation, product of inspiration,
and source of authority. And yet the work of the Holy
Spirit did not cease with the close of the canon. Although
Jesus and his apostolic interpreters represent the ultimate
in redemptive revelation (thereby justifying a closed canon), it has been necessary to interpret that truth for each
period of the church's history. The clarification and application of biblical revelation continues today, and it will as
long as God's creatures exist. In a secondary, derivative
fashion, therefore, the revelation and inspiration of God's
Spirit continues. Accordingly, from the standpoint of *theological interpretation* the canon has never been closed.
For this reason there is no basis in considering all of the
biblical writers and editors as qualitatively different from
postcanonical interpreters. Some of the psalms are simply

an exhortation to praise God because of his dealings with Israel. The psalmist repeats well-known facts and out of the fullness of his experience with God exhorts his fellows to greater lives of devotion to Israel's loving God. Some of the great hymns evidence the same kind of inspiration. Had Isaac Watts, Charles Wesley, Augustus Toplady, and Reginald Heber lived in the preexilic centuries of David and his successors and been *no more inspired than they were in their own day*, there is little doubt but that their hymns (which would have been different, of course, because the revelation of Jesus was still in the future) would have found their way into the Hebrew canon.

If the church had a more dynamic sense of God's inspiration in the twentieth century, it would be more effective in its witness and outreach. It is well and good to protect the distinctiveness of the Bible, but to think only in terms of its inspiration as absolutely different in kind from inspiration in our time is too high a price to pay. Christians today need to have the same sense of being God-motivated and God-sent as did the biblical writers and interpreters. In a genuine sense, the difficulty of interpreting God's record of revelation to this complex age requires as much of God's inbreathing and wisdom as did the process of interpretation in the biblical periods.

On the other hand, some well-intended interpretations are not valid extrapolations from Scripture. Therefore, the development of doctrine and teaching must continually be tested. Notwithstanding ambiguities, variations of viewpoint, and some admixture of error, the only valid criterion is the canon of Scripture. An honest, open tradition will update its legitimacy by periodically checking its conclusions against the word of Scripture.

The Scriptures, according to the traditional understanding of the church, *are* special (primary) revelation and therefore uniquely inspired. Technically speaking, however, the Bible is a record or witness to revelation, and as such it is the product of inspiration. This is not to deny the accuracy, authenticity, and trustworthiness of the Bible. Rather, it is to recognize that there are two different kinds of truth. Scripture is objective truth. Since it is rooted in history, the key events of redemptive history are to be investigated and authenticated, insofar as is possible, by the same criteria employed in checking all other historical data. Man's rational faculties can also investigate the logic and meaning of the teachings in Scripture. But a thorough study of Scripture by means of unaided human reason can never lead to the act of faith. The facts and teachings of Scripture do not possess the power to coerce trust and commitment on the part of the reader. Only as God's Holy Spirit seals the message of Scripture on the heart of the reader is he or she ready to respond and make revelation an actuality by exercising his or her will in an act of commitment to God.

Subjective truth has to do with reasons of the heart, whereas objective truth has to do with reasons of the mind. At any given moment a person cannot be actively engaged in both realms of truth, but this does not mean that the two are antithetical. As Emil Brunner observes: "The relation between the two kinds of truth is the same as that between the planes of existence: the higher includes the lower, but not vice versa. The personal truth of revelation, faith, and love includes within itself the impersonal truth connected with 'things,' and the impersonal truth connected with abstractions, but not vice versa."[5] Objective truth of itself cannot guarantee the reality of subjective truth, but subjective truth cannot occur without some minimal amount of objective truth. The Holy Spirit works in conjunction with the reading, preaching, and teaching of Scripture; therefore the objective truth of the biblical record is neglected or rejected at the peril of one's spiritual well-being.

True faith, therefore, is more than a blind leap into the dark. It begins in the area of objective truth with assent to the facts and teachings of Scripture. Otherwise the act of faith would amount to a credulous will to believe—a game of chance. The objective truth of natural revelation and of Scripture serves as the springboard of faith because it points in the direction in which one is to exercise his faith.

5. *Revelation and Reason*, p. 373.

Nevertheless, the act of trust and commitment into the loving arms of the Father is made only at the level of subjective, personal truth. Thus, in the Christian's walk with Christ it is a case of both objective and subjective truth. While the Christian experience, like true marriage, loses its dynamic without repeated experiences of subjective truth, it is by no means a continuous state of rapture, transport, or ecstasy. Rather, it is an alternation between the objective and subjective aspects of life. True worship may begin with objective truth (meditation about God and his will), but it should go on to subjective truth (being "lost in wonder, love, and praise"[6]).

The two kinds of truth are equally valid in the realm of authority. The ultimate authority of God's sovereignty was expressed in terms of specific demands upon his covenant people. His will was expressed in each generation by a series of interpretations and reinterpretations. However, many of the customs and regulations do not apply now, and so it is necessary to evaluate the commands of Scripture to determine what is still authoritative. This use of reason in the realm of objective truth does not make the ascertained will of God authoritative. The conviction that leads to submission and obedience comes only through the wooing of the Holy Spirit. In the subjective truth of personal encounter, God's will is made clear and authoritative.

If such convictions run counter to the standards and teachings of one's church or religious order, then the alternatives are to work for a revision of church polity or to seek another affiliation. Ecclesiastical authority has been exercised with varying degrees of rigidity. In spite of good intentions, in many instances the human authorities seem to have gone beyond the purposes of God by pulling up the tares (darnel) and thus ruining some of the wheat (Matt. 13:29). In more severe cases the religious authorities have been so confused as to think that the wheat looked like tares. Clearly, God will require an accounting of such miscarriages of his justice and righteousness. Inas-

6. "Love Divine, All Loves Excelling," verse 4.

much as ecclesiastical authority (whether Protestant or Roman Catholic) is fallible, it should be exercised with great caution and patience. Ultimately, authority is an individual, personal matter because everyone will be judged according to his willingness to know God's will and to obey it. Scripture still speaks today. The real question is whether we will listen and act diligently.

Bibliography

In addition to the books and articles cited in the notes the bibliography lists other sources consulted.

Abbott, Walter M., gen. ed. *The Documents of Vatican II* (New York: American Press, 1966).

Albrektson, Bertil. *History and the Gods* (Lund, Sweden: Gleerup, 1967).

Albright, William F. *The Archaeology of Palestine* (Harmondsworth-Middlesex: Penguin, 1949).

_____. "Recent Discoveries in Palestine and the Gospel of St. John," *The Background of the New Testament and Its Eschatology*, ed. by W. D. Davies and D. Daube (Cambridge: Cambridge Univ. Press, 1956).

Alonso-Schökel, Luis. *The Inspired Word*, tr. by Francis Martin (New York: Herder and Herder, 1965).

Aristeas. *Aristeas to Philocrates (Letter of Aristeas)*, ed. and tr. by Moses Hadas (New York: Harper and Row, 1951).

Athenagoras. *The Writings of Justin Martyr and Athenagoras*, Vol. II, Ante-Nicene Christian Library, tr. by Marcus Dods, George Reith, and B. P. Pratten (Edinburgh: Clark, 1867).

Augustine. *Christian Instruction*, tr. by John J. Gavigan, O.S.A., Vol. 2, The Fathers of the Church (Fathers of the Church, Inc., 2d ed., 1950).

_____. *Letters* (1-82), tr. by Wilfrid Parsons, Vol. 12, The Fathers of the Church (Fathers of the Church, Inc., 1951).

Bailey, Albert Edward. *The Gospel in Hymns* (New York: Scribner's, 1950).

Baillie, John. *The Idea of Revelation in Recent Thought* (New York: Columbia Univ. Press, 1956).

Barr, James. *Old and New in Interpretation* (New York: Harper and Row, 1966).

Barth, Karl. *The Doctrine of the Word of God*, Vol. I, Part 1, *Church Dogmatics*, tr. by G. T. Thomson (New York: Scribner's, 1936).

_____. *The Doctrine of the Word of God*, Vol. I, Part 2, *Church Dogmatics*, tr. by G. T. Thomson and Harold Knight (New York: Scribner's, 1956).

Bavinck, Herman. *The Philosophy of Revelation* (London: Longmans, Green, 1909).

Bea, Augustin Cardinal. *The Word of God and Mankind*, tr. by Dorothy White (New York: Franciscan Herald Press, 1967).

Benoit, Pierre. "La Septant est-elle inspirée?" in *Vom Wort des Lebens, Festschrift Max Meinertz*, pp. 41-49.

_____. "L'inspiration des Septant d'après les Pères," in *L'homme devant Dieu, Mélanges Henri de Lubac*, I, 169-187.

Berkouwer, G. C. *General Revelation* (Grand Rapids: Eerdmans, 1955).

Bornkamm, Günther. *Jesus of Nazareth*, tr. by Irene and Fraser McLuskey with James M. Robinson (New York: Harper and Brothers, 1960).

Briggs, Charles A. *The Bible, the Church and the Reason* (New York: Scribner's, 1893).

Bright, John. *The Authority of the Old Testament* (Nashville: Abingdon, 1967).

Brown, Robert McAfee. "Tradition as a Protestant Problem," pp. 430-454 in *Theology Today*, Vol. XVII, January, 1961.

_____. *The Spirit of Protestantism* (New York: Oxford Univ. Press, 1961).

Bruce, Alexander B. *The Chief End of Revelation* (London: Hodder and Stoughton, 1896).

Bruce, F. F. *Commentary on the Book of Acts, The New International Commentary on the New Testament* (Grand Rapids: Eerdmans, 1954).

_____. *Tradition Old and New* (Grand Rapids: Zondervan, 1970).

Brunner, Emil. *Revelation and Reason*, tr. by Olive Wyon (Philadelphia: Westminster, 1946).

Bultmann, Rudolf. *Jesus Christ and Mythology* (New York: Scribner's, 1958).

Burhenn, Herbert. "Pannenberg's Argument for the Historicity of the Resurrection," pp. 368-379, *Journal of the American Academy of Religion*, Vol. XL, No. 3, September, 1972.

Burnaby, John. *Is the Bible Inspired?* No. 9, Colet Library Series (London: Duckworth, 1949).

Burtchaell, James Tunstead. *Catholic Theories of Biblical Inspiration Since 1810* (New York: Cambridge Univ. Press, 1969).

Burtt, Edwin A. *The Metaphysical Foundations of Modern Physical Science* (New York: Harcourt, Brace, 1925).

Callahan, Daniel J., *et al.*, eds. *Christianity Divided* (New York: Sheed and Ward, 1961).

Calvin, John. *Commentary on a Harmony of the Evangelists, Matthew, Mark, and Luke*, tr. by William Pringle, 3 vols. (Edinburgh: Calvin Translation Society, 1846).

_____. *Commentaries on the Book of the Prophet Jeremiah and the Lamentations*, 5 vols., tr. by John Owen (Edinburgh: Calvin Translation Society, 1854).

Carnell, Edward J. *The Case for Orthodox Theology* (Philadelphia: Westminster, 1959).

Charles, R. H., ed. *The Apocrypha and Pseudepigrapha of the Old Testament in English*, 2 vols. (Oxford: Clarendon, 1913).

Childs, Brevard S. *Biblical Theology in Crisis* (Philadelphia: Westminster, 1970).

Clark, Gordon H. *Religion, Reason and Revelation* (Nutley, N. J.: Presbyterian and Reformed, 1961).

Coleridge, Samuel T. *Confessions of an Inquiring Spirit* (London: Adam and Charles Black, 1956).

Cullmann, Oscar. *The Early Church* (Philadelphia: Westminster. 1956).

Cunliffe-Jones, Hubert. *The Authority of the Biblical Revelation* (Philadelphia: Pilgrim Press, 1948).

Curtis, Olin A. *The Christian Faith* (Eaton and Mains, 1905).

Dillenberger, John. *Protestant Thought and Natural Science* (New York: Doubleday, 1960).

Dodd, C. H. *The Authority of the Bible* (New York: Harper and Row, 1929).

Epstein, I., ed. *The Babylonian Talmud*, 34 vols. plus index vol. (London: Soncino, 1935, 1936, 1938, 1948, and 1952).

Evans, Llewelyn J. "Biblical Scholarship and Inspiration," pp. 25-87 in *Inspiration and Inerrancy*, by Henry P. Smith (Robert Clarke, 1893).

Farrer, Austin. *The Glass of Vision* (London: Dacre, 1948).

Filson, Floyd V. *Which Books Belong in the Bible?* (Philadelphia: Westminster, 1957).

_____. *Jesus Christ the Risen Lord* (Nashville: Abingdon, 1956).

Forestell, J. T. "The Limitation of Inerrancy," pp. 9-18 in *Catholic Biblical Quarterly*, Vol. 20, 1958.

Forsyth, P. T. *The Principle of Authority* (London: Hodder and Stoughton, n.d.).

Fremantle, Anne. *The Papal Encyclicals in Their Historical Context*, exp. ed. (New York: New American Library, 1963).

Fuller, Daniel P. *Easter Faith and History* (Grand Rapids: Eerdmans, 1965).

Gaussen, Louis. *The Inspiration of the Holy Scriptures*, tr. by David D. Scott (Chicago: Moody, 1949).

Geiselmann, Josef Rupert. "Scripture, Tradition, and the Church: An Ecumenical Problem," pp. 39-72 in *Christianity Divided*, ed. by Daniel J. Callahan, *et al.*

Gladstone, William E. *The Impregnable Rock of Holy Scripture* (John D. Wattles, 1898).

Glueck, Nelson. "The Bible as Divining Rod," *Horizon*, Vol. II, No. 2, November, 1959, pp. 4-10, 118-119.

Grant, R. M. *The Letter and the Spirit* (London: S.P.C.K., 1957).

Harbison, E. Harris. *The Christian Scholar in the Age of the Reformation* (New York: Scribner's, 1956).

Harris, R. Laird. *Inspiration and Canonicity of the Bible* (Grand Rapids: Zondervan, 1957).

Harrison, Everett F. "Criteria of Biblical Inerrancy," *Christianity Today*, Vol. II, No. 8, January 20, 1958.

_____. "The Phenomena of Scripture," pp. 237-250, *Revelation and the Bible* (Grand Rapids: Baker, 1958).

Hebert, A. Gabriel. *The Authority of the Old Testament* (London: Faber and Faber, 1947).

_____. *Fundamentalism and the Church* (Philadelphia: Westminster, 1957).

Henry, Carl F. H. *The Protestant Dilemma* (Grand Rapids: Eerdmans, 1949).

_____, ed. *Revelation and the Bible* (Grand Rapids: Baker, 1958).

_____. *The Uneasy Conscience of Modern Fundamentalism* (Grand Rapids: Eerdmans, 1947).

Henry, Matthew. *Commentary on the Whole Bible*, 6 vols. (Westwood, N. J.: Revell, 1935).

Hills, Edward F. *The King James Version Defended!* (The Christian Research Press, 1956).

Hughes, Philip E. Review of *The Crime of Galileo*, by Giorgio de Santillana, in *Christianity Today*, Vol. IV, No. 8, January 18, 1960, pp. 33-34.

Kierkegaard, Søren. *Concluding Unscientific Postscript*, tr. by David F. Swenson with Introduction and notes by Walter Lowrie (Princeton, N. J.: Princeton Univ. Press, 1941).

Koestler, Arthur. *The Sleepwalkers* (New York: Grosset and Dunlap, 1963).

Küng, Hans. *Infallible? An Inquiry*, tr. by Edward Quinn (New York: Doubleday, 1971).

Künneth, Walter. *The Theology of the Resurrection*, tr. by James W. Keitch (St. Louis: Concordia, 1965).

Ladd, George Eldon. *The Blessed Hope* (Grand Rapids: Eerdmans, 1956).

Lewis, C. S. *Miracles* (London: Bles, 1952).

Lewis, Edwin. *The Biblical Faith and Christian Freedom* (Philadelphia: Westminster, 1953).

_____. *A Philosophy of the Christian Revelation* (New York: Harper and Row, 1940)..

Lohfink, Norbert. "Über die Irrtumslosigkeit und die Einheit der Schrift," *Stimmen der Zeit*, Band 174, Jahrgang 89, Juni, 1964, pp. 161-181.

Machen, J. Gresham. *The Virgin Birth of Christ* (New York: Harper and Row, 1930).

MacKenzie, R. A. F. "Some Problems in the Field of Inspiration," pp. 1-8 in *Catholic Biblical Quarterly*, Vol. 20, 1958.

Martyr, Justin. *The Writings of Justin Martyr and Athenagoras*, Vol. II, Ante-Nicene Christian Library, tr. by Marcus Dods, George Reith, and B. P. Pratten (Edinburgh: Clark, 1867).

Marxsen, Willi. *The Resurrection of Jesus of Nazareth*, tr. by Margaret Kohl (Philadelphia: Fortress, 1970).

McCarthy, Dennis J. "Personality, Society, and Inspiration," pp. 553-576 in *Theological Studies*, Vol. 24, 1963.

McDonald, H. D. *Theories of Revelation* (London: Allen and Unwin, 1963).

McKenzie, John. "The Social Character of Inspiration," pp. 115-124 in *Catholic Biblical Quarterly*, Vol. 24, 1962.

Metzger, Bruce M. *An Introduction to the Apocrypha* (New York: Oxford Univ. Press, 1957).

Mickelsen, A. Berkeley. *Interpreting the Bible* (Grand Rapids: Eerdmans, 1963).

Miller, Donald G. *The Authority of the Bible* (Grand Rapids: Eerdmans, 1972).

Montgomery, John Warwick. "Inductive Inerrancy," p. 48, *Christianity Today*, March 3, 1967.

Moran, Gabriel. *Scripture and Tradition* (New York: Herder and Herder, 1963).

_____. *Theology of Revelation* (New York: Herder and Herder, 1966).

Mowinckel, Sigmund. *The Old Testament as Word of God*, tr. by Reidar B. Bjornard (Nashville: Abingdon, 1959).

Nelson, J. Robert. "Hans Küng and the Indefectible Church," *Christian Advocate*, July 8, 1971, pp. 7-8, 18.

Newman, Francis William. *Phases of Faith* (London, 1850).

Niebuhr, H. Richard. *The Meaning of Revelation* (New York: Macmillan, 1941).

Niebuhr, Richard Reinhold. *Resurrection and Historical Reason* (New York: Scribner's, 1957).

Origen. *Selections from the Commentaries and Homilies of Origen,* tr. by R. B. Tollinton (London: S.P.C.K., 1929).

Orr, James. *Revelation and Inspiration* (Grand Rapids: Eerdmans, 1952).

Owen, H. P. *Revelation and Existence* (Cardiff: Univ. of Wales Press, 1957).

Packer, James I. *"Fundamentalism" and the Word of God* (London: Inter-Varsity, 1958).

Pannenberg, Wolfhart. *Jesus—God and Man,* tr. by Lewis L. Wilkins and Duane A. Priebe (Philadelphia: Westminster, 1968).

_____, *et al. Revelation as History,* tr. by David Granskou (New York: Macmillan, 1968).

Patton, Francis L. *Fundamental Christianity* (New York: Macmillan, 1929).

Pfeiffer, Robert H. "Facts and Faith in Biblical History," *Journal of Biblical Literature,* Vol. LXX, Part I, March, 1951, pp. 1-14.

Philo. *Life of Moses,* Book II, tr. by F. H. Colson in Vol. VI, *Philo with an English Translation,* Loeb Classical Library (Cambridge, Mass.: Harvard Univ. Press, 1935).

Pinnock, Clark H. *Biblical Revelation—The Foundation of Christian Theology* (Chicago: Moody, 1971).

Preus, Robert. *The Inspiration of Scripture* (Edinburgh and London: Oliver and Boyd, 1955).

Pritchard, James B., ed. *Ancient Near Eastern Texts* (Princeton, N.J.: Princeton Univ. Press, 1950).

Quenstedt, J. A. *Theologia Didactico-Polemica sive Systema Theologicum* (Lipsiae, 1715).

Rahner, Karl. *Inspiration in the Bible* (New York: Herder and Herder, 1961).

Ramm, Bernard. *The Christian View of Science and Scripture* (Grand Rapids: Eerdmans, 1955).

_____. *Special Revelation and the Word of God* (Grand Rapids: Eerdmans, 1961).

Reid, John K. S. *The Authority of Scripture* (New York: Harper and Row, 1957).

Richardson, Alan. *Christian Apologetics* (New York: Harper and Row, 1947).

Robinson, Henry Wheeler. *Inspiration and Revelation in the Old Testament* (Oxford: Clarendon, 1946).

Runia, Klaas. *Karl Barth's Doctrine of Holy Scripture* (Grand Rapids: Eerdmans, 1962).

———. "What Do Evangelicals Believe About the Bible?" *Christianity Today*, December 4, 1970, pp. 3-6, and December 18, 1970, pp. 8-10.

Sanday, William. *Inspiration*, Bampton Lectures, 1893 (London: Longmans, Green, 3d ed., 1903).

Sanders, James A. *Torah and Canon* (Philadelphia: Fortress, 1972).

Sauer, Erich. *From Eternity to Eternity—An Outline of the Divine Purposes*, tr. by G. H. Lang (Grand Rapids: Eerdmans, 1954).

Sayers, Dorothy L. *Christian Letters to a Post-Christian World* (Grand Rapids: Eerdmans, 1969).

Seeberg, Reinhold. *Revelation and Inspiration* (New York: Harper and Row, 1909).

Seynaeve, Jaak. *Cardinal Newman's Doctrine on Holy Scripture* (Universitas Catholica Lovaniensis, Series II, Tomus 45; Louvain: Publications universitaires de Louvain, 1953).

Simons, Francis. *Infallibility and the Evidence* (Springfield, Ill.: Templegate, 1968).

Smart, James D. *The Interpretation of Scripture* (Philadelphia: Westminster, 1961).

Smith, Henry Preserved. *Inspiration and Inerrancy—A History and a Defense* (Robert Clarke, 1893).

Smyth, J. Paterson. *How God Inspired the Bible* (James Pott, 1893).

Snaith, Norman H. *The Inspiration and Authority of the Bible* (London: Epworth, 1956).

Stonehouse, Ned B., and Woolley, Paul, eds. *The Infallible Word* (Nutley, N. J.: Presbyterian and Reformed, 1946).

Strong, Augustus Hopkins. *Systematic Theology* (Rochester, N. Y.: American Baptist Publication Society, 1907).

Tasker, R. V. G. *The Old Testament in the New Testament* (London: SCM, 2d ed., 1954).

Tavard, George H. *Holy Writ or Holy Church* (New York: Harper and Brothers, 1959).

———. *The Dogmatic Constitution on Divine Revelation of Vatican Council II* (Glen Rock, N. J.: Paulist Press, 1966).

Temple, William. *Nature, Man and God* (London: Macmillan, 1934).

Tertullian. *Apology*, tr. by Emily J. Daly, C.S.J., in *Tertullian, Apologetical Works*, Vol. 10, The Fathers of the Church (Fathers of the Church, 1950).

Thiele, Edwin R. *The Mysterious Numbers of the Hebrew Kings* (Chicago: Univ. of Chicago Press, 1951; rev. ed. Grand Rapids: Eerdmans, 1965).

Thiessen, Henry Clarence. *Introduction to the New Testament* (Grand Rapids: Eerdmans, 3d ed., 1943).

Tillich, Paul. *Systematic Theology*, Vol. I (Chicago: Univ. of Chicago Press, 1951).

Unger, Merrill F. *Introductory Guide to the Old Testament* (Grand Rapids: Zondervan, 1951).

Van Til, Cornelius. "Introduction," pp. 3-68, in Warfield, *The Inspiration and Authority of the Bible*, ed. by Samuel G. Craig.

Vawter, Bruce. *Biblical Inspiration* (Philadelphia: Westminster, 1972).

_____. "The Fuller Sense: Some Considerations," pp. 85-96, *Catholic Biblical Quarterly*, Vol. XXVI, No. 1, January, 1964.

Walvoord, John F., ed. *Inspiration and Interpretation* (Grand Rapids: Eerdmans, 1957).

Warfield, Benjamin B. *Biblical and Theological Studies*, ed. by Samuel G. Craig (Nutley, N. J.: Presbyterian and Reformed, 1952).

Warfield, Benjamin B., and Hodge, Archibald A. *Inspiration* (Philadelphia, n.d., reprinted from *Presbyterian Review*, April, 1881).

Warfield, Benjamin B. *The Inspiration and Authority of the Bible*, ed. by Samuel G. Craig (Nutley, N. J.: Presbyterian and Reformed, 1948).

Westcott, Brooke Foss. *An Introduction to the Study of the Gospels* (New York: Macmillan, 1895).

Wilson, Robert Dick. *Studies in the Book of Daniel—A Discussion of the Historical Questions* (New York: Putnam's, Knickerbocker Press, 1917).

Wolfson, Harry Austryn. *Philo*, 2 vols. (Cambridge, Mass.: Harvard Univ. Press, 1947).

Wright, G. Ernest. *God Who Acts* (London: SCM, 1952).

_____. *The Old Testament and Theology* (New York: Harper and Row, 1969).

Young, Edward J. *An Introduction to the Old Testament* (Grand Rapids: Eerdmans, 1952).

_____. *Thy Word Is Truth* (Grand Rapids: Eerdmans, 1957).

General Index

Acton, John, 210
Albrektson, Bertil, 66
Albright, William F., 161
allegory, 127, 129, 133-135, 137-138
Almain, Jacques, 97-98
Alonso-Schökel, Luis, 240, 307
Althaus, Paul, 62
Amenophis IV (Akhenaton), 35
apocrypha, 176
apostle, definition of, 112-113
Apostles' Creed, 119
apostolic succession, 113-115
Aqiba, 84-85
Aquinas, Thomas, 95, 231, 272
archaeology, 16, 223-224
Aristeas, letter of, 128, 166-167
Aristobulus, 128
Aristotle, 203
Assumption of the Virgin Mary, 107, 274-275
Athenagoras, 132-133, 141, 198
Augustine, 136-138, 142, 171-172
authority, 292-302
autographs
  definition of, 152
  inerrancy of, 144, 156
  loss of, 158-159
  of Book of Jeremiah, 150-152

  scriptural claims about, 152-156
  theological value of, 156-158

Baillie, John, 41-42, 49, 233, 297-298
Barr, James, 29-30, 66-68
Barth, Karl, 39, 49, 58, 63-64
Bea, Augustin Cardinal, 106
Belgic Confession of Faith, 141
Bellarmine, 103
Benoit, Pierre, 171-172
Berdyaev, Nicholas, 38, 64
Beza, Theodore, 145
Bible (see Scripture)
Biblical manuscripts, transmission of, 163-166
Billuart, Charles R., 228-229
de Brès, Guido, 141
Bright, John, 261, 300-301
Brown, Robert McAfee, 119
Bruce, F. F., 190
Brunner, Emil, 39, 42, 43-46, 48-49, 58-59, 63-64, 310
Buber, Martin, 38
Bultmann, Rudolf, 39, 56-58
Bunyan, John, 260
Burtchaell, James Tunstead, 147-148, 210, 229-230, 261, 274, 293-296, 302-303

321

274, 292
Pius X, 106, 293
Pius XI, 270
Pius XII, 106, 274
Plato, 127
plenary inspiration
  and duplicates, 243-244
  and Ecclesiastes, 251-254
  and Esther, 249-250
  and inerrancy, 254-259, 291
  and the canon, 242-263
  and the Song of Songs, 250-251
  and trivialities, 244-245
Polycarp, 116-117
Preus, Robert, 164, 200, 227-228
Prierias (Sylvester Prierias Mazzolini), 97-98
priestly tradition, 80
prophets, 78-79, 126
  as authors of Scripture, 246-249
pseudepigrapha, 176
Pseudo-Isidore Decretals, 272
Purim, Feast of, 249-250
Pythagoras, 127

Quenstedt, J. A., 143-144, 163-164
Qumran, 82, 177, 254, 262

Rahner, Karl, 204, 306
Ramm, Bernard, 284
reason
  and inerrancy, 217-219
  and revelation, 46
reasoning, deductive and inductive, 16-19
Reformation, 40, 98-100, 138-142
resurrection, 57-63
revelation
  and discovery, 31-34
  and doctrine, 42, 44-46
  and interpretation, 74-76
  and propositional truth, 46-50
  and reason, 46
  and salvation history, 65-69
  as communication, 50-52
  as variable element, 205-206
  associated terms, 21-25
  channels of, 25-27

idea of, 15, 19
in the Bible, 19-21, 29-30
primary, 70-71, 74-76, 85, 92, 116, 265, 306
secondary, 71-72, 74-76, 92, 116, 118
types of, 69-72
uniqueness of, 34-36

Sadducees, 82-83
salvation history, 65-69
Sanday, William, 206
Sanders, James A., 300
Sartre, Jean-Paul, 39
Sayers, Dorothy, 73
Schatzgeyer, Kaspar, 100
science, 32-33, 143
Scofield, Cyrus Ingerson, 109
Scofield Reference Bible, 109-110, 286
Scripture
  and tradition, 92-111, 115-116, 305-312
  as objective record of revelation, 49
  as redemptive history, 44, 52
  essentials in, 234
  theological variations in, 194-195
secularism, 31-32, 143
sensus plenior, 263
Septuagint, 128-129, 133, 136-138, 166-174, 191, 234
Shammai, 83-84
Simons, Francis, 273, 281-282, 285, 288
Simpson, Richard, 210
Smart, James D., 36, 296-297
Socinus, Faustus, 220
Socinus, Laelius, 219
sola scriptura, 98, 100, 119-121
source material, 159-162
stoicism, 127
Syllabus of Errors, 105, 209
Synod of Dordt, 141

Tavard, George, 94-103, 117, 122
Temple, William, 41
Ten Commandments (*see* Decalogue)
Terreni, Guido, 96
Tertullian, 93, 133-134, 271

Scriptural Index

BS480.B363 1973
SCRIPTURE, TRADITION, AND INFALLIBILITY

3 3001 00020 7554